Praise for **NFL Confidential**

"The author is frequently a good observer of everyday life among professional football's proletariat, and he gets some important things said."
—*New York Times*

"An obscure offensive lineman writing under the pseudonym 'Johnny Anonymous' leaves no scandal unexamined in his damning new book."
—*Daily News* (NY)

"It's unusual to hear a current NFL player criticize the league, let alone talk frankly about its handling of concussions or its response to domestic violence scandals."
—NPR

"Unlike the glossy, self-promotional tell-all memoirs of former gridiron star players and coaches of the National Football League, this hard-hitting sports confessional by a current pro-baller, who has decided not to come out from the shadows, will stick in the craw of the NFL front office. . . . This wicked football expose, written by an active player who 'hates' the sport, is a ticking time bomb."
—*Publishers Weekly*

"If you love football, you'll still enjoy this book. . . . Pick this book up if you need a straight-forward read about the life of a career back-up in the NFL."
—Gang Green Nation

"At times disturbing and bitter, but also hilarious and moving. And it rings very, very true. . . . His perspective as someone who comes across as one of the more intelligent players in the league is often refreshing. . . . He strips the illusion of glamour from being an NFL player."
—Blogging the Boys

NFL Confidential

NFL
[CONFIDENTIAL]

True Confessions from
the Gutter of Football

JOHNNY ANONYMOUS

DEY ST.
AN IMPRINT OF WILLIAM MORROW *PUBLISHERS*

DEY ST.

NFL CONFIDENTIAL. Copyright © 2016 by Nunn of Your Business Productions LLC. All rights reserved. Printed in the United States of America. No part of this book may be used or reproduced in any manner whatsoever without written permission except in the case of brief quotations embodied in critical articles and reviews. For information address HarperCollins Publishers, 195 Broadway, New York, NY 10007.

HarperCollins books may be purchased for educational, business, or sales promotional use. For information please e-mail the Special Markets Department at SPsales@harpercollins .com.

A hardcover edition of this book was published in 2016 by Dey Street Books, an imprint of William Morrow Publishers.

FIRST DEY STREET BOOKS PAPERBACK EDITION PUBLISHED 2016.

Designed by Shannon Nicole Plunkett

Library of Congress Cataloging-in-Publication Data has been applied for.

ISBN 978-0-06-242243-9

16 17 18 19 20 DIX/RRD 10 9 8 7 6 5 4 3 2 1

CONTENTS

A Message to My Beautiful Readers   ix

1. Training Day   1

2. It's Flashback Time   25

3. Knee-Deep in It   41

4. The Reaper   67

5. My Glorious Backup Dream™   91

6. Fuck   111

7. Center of Attention   129

8. Celebrity Homecoming   151

9. The Meaning of Irony   171

10. Miss Me When I'm Gone   187

11. Losers   201

12. Winner   221

    Epilogue   235

A MESSAGE TO
MY BEAUTIFUL READERS

At the beginning of the 2014 season, I started keeping a detailed journal about my life as an NFL player. I carried around the notebook the team issues to all the players to write down crap about plays, and I wrote about other stuff instead. Fun stuff, scary stuff, controversial stuff. Real stuff. Everything that went on in meetings, in the locker room, on the field, as it happened.

My coaches thought I was the most diligent note taker they'd ever seen.

There's one simple rule you're gonna have to follow if you want to be a part of all this. You can never know my real name. I know, tragic, right? Don't worry, it's a normal, boring white-man name. But if you found it out, the League would find it out. And they'd destroy me.

Now if I wanted to be safe, I'd get everything approved by the NFL, and you'd get a completely whitewashed, totally inaccurate, and extremely dull story about life in pro football. And sure, you'd also get my real name.

To hell with being safe. I'm gonna be honest.

What should you call me? Honestly, I don't really care. I'm not a Brady, I'm not a Peyton, I'm not a Sherman, and I sure as hell don't have a stupid fucking nickname like Johnny Football. But if you gotta call me something, fine. For once in my life *I'm* gonna get the stupid nickname.

Call me Johnny Anonymous.

Oh, and I changed a bunch of other crap too. Names, timeline, details, the usual. All so you can't figure out who I really am. Go ahead, try. I dare you. Catch me if you can.

NFL Confidential

Chapter 1
TRAINING DAY

Friday, July 25, 2014

My first day of training camp with my brand-new team starts in exactly forty-five minutes. And I'm feeling pretty fucking good.

It's a gorgeous morning. I'm driving my truck through my new, sprawling, filthy city, the sun is shining, and football is everywhere.

God bless America.

A giant billboard for the team just inside the city limits. The wall of an old brick building, painted with the team's faded logo. Posters and flags in every storefront window, jerseys on the kids, jerseys on the dads, even jerseys on the moms, unless they're headed to work, in which case hats are acceptable. I turn on the radio, and every station is talking about the upcoming season. Not just the sports talk radio crap, but all the other stations too. Classic rock, rap, easy listening, all of them going on and on about football, *football,* FOOTBALL!!!

And I'm feeling like what I do *matters.* Like I'm gonna be a part of something big. Something bigger than any single player, fan, or coach. Something meaningful. Something important.

I see the football everywhere, and I feel like I'm somebody.

I pull my truck into the parking lot at my new team's complex. It's 8:45 A.M. I'm right on time. I open my door and step out, all six feet, three inches and 279 pounds of me. I look around, and what I see makes me feel even bigger, even better.

It's massive. Offices, courtyards, conference halls, indoor training facility, practice field. It's modern, pristine, with this giant arched entrance, stone pillars and gorgeous bubbling fountain, and big shiny windows. It's like a temple of football. But this is the NFL, the best of the best, the biggest of the big, the richest of the rich, and I'm an NFL player, so I should expect nothing less.

Right? *Right?* Fuck yeah!

I walk down the sidewalk to the big glass doors, and just outside is the special teams coach, standing with his teenage daughter. Now I'm not the kicker, I'm an offensive lineman, but I did spend a lot of time with this guy during the summer session just a couple months ago. Still, I'm impressed that a coach is waiting to greet me at the door on my first day. That's a pretty classy touch from my new organization.

"Hey, Doug," I say, calling him by his first name because you never call a coach "Coach" in the NFL. "Great to see you again! How was your break?"

"Hey, look who it is!" he says, a big warm smile on his face. "Alyssa, I want you to meet Keith, Keith Nunn. How's it going, Keith?"

There's just one small problem. My name is not Keith. Not even close.

I pause, clear my throat awkwardly.

"Johnny," I say. "My name is *Johnny*."

Doug's gigantic, tooth-filled grin vanishes instantly. His daughter gets that look on her face that only a mix of embarrassment, parents, and adolescent hormones can create. I almost feel bad for her.

"Daddy!" she says. "*Jesus!* He's your own player, and you don't even know his name?"

"Oh," he stammers, confused. "Oh—oh, right. Johnny. Of course. Well. Okay. Um. Welcome, Johnny. And I'll, you know . . . *Okay, see you!*"

He pumps my hand furiously without looking me in the eye, physically grabs his daughter by her narrow shoulders, and walks away as fast as he can go.

I stand there, fuming. My name is not Keith, or even Keith Nunn. Fuck, I don't even *look* like a Keith. In fact, no offense to all you Keiths out there, but Keith is one of the stupidest fucking names in the human language and just saying it leaves a bad taste in my mouth. Did I mention I look nothing like a Keith?

And then I realize the truth. They don't give a fuck who I am. I could be a Keith, I could be a Johnny, I could be a Steve or a Carlos or a Tyrone. I mean nothing to them.

I'm an NFL player, so I should expect nothing less.

YOU CAN BREAK NFL PLAYERS down into three categories.

Twenty percent do it because they're true believers. They're smart enough to do something else if they wanted, and the money is nice and all, but really they just *love football*. They love it, they live it, they believe in it, it's their creed. They would be nothing without it. Hell, they'd probably pay the League to play if they had to! These guys are obviously psychotic. Gronk is the obvious prototype here, but you also got a lot of your star quarterbacks like Peyton Manning or Brett Favre, people who fear life after football so much that they stay in the game way too long.

Thirty percent of them do it just for the money. So they could do something else—sales, desk jockey, accountant, whatever—but they play football because the money is just so damn good. And it is good. The least you can make as a rookie in the NFL in 2014—the least!—is $420,000. The guys in this category aren't the big stars. We're talking about most of the special teams guys, some offensive linemen, maybe a few backup linebackers here and there. I could tell you names, but trust me, you wouldn't have a clue who they are, and they like it that way.

And last of all, 49.99 percent play football because, frankly, it's the only thing they know how to do. Even if they wanted to do something "normal," they couldn't. All they've ever done in their lives is play football—it was their way out, either of the hood or the deep woods country. They *need* football. If football didn't exist, they'd be homeless, in a gang, or maybe in prison. I could give you tons of examples here, but if they ever learned my true identity, it wouldn't be good for my health.

Then there's me.

I'm part of my own little weird minority, that final 0.01 percent. We're such a minority, we don't even count as a category. We're the professional football players who flat-out *hate* professional football.

Resent it. Loathe it. Hate what it does to our bodies, how it breaks us down, tearing our ligaments, shredding our knees, turning us into old men while we're still in our twenties. Hate what it does to our minds, how it makes us forget things like where we put our keys and eventually who the hell we are. Hate what it does to our lives, how it separates us from our friends and family, treats us like high-priced slaves who can be bought and sold, telling us it loves us one second, then tossing us out like trash the next. Hate the whole *idea* of "Football as a Way of Life." All the garbage about us being "warriors" on a "battlefield," that somehow we're Real Men or Heroes because we play this stupid game with a little scrap of leather on a hundred yards of fake grass.

I'm a member of a club that's so damn small and so damn secret I don't even know if there are any other members, which I guess makes me the very lonely president. At least the dudes in *Fight Club* got to beat the shit out of each other in a dirty basement. All I get to do is roll my eyes and make sarcastic remarks to myself.

Sure, sometimes even I get caught up in all the bullshit of pro football. All the fake glory and forced glamour. Just like a few minutes ago when I was driving into my new city. There's a reason the League I work for is so popular, so powerful. It's an expert at manipulating people. Players, fans, coaches, even me.

But once I'm out of the League, I'm out. I'll never play another game. I'll never watch one, in person or on TV. I'll never even touch a football again. If some douche decides to whip one at me, I won't even catch it, I'll just step aside and let it bean the sorry fucker behind me in the face.

And that—all that hatred, all that contempt, all that bottled-up rage toward football—is how I came up with my dream.

That's right, I have a dream. It's a beautiful dream. It may be the boldest dream in all human history in just how completely and totally un-ambitious it really is.

I'm going to be the Best NFL Backup Ever™.

(See how I trademarked that? Yeah, don't you forget it.)

Now, let me guess. I tell you I'm just a backup, and you laugh, right? Hahaha. What a scrub. What a nobody.

Well, fuck you.

As an NFL backup, I'll get paid hundreds of thousands of dollars to stand on the sidelines in gigantic stadiums with roaring crowds all around me and do absolutely nothing. Nothing.

Let me repeat that for you, okay? NOTHING.

But you know what's best of all? Just *maybe* the only thing in the world that could ever be better than money for nothing?

I'll do it by beating the NFL at its own game. Literally. I'll take their fucking money, and they'll thank me for it. Praise me for being the football true believer I'm not.

I'll convince all the coaches, the management, hell, even my own agent that I actually *care* about football. That I live it. That I bleed it. But the whole time, I'll be lying, laughing at them through my mouth guard. All to prove to myself, to this League, to the whole world, that I'm bigger, stronger, smarter—that I'm *better*—than all of this.

But it won't be easy. Fuck, I haven't even made the goddamn team yet. Until the end of camp, I could get cut at any moment. And there's a good chance I will.

That's right. I'll be one of a total of ninety players in training camp fighting for fifty-three spots on the final roster. Sound bad? It gets worse. There are already twenty-two starters, guys who are pretty much guaranteed a position. Not to mention the high draft picks from the last couple years, three specialists, and the backup QB. That leaves the rest of us fighting over what's left. Thirty-one openings for sixty-eight guys.

Oh, and it gets even worse. I'm third string.

Third. Fucking. String. Do you have any idea just how shitty that is? I'm not even the backup. I'm the *backup's* backup. Now I'm no genius when it comes to math, but even I can tell you that my odds suck dick.

And guess what, you lucky bastard, it gets *even* worse. This is my second team in three years. I was cut loose by my last team at the end of last season. It all came down to politics, lost my spot to a kid who shared an agent with my coach, nothing to do with how well I played, but none of that matters now. I'm damaged goods. I interviewed with four different teams before I finally got a shitty offer from this one.

Training camp lasts five weeks. There are two rounds of cuts. If I get cut this time, my career is over. No one will want to touch me with my history. So I'll have to fight harder than I ever have in my life just to achieve my dream of highly paid, professional mediocrity.

But when it's all said and done, when I finally win—because I will win—I'll get exactly what I want: a big fat paycheck from the NFL, all on my own terms. It's gorgeous. The ultimate con. A football Frank Abagnale.

That's why I'm here. That's why I'm gonna shake off the humiliation of my own coach not knowing my name, and I'm gonna walk right into that big shiny building and subject myself, at least temporarily, to even more abuse. Because I have a dream.

Money for nothing, and revenge for free.

I HEAD DOWN THE HALLWAY to the locker room. Even the hall has perfectly groomed carpet, the team logo stitched everywhere, you know, just in case we forget where we are.

Everything you do at training camp is a test. Everything.

Some of it is obvious. The drills, the practices, the weigh-ins, the quizzes about plays and coverages and rules. But even the stuff they don't call a test is also a test. The way they shake your hand—or don't. The way they look you in the eye when they pass you in the building—or don't. The way they call you by name—and get it completely fucking wrong.

I get to the locker room. It's the size of a small warehouse, but instead of racks of cardboard boxes filled with that crap your work sells, there's an endless mass of lockers as big as walk-in closets. More bright carpet in the team's colors, more logos. It's like a funky cross between a high-end finished garage and your mom's dining room circa 1989. It cost a few million dollars to build instead of a couple thousand, but somehow it feels just as cheap.

"Hey, sweetie pie," I say to some random defensive back. "How was your break?"

I love doing that, calling guys "baby," "sweetie," "cutie," that kind of shit. Of course everyone on the team—on *any* football team—is so knee-jerk homophobic it automatically freaks them out, and I fucking love freaking football players out. So easy, so much fun.

"Fuck that gay shit, man," he says and keeps walking.

"You got it, baby," I say to the man in the giant room filled with half-naked dudes.

You know that famous scene from *Goodfellas*? The one where the main guy walks into the Italian restaurant, and he lists off all the different mobsters one by one. There's the guy who always says everything twice, so they call him Jimmy Two Times. Then there's the guy with the flattened-out face, so they call him Freddy No Nose, and then there's Frankie Carbone, who's got a rug of curly black hair and bushy black eyebrows and looks more Italian than Chef Boyardee.

And you barely even need to hear their names, right? Because as soon as you see them, you know who they are. You know their type.

That's what it's like when I walk into an NFL locker room. It doesn't matter that this is my first day of camp. It doesn't matter that this is a brand-new team or that I barely got to know any of these guys during the summer session. I look around, and I just *know*.

Over on the left I see the specialists all hanging out—the kicker, the long snapper, the punter. They're the Average-Looking White Guys, the closest thing you get to normal schmoes who just happen to play pro football. They play a lot of golf and have way too much time on their hands and they're always together. I mean, if all you had to do every day was kick a couple balls while the rest of the animals on the team are dying on the field, you better stick together, right? And one of them, at least one, is always some quirky free-spirit jackass. No shit, just as I'm thinking this, Ollie the long-haired kicker pulls out a kazoo and starts playing "Enter Sandman" by Metallica. Even worse, he's pretty damn good.

"Yo! Y'all wanna know the *hardest* thing to do in the League?"

This comes from a locker in the corner. This is the Preacher. These guys are generally outside linebackers or tight ends, just smart enough to make sense but not to actually know what the fuck they're talking about. This one happens to be named Jovan. And yeah, he's a tight end.

"It ain't catching a ball, it ain't making a tackle, it ain't even winning games—it's *stackin' them racks!*"

In case you don't spend a lot of time around the Ebonically gifted like I do, that means money. If no one shuts Jovan up, in about five minutes he'll end up screaming incoherently, and even the rookies will stop listening to him.

"Man, Jovan, shut the *fuck up!*"

Thank God. That's the Old Vet. Now usually the Old Vet doesn't get involved in dumb locker-room crap. But this dude is Jeb. Jeb is on the offensive line like me, but unlike me, he's a star with a massive multiyear contract. So not only is he ancient by football standards—meaning thirty-four—but he also doesn't put up with bullshit. Why should he? He's untouchable. He's also bald, six foot five, 335 pounds, with enough ink on his arms to fill a comic book. He's fucking terrifying. Most white guys won't fuck with the loud black guys on the team. But Jeb doesn't give a shit. He'll fuck with anything that moves.

To my right, I pass by the Samoan, another offensive lineman. This guy is a Meathead with a special ethnic twist. His name is Teddy. I'm pretty sure that means something cool in, like, Samoan or something.

This massive bastard is one of my favorite guys on the team. A little simpler than most . . . six foot three, 320 pounds of muscle, so deep island he should be out spearing fish and wrestling whales. But throw a pair of pads on him and he'll tear a hole in a defense without even *thinking* about it. Mostly because he can't. And that lack of a brain makes him an easy target.

"Hey, Teddy, what shape is a stop sign?"

A bunch of O linemen are huddled around Teddy with eager looks on their faces. The guy asking the questions is Antonne, the starting center. The Alpha. He's the line's official leader. He's got a thick black beard and dreads down to his shoulders.

"Uhhhhh," Teddy says. "Uhhhhhhhhh."

Teddy stares straight ahead, his forehead all crinkled up like he's concentrating harder than he ever has in his life.

"Come on, man! Think! You can do it!"

Teddy's eyes finally open wide like he's been hit by a ray of light from above.

"An octagon?"

"Yes!" Antonne shouts. The other guys cheer, fist bumps all around. "Now how many sides does an octagon have?"

More wrinkles on Teddy's brow.

"Uhhh . . . six?"

A massive groan as the guys all bust out laughing. Offensive linemen consider themselves the smartest guys on the team. As an offensive lineman, I can say that this is true. But every rule has its exception.

Suddenly from my left—

"Hey, you think it's cool to have a few girlfriends?"

Without even looking, I already know this is a wide receiver. The Diva. Arrogant, outspoken, selfish. They spend money like it's their job, on jewelry, a couple Benzes, Gucci backpacks—backpacks?—and typically have no shame. On top of that, they're the funniest guys on the team. When I do turn around, I see which receiver it is: our star, our franchise guy, Dante. He's so talented the team's built its whole offense around him, and no joke, he's juggling texts from women on three different smartphones right now.

"Dante! How about you have a *relationship* with the *mother* of your damn *baby*?" Jeb the Old Vet shouts.

"I do have a relationship with her," Dante says. "Seventy-five thousand dollars a year!"

Everyone cracks up, especially the other receivers and the defensive backs, who are basically shorter and uglier versions of receivers except on the other side of the ball and with even less shame, if that's possible.

The only guy not laughing is our starting QB, Brody. Not even a chuckle. What can I say about the quarterback? Nothing, really. Everyone knows your prototypical quarterback. Leadership blah blah blah. They're all the same. The Bores.

I finally get to my own locker. It's just a few spaces down from Dante's and Jeb's lockers, which means I'm gonna have to deal with a shitload of texting and arguing. Fantastic.

Your locker is a little like your sanctuary in the NFL. It's your territory, the only thing that almost feels like it's yours, even though in reality the team can take it away from you whenever it wants. After practice when everyone is too tired to move, I've seen guys sleeping in front of their lockers, right on the floor. Throw down a towel, maybe a duffel bag for a pillow, and you're all set.

It's weird to think that if I don't make this team, this locker could be my last one.

I scan the room, searching for the one guy I haven't found yet. They're all here. The Brownnose, the Fuckup, the Asshole, the Complainer, the Fighter. Every last one of them, just like I knew they would be. But not him.

Then I spot him. Over in the corner, sitting all by himself. When it comes to my future, he's by far the most important player on this whole team. His name is Paulson, and he's the second-string guard/center for the offensive line, the dude right ahead of me on the roster. He's a big black dude with neatly trimmed hair and thick-rimmed glasses, and right now he's quietly reading a ratty old book, not talking to anyone.

That's right. My mortal enemy is the Likable Nerd.

If I want a shot at being the Best NFL Backup Ever™, I need to beat Paulson out for his spot. Plain and simple.

He's been with the team the last two years, but last season he suffered a groin injury that knocked him out for a few games. That's why they brought me in. He's made a "full recovery," but the team wants a human insurance policy—at least through the end of training camp, when they'll have to let one of us go to make quota.

The ugly truth is that if I want to make this team, I'll have to be good enough to take this guy's job. It's absolutely disgusting, but it's nothing personal. It's business.

In this League, it always is.

THERE'S NO ONE HOLDING YOUR hand during training camp. No one actually telling you where to go and what to do every single second. Before we all got here, they sent us an e-mail with our daily schedule. It's up to us to make it to the right place at the right time.

Thing is, most of us don't really bother reading it till the last minute.

"Man, one fag joins the NFL and we gotta have a fucking *meeting*?" Dante says as he finally scans the e-mail.

Yep, we're talking about Michael Sam. He's gay, in case you didn't get a chance to watch him kiss his BF on draft day. And right now, he's in St. Louis, at the Rams' training camp, trying to make the final roster, just like we are. And everyone in the country thinks he and his gayness are a big fucking deal.

So our team has decided to hold a meeting, a class really. On sensitivity.

That's right. On the very first day of a camp where we'll spend the next five weeks mangling one another, we are about to undergo sensitivity training.

It's no secret there's a ton of homophobia in this business. I mean, you've got a sport full of southern conservative hillbillies, black dudes who devour rap culture, and players from both races who call themselves born-again Christians. Then you pay all these guys a shitload of cash to act like hypermasculine warriors, all while wearing tights and showering together. Are we surprised there's some sexual insecurity?

Obviously I have no problem mocking that insecurity; I mean, I call defensive backs I don't even know "baby" just to freak them out. And I honestly don't give a shit if someone's gay, player or not. Now, I'm not gonna sing "Kumbaya" for social harmony or something, but if you're a dude and you want to diddle another dude, that's your business. But it should stay *your* business.

For all of us, even a vaguely smart smart-ass like myself, the whole kissing-in-public thing went about twenty steps too far. To put it delicately, it was fucking gross. The locker room is supposed to be a place where guys on the team can let their guard down, relax, be themselves. And, yes, be naked without feeling like it's a "gay" thing.

On my last team, one of our practices got held up because our star running back was taking too long in the locker room. Every player on the offense started screaming for him to hurry the fuck up and get outside—so he did. He walked to the door of the facility buck naked, his dick swinging out in front of everyone.

"Sorry, guys!" he shouted. "Just need a few more minutes!"

This dude was probably one of the most homophobic motherfuckers on the whole team, but around us he felt totally comfortable literally letting it all hang out. We almost died laughing.

It's safe to say this would not have happened with Michael Sam on the team.

Is it ironic that in order to allow the rest of us to feel like ourselves, we need gay guys to pretend to be who they aren't? Of course.

But this isn't theory, this is football. And the idea that you're gonna change any of us by making us sit through an hour-long class is a total fucking joke.

Do you honestly think the League gives a shit about "equality" or any of that other stuff? Of course not. They care about money. They just make us do this nonsense to cover their asses from media backlash and potential lawsuits. That way we can get back to doing what really matters: destroying one another on national TV so the NFL can make bank.

Everyone files into the room; I grab a seat near the door. It's kind of set up like a college class; you got the lecture hall with the desks and the whiteboards and everything, except all the students weigh over two hundred pounds, a lot of them make more money than the teachers, the "desks" are plush leather recliners, and all we do is play football.

Actually, that still sounds like a whole lot of my college classes.

Sitting by the back wall, there are even a bunch of coaches. I see the quarterbacks coach, the safeties coach, the receivers coach, and the special teams coach who got my name wrong. Fantastic. At least they gotta sit through this shit too.

"Okay, excuse me? Excuse me! Can I have everyone's attention?"

I turn to the front of the room. A guy who's in pretty good shape for someone in his midforties is standing next to the whiteboard, marker in hand. He has leathery white skin and spiky blond hair and he looks like an extra from a Nickelback video. How the fuck did a former player get into sensitivity training?

"Hey, fellas! How is everybody!"

He doesn't really ask us so much as shout it at us. We reply with blank stares. Every single player has a notebook and pen, given out by the team. Somehow I don't think many notes will be taken today.

He tells us he's a former player, just like I thought. Used to be a linebacker for Indianapolis for eleven years, now he travels the country speaking to athletes about important shit like workplace relations and world peace. That actually sounds worse to me than playing football.

"All right, so we all know times are different," he says. "We got different kinds of people, all right? And they got different points of view. Even, you know, lifestyles. And as a former player, I understand it can be, like, stressful, all right?"

He stops for a second. Looks at us like what he's about to say is really, really important.

"I want you to know . . . *I get it!*"

Absolute, perfect silence.

"All right, fantastic!" the instructor says, not bothered at all by this total lack of interest. "Now I got an exercise for us, all right? I want us to come up with *ten different words* that we can use to describe what it means to be a successful teammate. Anyone have any ideas?"

Silence.

"Anyone?"

Nope.

"All right, so let's get some volunteers up here. How about that?"

That sounds fucking awful. Suddenly every one of those notebooks is open, and every single player is writing down the most important words ever written by man. He grabs two sorry fuckers out of the crowd, some third-string white guy on defense I don't know, and Jovan. The Preacher. This is probably the first time in his life he's ever been speechless. I cherish it.

"All right," the instructor says as his two "volunteers" stare at their feet. "Who wants to go first? Give me one word to describe how to be a successful teammate."

We all sit there in silence, I shit you not, for a solid seven seconds before it dawns on these two geniuses that unless they actually say something, this torture will never, ever end.

"Uh . . . Respect?" the third-string guy finally, mercifully says. It's barely a low whisper, but the instructor reacts like he just heard the first five chords of "How You Remind Me."

"Excellent!" the instructor shouts. " 'Respect' is a perfect example of a great quality for a successful teammate to have. Here, why don't you write it down on the board for us."

Third String takes the marker and scrawls "Respect" on the whiteboard. His handwriting actually isn't that bad.

"Fantastic!" the instructor says. "Love it! Let's get a second word up there, all right? We're really on a roll!"

Now that his successful teammate has actually contributed something to the board, I can tell Jovan's competitive juices are flowing. He doesn't need to be asked twice.

"I know," he says. "Tolerance!"

"*Excellent,*" the instructor says, beaming.

Jovan grins, proud of his accomplishment. The instructor holds out the marker to him.

"Here you go! Add it to the board."

Jovan reaches for the marker, then hesitates. He looks confused. He turns to the audience as if asking for help. We have none to give. He turns back to the instructor.

"I don't know how to spell it," Jovan says.

He looks at the third-string guy, who just shrugs.

"No problem at all," the instructor says. "I got you!"

He takes the marker and walks over to the board. He writes a big "T," then stops. He stands there for a second before putting the marker down.

"You know what?" he says. "I don't know how to spell it either."

I'll admit that this comes as a bit of a surprise. Everyone in the hall stares as the instructor pulls his smartphone out of his pocket.

"I guess we'll just have to google it! So, uh, that was 'tolerance,' right?"

Suddenly I hear a loud *pssst!* from behind me, on the other side of the room. It's Dante. He's snuck up next to the receivers coach, the man who is technically his boss—and who is currently fast asleep in his chair.

It's not a subtle sleep either. His head is bent down, resting on his arms, and his gum is resting about three inches from his mouth. The other coaches don't even notice. They're too busy texting and e-mailing people to care.

As the other players watch, Dante pulls out one of his three phones, moves in closer to the peaceful, horizontal head, and smiles a nice big smile for a selfie with his comatose coach.

Click.

Even Jeb the Old Vet is having a hard time not laughing.

"All right!" the instructor says at the front of the class. "On to the next word!"

OUT OF ALL THE COACHES we have, and we have a ton—no shit, at least twenty-two by my count, and they coach everything from our tight ends to how we tie our damn cleats—there are two who have more control over my fate than all the others. Whether I'll make this team, or whether I'm done with football forever.

They're the gatekeepers of My Glorious Backup Dream™. Their names are Jack and Lopez. And right now, on our spotless, fluorescently lit indoor practice field, they're here for the sole purpose of judging us in our first official test of camp, the conditioning test. In other words, they're gonna run the shit out of all the offensive linemen and see who collapses first.

God, I love this test.

"Jack" is our head coach, Jack Loeffler. Yep, even the head coach gets called by his first name. Jack is standing in the center of the pack of coaches on the sideline, studying something on an iPad because he's one of those coaches who are all into "technology," which I guess makes it a lot easier to watch porn than if he used a clipboard.

He's tall with a big, pasty bald head and a jet-black goatee. It looks weird. I think he dyes it or something. Jack's not a yeller, not even much of a talker. He does all his communicating with his eyes. Sharp, black eyes that can crush whatever he's looking at.

Standing next to Jack is Lopez. He's my position coach, the guy who directly oversees me and the other O linemen. He's fat, and he's always chewing on something. Gum, a pen, whatever. Right now, it's a paper clip.

It's Lopez's first year with the team—*and* his first year coaching in the pros. He had a long, successful career coaching college, at some of the biggest programs out there. USC, Florida. But that doesn't mean shit once you get to the NFL.

Lopez's eyes are the complete opposite of Jack's. Cold, brown, blank. As you probably guessed, he's Latino or something, but a completely whitewashed American, even speaks with a southern accent, which doesn't stop guys from making cracks about tacos and burritos and a hell of a lot worse behind his back. I look at him, staring at nothing, chewing on that damn paper clip, and I can't get a good read on him. It's weird. Reading people is my specialty.

For the sake of my career, my dream, I need these two coaches to notice me, a third-string player they couldn't give two shits about. And this conditioning test will give me one of my best shots all week.

The test is simple: run ten half-gassers in a row. That's the width of the football field and back, ten times, with only twenty seconds to run each of them, and a thirty-second break in between. But for most linemen, that's absolute torture, because most linemen are fat and slow. I, on the other hand, am tall, lean, and fast as hell. For me, this test will be easy as shit. It damn well better be.

All sixteen O linemen line up along the broad, green turf. We stand shoulder to shoulder, a few yards apart, waiting for the start. It isn't supposed to be a race, but we're all running at the same time so of course it is.

The whistle blows and we all take off.

When I hit the sideline, I'm already six feet ahead of the pack. I don't even have to turn my head and look. I can feel it, feel everyone staring at my back and knowing that it doesn't matter what they do, how hard they try, they will not be able to catch me.

Catch me if you can, I think. I almost laugh. I'm a pretty funny guy.

None of them do catch me. Not even close.

By the time we finish our last half-gasser, I've beaten everyone by a solid ten yards. Ten yards. That's a first down. The closest player to me is Antonne, the center, our unit's leader, and he's huffing and puffing like he might puke at any second.

And Paulson? The second-string guy I'm supposedly backing up? The guy who has *my* spot? He's the last person to cross the line.

I come to a stop, and I feel fantastic. It's the first time I've felt like myself since I got here this morning. The first time I've felt in control.

"Yeah, baby!" I say for no reason other than that it feels nice to say.

And you know what? None of it even matters.

The coaches aren't even looking in my direction. Jack's already on the other side of the field, talking to the receivers, like my test didn't even happen.

And Lopez? He makes a beeline right to Paulson. To congratulate him. That's right, Paulson looks like he's about to collapse, all bent over at the waist like he's about to take a dump right there on the turf, and motherfucking Lopez slaps him on the back like he just won the Boston Fucking Marathon.

"You looked awesome out there!" he says with that stupid southern accent.

And it hits me. I could've run the fastest half-gasser in the history of professional football, and the gatekeepers wouldn't have even noticed. They were watching Paulson the entire time. They had eyes only for him. They didn't care if he was fast, they just wanted him healthy. He was the backup, and I was third string. As long as Paulson could move, he was their guy, not me.

It's worse than I thought. It won't be enough for me to be good. If I want to make this team, I can't just pass all my tests or even dominate them. I need Paulson to fail.

I still have a billion more tests. And the one I'm about to take back in the training room, the last test of my very first day, is one I already know I'll fail. To take it, I won't have to run, lift, or hit anything.

I'll just have to step onto a scale.

HERE'S THE REALITY OF MY situation: even if I do make this team, even if I do achieve my golden dream and become the Best NFL Backup Ever™, I will never ever, *ever* be a starter in the National Football League.

And it all comes down to one reason: I'm too damn skinny.

By "too skinny," I mean I'm six foot three and 279 pounds with a completely empty colon. Yeah, tiny, right? I should've been a ballerina. But think about the weights of the starters. Jeb, the Old Vet who's the star of our line, is 345 pounds. Hell, Teddy, the Meathead Samoan, weighs 320 pounds, and he's second string!

See, the whole purpose of the offensive line is to form a moving, human wall to protect your quarterback or create space for your running back to run. And coaches want the human blocks that make up that wall to be as big as possible. Speed is nice, but size is everything. And 279 pounds is not "everything."

For me, the magic number, the Holy Grail of weights, is 285 pounds. Sure, even that's small, but somehow, at some point in time, the Football Gods decided that 285 pounds was the very least an offensive lineman could possibly weigh. I can't even tell you where I first heard it. It's just something that's echoed around me since I first started playing in high school. Gotta get up to 285. If you could only just be 285. Everything'll be cool at 285. 285. 285.

That number has haunted me for every weigh-in I've had over the last eleven years. And it's still haunting me now, for my first weigh-in of camp.

I get to the training center and I strip down to my shorts. The floor is cold on my bare feet. I'm in a group of ten other guys. The last group hasn't finished yet, so the line is all backed up.

I'm nervous. Not only have I not eaten anything since lunch, but I had to come here straight from cardio. I bet I sweated out at least five pounds in water weight running around on that damn field. A few minutes ago I took a piss, and it came out like corn syrup.

The truth is that my body, in its natural state, would never go an ounce above 211 pounds. I have a skinny frame; it's just how I'm built. You look at my sister and my dad, and you'll see I come from a family of beanpoles. Even my mom was five foot eleven and thin as a rail, like 140 pounds, and that was before the cancer. Like most normal human beings, my neck really, really wants to be thinner than my head. But football wants my neck much, much thicker.

Every day of my off-season is spent basically defying nature. For most guys in the NFL, the off-season is just what it sounds like—off. They relax, they eat what they want, and a workout for them is playing a game of pickup basketball with some friends or maybe a few holes of golf. They're freaks, naturally superior athletes who just don't have to work very hard. For a handful of players, the only exercise they get is walking from the sofa to the fridge. If anything, some of them get *too* big, *too* fat, gorging on junk food and slacking off, exercising like crazy and eating nothing but protein shakes to get back in shape the week before camp starts.

Not me. I have to work my ass off, not to be superior—just to *maintain* my size. If I stop training and eating about five thousand calories a day for anything more than a week, I literally shrink. I'll lose twelve pounds in four days, not because I'm starving myself, but because I'm just being normal.

Five days a week I follow a strict regimen of lifting and cardio and eating. I lift to put on muscle, because muscle is heavy. Benching 320 pounds is a warm-up. For a regular set of ten reps, I'd say my max is at least 495. So I lift a lot, and I put on a lot of muscle, and that makes me heavy. But to be a football player I also have to be mobile, right? I can't just be a mountain of muscle. So if I'm not lifting, I'm conditioning, working on speed, footwork. But working on speed and footwork just makes me burn calories, which makes me lighter again. So when I'm not lifting or conditioning, I'm eating. And eating.

And eating.

Just to keep myself around 265 pounds (not even 279!) I eat four meals a day, plus three protein shakes. Every third day I add an entire large frozen pizza. To get myself up into the 270s, I wait until two weeks before training camp begins, and I just gorge myself for fourteen straight days. Meat, vegetables, meat, pasta, rice, bread, pasta, meat, pasta, pasta. Why do I wait till I only have two weeks left? Because if I ate like that all year long, I'd probably die. My body just wouldn't be able to take it. All you suckers who have to suffer through low-carb diets? I laugh at you. I *wish* I could eat like that, just for a day.

And even with all that, even with optimizing and overwhelming every single one of my body's metabolic processes in a way that is completely, psychotically unhealthy, at 279 pounds, I max out. That's it, no more. I just physically can't go any higher.

But I have to. Without those extra six pounds, as far as the League goes, I am absolutely worthless. If I want my career, somehow I *have* to get to 285.

The massive D lineman before me finishes up. Yeah, *he's* not gonna have any issues, the fucker. It's finally my turn to weigh in.

One of the trainers, I think his name is Danny, stands next to the scale with an iPad as I walk up. I force a laugh.

"Look at you, you lucky bastard," I say. "You get to weigh me today!"

I'm not sure what I expect to gain by making awkward small talk with this guy. Like suddenly he's gonna add an extra ten pounds to my report if he likes my lame-ass joke?

Taking a deep breath—air must weigh something, right?—I get on the scale. I slowly reach my hand out to the wall in front of me. *If I can just create some downward pressure . . .*

"Hands at your side, Johnny."

The numbers flash green on the scale's digital readout. It finally lands on 272 pounds. I was right. The sweating from my triumphant, absolutely worthless performance in the cardio test absolutely killed me.

We stand there in silence as Danny types my weight into the iPad. There's no yelling, no angry looks. He just looks at me and says: "Gonna have to get that weight up there."

And that's it. I've officially been put on notice. He doesn't even have to say the number 285. We both know what it is.

"Yep," I say.

I head to the locker room, grab my stuff. I don't talk to any of the other players. I feel like an outsider. Nobody looks me in the eye. Nobody even acknowledges my existence. This is life as a third stringer. We're expendable, we could be gone at any time. Why would anyone waste their time?

I failed the weight test. But the good news—I guess?—is that I have another one tomorrow. I'll have to weigh in at least once a week, sometimes more.

But here's the thing. Here's what makes this all such a mind-fuck. Even if I do reach 285 pounds, hell, even if I somehow, some way miraculously made it all the way up to 295, my team can do *whatever it wants*.

My coach can tell me to be 285 pounds, then hire me at 281. He can tell me to be 285 pounds, then fire me at 297. He can do whatever! My contract has no guarantees. As hard as I try to control this whole ridiculous process, as a third-string player I have no control. None.

My whole world is one big maybe. Maybe one day, if I'm a tiny bit too light one too many times, maybe, just maybe, the training staff will report me to Lopez, who'll have a conversation with Jack, who'll mention it in passing to the general manager. And then, maybe, they'll cut me.

Or maybe I'll be just fine. Who the fuck knows? Not me.

IT'S THE END OF THE day. I walk out the building to my truck. My phone rings as I'm getting in. It's my girlfriend, Kate. As I'm answering, I notice that my dad tried calling a couple times during the day too.

"Hello," I say.

"Hey!" she says. "How was your first day?"

I can hear the forced excitement in her voice. She knows how shitty my situation is, so she's trying to compensate, trying to be helpful. I have to admit, right now it's just annoying.

"Fucking sucked," I say.

"Oh. That's horrible."

There's a pause. Kate and I met in high school, been dating on and off since then. She still lives in our hometown, a few hundred miles away.

"Um," she says. "Do you wanna talk about it?"

"No, not really," I say. Then, forcing myself to be nicer because I know that none of this is her fault, "Look, I'm just really tired. My brain feels like absolute death."

"I totally get it," she says.

"I'll call you tomorrow, okay?" I say. "Promise."

"Great!" she says. "Sounds good. Love you!"

"I love you too."

I hang up the phone, pull my truck out into the street. I wish I could open up to her, I really do. But I don't want to talk to anyone right now. I'm stuck in my own head, agonizing over what the goddamn coaches thought of me, terrified that I won't make this fucking team.

I know, I know. I'm not supposed to give a shit about this anymore. That's supposed to be the beauty of my dream to be the Best NFL Backup Ever™. I'm supposed to succeed on my own terms, not the League's.

And I want to let it go, more than anything.

But that's what the NFL does to you. It treats you like shit, then leaves you wanting more. It tells you you're worthless, then makes you beg for another chance to win its love. It's like being trapped in an abusive relationship. You hate it, but somehow, for some reason, you still need it.

That's what I hate most about football—that despite all the bullshit, I still care about football.

Confused? Does that all seem a little contradictory? Or just plain fucked up?

Congratulations. You're starting to understand what it means to be a player in the NFL.

Chapter 2

IT'S FLASHBACK TIME

You're probably wondering how the hell a guy who hates football wound up playing it at its highest level.

Okay, fair question.

It all started with my mom. You know how everyone believes that *their* mom is the kindest, the most loving, or the most beautiful?

In my case, it's the truth.

My mom was tall and thin, but soft, feminine. She had a bright, quick smile and curly, shoulder-length brown hair. She loved crafts. Knitting, sewing, crocheting. But her favorite, by far, was arranging flowers, the artificial kind. Silk roses, dried berries, rayon tulips. Our living room was a big, beautiful, polyester Garden of Eden.

We lived in a small town in central Ohio. My dad, my older sister, my mom, and me. I didn't have one of those tough-luck upbringings you hear about in the NFL. My dad sold real estate, my mom was a home-maker, and my sister and I fought all the time, just like all brothers and sisters. We were a small, middle-class family in a small Midwest town.

My mom was the glue that held us together.

I like to think I was her favorite. Was I really? I'm not sure. She was one of those people who had a knack for making everyone feel like they were her favorite. But yeah, I was.

I was a real mama's boy. I don't just mean soft, although I was definitely soft—makes me sick just thinking about it now—I mean I seriously spent all my time with my mother. Even as I got older, right around that age when it was kind of strange for a kid to be hanging out with his mom, I still just hung out with my mom. She really was my best friend.

Every week we went shopping together. It was our thing, just the two of us. We'd go grocery shopping, and we'd stop at Michael's, Tuesday Morning, and a million other craft stores. We'd walk down the aisles, my mom in the lead with her long list of things to do, places to go, and bargains to hunt. And I'd be right behind her, loaded up with shopping bags. If I wanted her to buy me a toy, I knew not to ask for anything, not to whine or push too hard, because then she'd never say yes. My favorites were Legos and Hot Wheels. It was a world that was very comfortable, and very safe.

When I was eleven, my mom got cancer.

Sorry, was that abrupt? Well, now you understand how it felt for me and my family.

My world didn't just change. It came to an end.

My mom fought the cancer as hard as she could. But it spread fast, to her lungs, her breasts, her brain. She couldn't stop it, we couldn't stop it. I couldn't stop it.

Toward the end, we didn't want my mom to suffer in some strange, foreign hospital bed, so we turned my dad's home office into her hospice room. Carried his desk, the filing cabinets, the chairs and bookshelves into the basement and lugged in a big, adjustable bed, a giant whirring ventilator, and armfuls of silk flowers. We said the move was for her, but it was just as much for us. We couldn't bear not having her close. We knew she would be gone soon.

My mom wanted to pass peacefully, with dignity, without desperate interventions, without last-minute resuscitations or intrusive procedures. But I still remember the day the ambulance came and took her to the hospital, the men in white coming into our home and carrying her out on a stretcher and past my dad.

He looked at me and my sister, his face pale, his eyes rimmed in red.

"I did a bad thing," he said. "I called the ambulance to help. I just want her around for a little while longer." She was back the next day, still alive. I don't know what exactly it was they did to revive her, and I'll never ask my dad. Whatever it was, it was worth it. We had her for ten more days.

My dad, my sister, and I were all there, in her room, when she did finally leave us. A candle was lit next to her bed. It flickered when she passed away. We knew it was a sign.

The following weeks, the office went back to being an office. And we all tried to move on. My dad tried to talk to us about her death a few times, but the conversation would always just end with silence and a shrug, with us trying to go back about the business of our lives. It didn't work.

With my mom gone, there was a void, and I needed to fill it with something, anything to make the pain go away.

Five months after my mom died, I started high school. I decided to join the football team.

IT WAS MY FIRST DAY of practice, thirty minutes before I had to join the squad for summer two-a-days, and there was one tiny problem.

My dad and I could not figure out how *the hell* to get on my shoulder pads.

"Uh, I think maybe you do something with this strap?" he said as he fumbled with it.

"Of course you do something with the strap!" I said. "It's there for a reason! We need to figure out what that reason is!"

He lost it.

"How should I know?" he shouted, tugging on the thing as hard as he could. "I play golf!"

Neither one of us knew a damn thing about the game of football. All the other kids on the team had been playing since junior high, at least. A lot of them since even younger, on peewee teams. They all had brothers who played football, fathers who played football, some of them even had grandfathers who played football. My granddad claimed he had played football in high school, but no one believed him. And my dad?

"*I play golf!*" he said in a full-on panic, dropping the strap.

We finally just decided to place the pads on my shoulders—we hoped they were at least facing the right direction—and forget about all the goddamn straps. When I got to practice, I nervously tapped one of the coaches on the shoulder, and he had to put on my shoulder pads for me as my teammates laughed.

Welcome to football, Johnny Anonymous.

My first season of football was probably the only year of my life I didn't have to worry about my size. I was on the freshman team, which is like the younger stepchild of the JV. I was skinny as hell, but so was everyone else, and I was already almost six feet tall, so I was actually bigger than most of the guys.

During that first week of practice, though, I found out fast that size didn't mean shit. Even though I was bigger than everyone else, I was still getting my ass kicked.

I was just too nice.

Smaller kids on the line were demolishing me, shoving me into the dirt, and I wouldn't even push back. When they laughed and made fun of me, I wouldn't say a word. I'd just go home and tear up in my room, alone. I was still a mama's boy after all.

"Dad," I said after my third day of getting dominated, "I don't think I can do this."

My dad sighed.

"It's okay to be afraid," he said. "But not to quit. Our family doesn't quit. Tomorrow, when you put that helmet on, I want you to let it out. Turn it on. Like flipping a switch."

Maybe my dad was a golfer, but he was still a dad, and a good one. We were all in a vulnerable place after my mom's death, and he knew how important it was not to give up something I started. We had to keep fighting, both of us.

The next day, when I put on that helmet, I flipped the switch. I turned it on.

I went out onto that field, lined up across from a guy who had crushed me into the ground, laughing, just the day before. And when that whistle blew, when our center snapped the ball, I grabbed that fucker across from me and I just *flattened* him. Drove my fists into his chest plate with a satisfying crunch and laid him out on the ground.

Damn, that felt good.

Yeah, the move was totally illegal and I would've been flagged for a hold in any legitimate game. But *damn* that felt good.

At that moment, I knew I was really, really going to like football.

I didn't understand it then, didn't start to piece things together until years later, but I know now that I was tapping into my anger. The anger that welled up after my mom was taken from me. It was still there, hanging over me like a shroud. And I needed to release it. Football became that release.

From there on out, I learned how to use that anger. When I played in games, I played angry. When I practiced, I practiced angry. When I lifted weights, I got angry at the motherfucking weights. Every single drill, every single snap, every single rep, I was angry. Now don't get me wrong—I was always in control. No one had more fun than I did on a football field. But I knew how to turn it on, and there was a never-ending reservoir to tap into.

And when I was done lifting, or practicing, or playing, I tucked the anger back inside me, nice and neat and smiling and polite, till I decided to bring it out and use it again. No one but me and my dad would ever know.

For the first two games of my freshman season, I sat the bench. By the fifth game, I was starting. By the time I was a sophomore, I was so good that I skipped JV and went straight to varsity. I started every single game for the rest of my high school career.

My mom would've been proud.

IT WAS MY SOPHOMORE YEAR in high school and I was at yet another football party.

This was at my friend Scott's house. Scott lived with his dad, who was divorced, so the place had a bachelor-pad feel to it. The lighting was dim, the sofa was covered in cracked black leather, and there were a lot of mirrors and weird tapestries on the walls. It was pretty hot for Ohio.

Scott's dad was out, so a bunch of us were hanging, drinking beer and watching *Top Gun* on DVD. That's right, *Top Gun*. How the fuck is this movie not going to appeal to football players? You got Tom Cruise flying jets and killing communists, banging hot blond chicks, and weeping over the dead body of his best buddy—what more could you want? It was Scott's favorite flick, still is to this day.

The night was typical for us back then. We weren't bad people. We were just young; we had fun and we did what we wanted. I stayed out late and drank a lot of beer. I skipped a bunch of class even as I took AP classes, and still somehow got A's. I did doughnuts on the football field in my used Ford one day, and the next day did wind sprints till I puked on the exact same field.

I was a football player in a small town in Ohio. People let me do whatever I wanted because I was great at playing a game. I was a punk, because no one ever told me no. Not my teachers, not my friends, not even my dad, who was still kind of figuring out how the whole single-fatherhood thing worked.

Then I met Kate.

At Scott's place, while all of us were living the life, drinking, laughing, watching Maverick and Goose kick ass and play beach volleyball, one person, this tiny little blond girl, was sitting in an office chair in the corner of the living room. Just spinning round and round and round, in her own tiny-little-blond-girl world.

My first reaction was extreme annoyance.

I didn't know this girl, had never met her before. Scott told me she was a freshman, the younger sister of some guy on the team. Whatever. I mean, didn't she understand where she was, who she was hanging out with, what was going on here? We were the *cool kids*. We were *football players*. We drank beer and cut school and one of our dads was out of town and we had complete access to this amazing house draped in leather and tapestries and we were having a party and she was supposed to be impressed, goddammit!

Then she kept doing it, kept spinning, and I decided it was kind of incredibly cute.

I stood up from the cracked black leather sofa, beer in hand, and swaggered over. I was Big Bank Hank. I was the shit, and if anyone could put a stop to this ridiculous, out-of-control cuteness, it was me.

"Hey," I said, in my most reasonable-yet-authoritative cool-guy-football-player voice. "Stop the spinning, okay? Come on over and hang out."

She looked up at me with the most incredible blue eyes and without a care in the entire world and said: "No. I'm bored and this is more fun."

And she kept spinning.

I was hooked. Someone was finally telling me no, and I was flustered. I actually didn't know what to say. I hadn't planned this far ahead. I didn't think I'd have to. Then it hit me.

"Hey, aren't you a cheerleader?" I asked.

"Yep," she said. She finally stopped spinning, looked me right in the eye.

Yes! I thought. *Now I had her!*

"Well, you know, I'm on the football team."

Now she laughed. I mean really laughed. Not a chuckle, or even a large giggle. We're talking a loud, full-bodied, tilt-your-head-all-the-way-back-and-let-it-all-the-fuck-out laugh.

"So?" she said. "Football *sucks!*"

Kate took another spin in the office chair, and now I wasn't just hooked. I was in love.

Kate was not. She liked me, she said, but she "just wanted to be friends." The five most dreaded words in the adolescent male vocabulary, and she knocked me over with them—me, a football player! For once, I was faced with a challenge that couldn't be solved by violently over-powering my opponent.

So I did the next best thing. I became a relentless romantic. I took her out to dinner, I took her out to movies, I bought her flowers, and I bought her more flowers. I single-handedly kept our local florist in business with all the red roses I bought for Kate. A dozen red roses, every single day for two straight weeks, waiting for her by her locker at school. I was in love, and I would not be stopped. Except by her.

We talked, we wrote each other notes, we spent almost all our time together, did all the things high school couples are supposed to do, but she still said no. She didn't want to date, she just wanted to be friends. And her girlfriends? They hated my guts. They thought I was just a big, arrogant, athletic douchebag, and they let me know it. Repeatedly.

Maybe I used to be that guy, but around Kate, I wasn't.

Kate thought that underneath all the shit, I was a good person. The arrogant me wasn't the real me. Football had made me that way.

And because she believed it, I believed it too. Slowly, over time, it became the truth. The humble, grounded, sensitive person I had been before football, before my mother died, before I had learned to tap into my anger so effectively started to come back.

Homecoming was around the corner. My small town in the middle of America celebrated the way all small American towns celebrate, with a parade. Kate and the rest of the high school cheerleaders would be marching in the parade. The football players would *not* be in the parade, but I decided that wasn't going to stop me.

In the middle of Main Street, as the marching band banged their drums and blew their horns, as the cheerleaders shook their pom-poms and the floats floated by, as the entire town watched and cheered and snapped photos, I sprinted out into the center of it all, holding two dozen roses and a final, desperate plea in my pathetic teenage heart.

I literally stopped the parade.

"Kate," I said, as her friends and the school and the whole damn town looked on. "Will you go to Homecoming with me?"

I got down on one knee and held out the roses.

I looked like a total fucking idiot. She absolutely loved it. Her jaw dropped. Her cheeks flushed red. Her eyes filled with tears, the good kind.

"Yes," she said, laughing. "Yes, I'll go!"

Yes. That was all I needed to hear.

MY SOPHOMORE YEAR OF COLLEGE. My second game as a starter for one of the top programs in the country. We were up against a shitty team from a smaller conference, one of those creampuff matchups that big teams schedule early in the season to pad their records.

And I was owning the defensive lineman I was playing against. Dominating him in a way I had never before experienced.

I wasn't just beating him, wasn't simply overpowering him. Over the course of the game, as I kept driving, hitting, pushing and driving, I had broken his will. His spirit, his ability to resist me, was simply gone. And we both knew it. I could actually see the exact moment it happened, the *exact* moment I crushed him. Something about his eyes. He looked at me as if to say, *Okay, you win, Johnny. Put me wherever you want. I give up.*

For the three hours of that game, I had stolen his soul. I controlled him. He was my puppet.

It reminded me a lot of what it felt like to play ball for a major college program. It reminded me a lot of my life.

Back in high school, football was fun. Just me and a few buddies goofing off with a worn-out old ball on a ratty, crabgrass-covered field. It was my escape from the real world, the way I managed the pain of my mom's death and felt like a normal, stupid kid for a few hours of the day. Football was simple and pure, and I loved it.

Not anymore. The game wasn't a game, it was a full-time job.

Nothing in my life was left to chance. Nothing. From the moment I stepped onto campus, every minute of every day was scheduled, choreographed, and controlled by the program. There was an entire team of people who existed only to make sure *our* team didn't fuck up. They made sure we ate the right things. That we lifted the right weights. That we went to the right classes at the right times in the right places. They definitely made sure we turned our homework in. And if we couldn't do it, they'd do it for us.

Kate was gone, at another school hundreds of miles away. She had wanted to join me, attend my college, even just live nearby, but I said no. It wasn't that I didn't love her, I did. But I wanted her to live her own life. I didn't want to be responsible for her happiness. Honestly, being a professional college football player was the only thing I had time for.

And it was slowly destroying me.

THAT SEMESTER I TOOK a psych course. I wrote a paper on head trauma in football. I almost wish I hadn't. I saw photos of brains covered in black, tarlike lesions that had built up over time, blocking synapses, causing mental disease, anxiety, Alzheimer's, memory loss.

As a player, I had always thought that as long as I didn't suffer any concussions I'd be fine. Now I learned that was bullshit. What mattered was the little stuff, the constant, low-level pounding my head had been taking for years. On every play, with every hit big or small, my brain was getting scrambled like an egg yolk inside its shell. I could go my whole career without suffering a major head injury. I could wear a state-of-the-art helmet, block with my arms and body instead of leading with my head, play the game as "safe" as possible. And it wouldn't matter. If I kept going, I'd be screwed.

At least that's what I wrote in my paper. In real life, I laughed it off. I was young, I was invincible.

At the end of the season, my buddy's parents came into town to catch one of our games. We all went out to dinner. Nothing fancy, nothing unusual. Just another night with some friends. As we were finishing up, we started coordinating plans for the evening.

"Johnny, what's your cell?" his dad asked me. "We can text you later."

I opened my mouth. And realized I had no fucking idea what my phone number was.

None.

I had had this same number since I was thirteen. I sat there, closing my eyes, peering back into the depths of my head and firing every single neuron in my brain, and that number just wasn't there anymore. It was gone.

I was nineteen years old. I wasn't invincible anymore.

I HEARD THE SOUND THROUGH all the shouting of the coaches, through the grunting of the players, through the smashing of our pads as we crashed into each other. I could hear it through all the noise.

Pop.

It didn't really hurt, which was surprising. But that sound, that noise, was the strangest, most terrifying thing I had ever heard.

Pop.

That's all it was. I heard it during one of our spring practices my sophomore year. I made an awkward cut on a drill, and that was it, it just happened. As soon as I heard that sound, I knew my junior season was pretty much over. I had torn my right MCL.

I worked my ass off to rehab my knee. I focused every last drop of rage and frustration I could find, and I worked harder than I ever had before. Sure, the game wasn't fun anymore, but the best way to motivate me is to piss me off. And that injury *really* pissed me off.

I was back to starting by the sixth game of my junior year. It was a fucking miracle, if I do say so myself.

The following game, I tore my left ACL.

Pop.

My entire junior season lasted a total of one and a half games.

BY MY SENIOR YEAR, I was completely healthy. That's when the strangest thing of all happened.

I couldn't find the anger.

It had happened slowly, gradually. In high school, I played every snap angry. It didn't matter if it was a big game, a little game, a practice, or a game of two-hand touch. I reached inside, tapped into that eternal reservoir of rage, and focused it into a laser beam on the field.

Then, my freshman year of college, it started to change. I could still get angry for the games, but practices? Fuck that. I just didn't have it in me. By my sophomore season, I was able to harness my anger for the big games. But forget about any of the smaller stuff. And by my senior year, I couldn't even get angry for the big games. The big plays, yes. Fourth and one. A goal-line stand. A last-minute drive.

But the rest of the time? I was just doing my job.

As I grew older, I started to understand myself better, and where my anger was coming from. I figured out how to express it in ways that didn't involve physically obliterating other people or myself.

I talked to my dad on the phone every day. I was closer to him than I was when we lived in the same house.

I got back together with Kate. After over a year apart, I realized what I had lost—my anchor, the one person who had grounded me. At the start of my junior year, in the depths of rehabbing my knee, I got into my old, piece-of-shit Ford and drove all night to her college. I showed up at her apartment and begged her to take me back. I couldn't get down on my hands and knees, but I still begged.

And even though I couldn't see my mother anymore, couldn't actually speak to her, I felt her presence.

Before all my games, during every national anthem, I'd picture her in the stands, watching me under one of her homemade blankets, and I'd feel her with me. Swear to God, sometimes a breeze would blow at just the right moment, and I'd know my mom was watching.

In a weird way, even as I lost my anger, I played better. Smarter, faster, more balanced.

After spending most of the previous year injured, my senior season was the best I had ever played. I was honored as one of the top five linemen in the country. I skipped the award ceremony, sure, but the plaque looked great in my dad's basement.

WHEN I GRADUATED, YOU PROBABLY think I was at a turning point, right?

That I agonized over whether or not to join the NFL. That I thought long and hard about all the permanent damage I was doing to my body and my mind, and I wondered if there was a point to it all now that I was at peace with losing my mom.

But I didn't. I never once considered quitting football. Silly me.

I had worked way too long and way too hard to give up now. I had practically killed myself. Hell, I *was* killing myself. I had done a job for the past four years without getting paid beyond free tuition and a tiny stipend to live off. It was time to get paid for *real*. And if I didn't have the same intense rage to drive me on the field, so what? I was still better than everybody else, right?

Then the talk started. People doubted me, saying I wouldn't be able to cut it in the pros. Scouts said I was too skinny, that I didn't have pro size. I was still six foot three and 270 pounds, and that growth spurt I was waiting for was never gonna happen. They also said I was injury-prone, that my stitched-together Frankenstein knees were just waiting to fall apart. I wouldn't even get drafted, they said. And I sure as hell was never gonna start.

Well, fuck that.

If anything could make me angry again, it was that kind of bullshit. I was gonna get drafted, I was gonna make a shit-ton of money, I was gonna be a starter in the NFL.

ALL I EVER HEARD MY first two years in the League was how much my team loved me. The head coach, the offensive-line coach, the general manager who had made a huge bet on me by picking me in the sixth round of the draft. All of them made me feel like I hadn't just found a team, hadn't just found a job, I had found a home. For the rest of my life.

"We really like you, Johnny . . ."

"You're the future of this team, Johnny . . ."

"For as long as you're in the NFL, we want you to play for us, Johnny . . ."

And I believed them.

The player I was backing up on the line was really good and really old. I mean, he was thirty-two! In lineman years, he was one foot from the grave, and no more than two years from retirement. I was the heir apparent. The team was training me, grooming me to take his place when he was ready to step down. They needed me just as much as I needed them.

So I worked like hell. I pushed myself. I paid my dues. I shrugged off the politics, ignored the way they treated me like a commodity, and I worked on getting bigger, better, stronger. I found anger in places inside me I didn't even know existed, and I let it loose on the field, practice after practice, drill after drill, rep after rep. And if I couldn't find the anger, I manufactured it, and I worked anyway. I made myself what my coaches wanted me to be.

All because I believed I was gonna get my shot. My first two years in the NFL, that's what I lived for. Until it was gone.

"THEY'RE GOING TO CUT YOU," Bernie said in a low voice.

"What the fuck are you talking about?"

"I'll explain the details later. They'll call within the hour. I'm sorry, Johnny."

He hung up the phone.

Part of me thought Bernie was just trying to fuck with me, but my job provided his income. He'd been my agent since I finished my college career. Believed in me when everyone else was questioning my size, my injuries, my ability to make it in the League. He'd been there since the beginning.

Within fifteen minutes, I got the call. The general manager wanted to talk to me, and there's only one reason the GM talks to a guy like me. It was over. It was over and there was nothing else to do.

Kate was visiting. We had been celebrating the end of my second successful season in the NFL. I looked at her, and I didn't have to say anything. She knew. She started crying. I gave her a kiss and left.

I drove to the facility in the truck I had bought two years ago with my signing bonus. Radio off. Phone off. Nothing but me and an awful, empty feeling. I thought about my mom and how I had failed her.

I walked into the building, stapled on a smile. I knocked on the GM's office door. He was sitting there, behind his big desk. He wouldn't look me in the eye.

"Johnny, I'm gonna be honest. I've never said this to anyone before. This may be the worst decision of my career. But I have to let you go."

This was the same man who had told me no less than a hundred times that I was his guy. That I would have a place on this team for the rest of my life.

"Why?" I said. "What happened? Did I do something wrong?"

He hesitated. Still avoiding my eyes.

"It's complicated," he said, sighing. "It is what it is."

I shook his hand. It was cold and limp.

"This isn't the end," I told him. "This isn't the end."

I walked out of his office. Minutes later, I called Bernie.

"Tell me," I said.

"They found another kid to take your place, a rookie," he said. "Kid sucks. But he's got the same agent as the offensive-line coach."

For a moment, I was silent.

"Are you fucking kidding me?"

"Look, I'm sorry," he said. "That's the business."

Ten years of work, of anger, injuries, and sacrifice—of football—meant nothing. I was disposable. I had been betrayed.

And I would never, ever forget it.

"Yeah," I said. "That's the business."

I KNEW WHAT I HAD to do.

My agent scrambled to find me another team. I went and worked out for three of them. I met with their general managers, with their coaches. I told them everything they wanted to hear. They told me everything I wanted to hear.

They gave me the Old Coaching Handshake that all old coaches give, squeezing my fingers like they wanted to break them off, pulling me in for a manly hug, and slapping me hard on the back so they could test just how strong I was, just how solid. Because we were all men here, weren't we? Real Men. Honest Men. Men of Integrity.

Men of Football.

They were all liars. But this time, I was lying too. And I was lying better than them. I didn't give a shit about them or their stupid game. I just wanted to take their money and do as little work for it as possible. Hey, that's the business, right?

After my last meeting with my now current team, I knew I had them. I wasn't starting out big, nothing was guaranteed. I wouldn't even start out at second string, I'd be third. But I got myself and my lesion-covered brain in the door. I got my shot. That was all I needed.

After the meeting, I called up my dad, the same man who had dropped me off on my first day of practice in the ninth grade, and who felt just as betrayed by the League as I did.

"Well?" he said. "Did we get 'em?"

"Yeah," I said. "I'm gonna be the Best NFL Backup Ever."

My Glorious Backup Dream™ was born.

Chapter 3

KNEE-DEEP IN IT

Day Two of camp. Fuck.

At 7:25 A.M., my cell's alarm goes off. I wake up in my hotel room, a standard, bland deal that the team puts us all up in. To save us the money, they say, but really it's to keep track of who's going out most. They call us guests; really, we're prisoners.

Like most men in America at this time of the morning, I have to take a shit, and this one is a beast. Usually, that would be no big deal. Plop down on the can, grab a magazine, let the animal out of its cage, and be done with it. In fact, for most of my life it's a pretty awesome way to start the day.

Not so much right now. In training camp, my shit is a huge fucking deal.

Now look, I know that sounds a little extreme. I'm a fucking backup! Who cares? But it's true. This dump is really, really important. Why? In training camp, my weight is really, really important. And I'm going to have to hold on to every last ounce of this shit if I'm gonna make my weight today.

That's right. This is how I'll get from my maxed-out weight of 279 to the NFL's magic number of 285. This is how I'll beat their test. By adding a few precious pounds of morning turd.

Ridiculous, right? Yeah. Dangerous? I'll let you know. But what would *you* do to qualify for a salary of $570,000, the League minimum for a third-year player like me? What would *you* sacrifice to add six pounds a day if each pound was worth almost $100,000? How far would *you* go to beat the NFL at its own game?

About a quarter of all NFL players have some sort of weight issue. Mostly it's little, ticky-tacky shit. I love hearing a guy who's 250 pounds bitch because the trainer told him he has to get up to 253. Yeah, my heart really goes out to you, buddy. All those dudes do is guzzle a bunch of the protein shakes the team pushes on us—seriously, almost all the teams have a deal with some kind of protein supplier, and they practically force the artificial chocolaty goo down our throats—and they're good to go for their weigh-in.

But a few of us need to go to extremes. In training camp last year, I met a player who was six foot seven and 370 pounds, with a full gold grille in his mouth that probably added an extra five pounds just for good measure. To quote Chris Farley, he had what doctors would've called "a little bit of a weight problem." His solution? Before every weigh-in, he'd put on two or three layers of sweatshirts and -pants and sit in the sauna three straight hours, as if he could sweat his fat out right through his pores. Not only did it barely put a dent in his weight, but when he took the League's drug test, the only piss he could squirt into the cup was a deep-brown tarlike sludge with hints of red in it.

Yes, he actually showed me the piss, and, no, he did not make the team.

Yesterday, after an afternoon of training, I weighed in at 272 pounds. Fuck. That's thirteen pounds under. That's a fail and a "fuck you, go home." So last night, I got to my room and ate. And ate. And ate. So much chicken and rice it might be illegal. The staples of my high-everything diet.

When I wake up, my colon feels like it's going to explode, like there's a midget punching me in the gut with every step. But I hold that little man in. He's not going anywhere.

And guess what? Before I can weigh in, I need to eat some more. So I head to the team cafeteria for breakfast. I walk up to the big double doors and swing them open and guess who's sitting there, all by himself, just watching and waiting?

The head coach. Jack.

He's got a playbook in front of him, pen in his hand, all to make it look like he's busy working on plays, but he's not. He's looking directly at the door, at every single one of his players as they walk in to get their food. He's there to size us up, see if we're worthy of his presence. One by one.

He stares right through me. Past me, actually. Those sharp black eyes of his already searching for the next player, telling me I don't exist.

I grab my breakfast. Whole-grain pancakes. Stacks and stacks of them. Covered in syrup and brown sugar. The sight of it makes me want to puke.

The cafeteria is almost full. Players at different positions have different daily schedules, but we all eat breakfast at the same time. Remember your high school cafeteria, with all the different cliques separated and sitting at their own tables? That's what this is like—different positions tend to stick together. So there's a table of offensive linemen, a table of defensive linemen, a table of skill players, the receivers and corners and safeties, and so on. It also just so happens that a lot of guys within a given position tend to be of the same race. Offensive linemen trend white, defensive linemen trend black, and skill players don't trend at all—they're all black.

Now is it coincidence that somehow black guys and white guys always seem to end up with each other? How should I know, I'm no sociologist. But sometimes I'll notice white D linemen mysteriously finding their way to the O-line table, and black O linemen subtly edging their way to the skill table. Completely random, I'm sure.

Then of course you got the special teams guys, who are always white but are really a race all to themselves. I walk by their table, and they're deeply engaged in one of their typical conversations.

"Hey, you think you can scream so loud you pass out?" Ollie the kicker says.

"I don't know, I never tried!" replies Greg the punter.

"Count of three, okay?" Ollie asks.

"Okay!" Greg says.

"One-two-three-SCREAM!"

Not a peep from either of them.

"Wait, why didn't you scream?" Greg asks.

"I don't know," Ollie says. "I changed my mind."

God bless them. Usually I would stop and say hello, but not this morning. This morning, I'm on a mission.

I sit at a table by myself and start cramming the pancakes in my mouth, one bite after another, forcing it down my throat as I feel the pressure inside me building.

Then, just when I'm about to pop, just when it feels like I might actually, physically explode from the pressure, I calmly leave the cafeteria—and I straight up *sprint* to that motherfucking locker room. Throw open my locker, strip off my clothes—and I'm still not done yet. Nope.

Before I step on that scale, I guzzle water.

One bottle. Twenty ounces.

Two bottles—holy fuck, I think I might vomit—another twenty ounces.

And . . . three. Three full bottles of water.

And I finally, finally, get on the scale. I pinch my cheeks to hold everything in.

And I'm 284 pounds. Seriously, I'm not joking. After all that, after all that eating and guzzling and not shitting, I only make it up to 284.

It's not a surprise. I've done this a hundred times before, at hundreds of other weigh-ins as a professional and a college player, and I almost never get past 284. Okay, maybe if I have a huge, *huge* dinner the night before, I might reach 285. But I usually fall short. Just shy of 285, that magic, evil fucking number.

Danny the assistant trainer looks at me, nods, and punches in some numbers on his stupid iPad. He says nothing. I wish he'd at least give me a high five; I just killed myself for that number. But for all I know, the coaches will never even read Danny's report. For all I know, his finger slipped and he typed 184 instead of 284. For all I know, the GM decided to cut me last night while I sucked down that third chicken breast.

Maybe I should start paying Danny off.

I run the short distance to the bathroom. It's still early in the morning, so the rows of stalls are all empty, and it isn't hard to find one that's pretty clean. I sit down on the toilet. My shrine. It's quiet and peaceful, serene, really.

I unleash the beast. I literally shit an entire five pounds out of a very, very small hole in my ass. When I'm done, I can actually feel the difference in my body. I'm lighter. I'm faster. I can move more easily. I'm a whole new person.

Life is good. Next week, I'll do it all over again.

"WHAT THE HELL AM I doing here, man?" Coulter says. "I should be back home, you know? Being a father to my kids."

We're in the training room, soaking in the hot tub. Me, Paulson, Coulter, who's a starter on the O line, and a linebacker with dreads who I don't know. Yeah, it's a big tub.

It might sound relaxing, but it's not. Just a ten-minute soak to warm up our joints before we work out and practice this afternoon. That's right. No more bureaucratic shit, no more HR sensitivity meeting BS. We do what we came here to do. Play football, make the team, fight for our professional lives.

Coulter's words hang there for a little. Coulter's got big sideburns and a scraggly goatee, and he's wearing a baseball cap. Kind of looks like a biker. None of us says anything. I look at Paulson, my competition. His face is blank. Finally Coulter laughs.

"Sorry," he says. "I don't want you guys to stoop to my level."

The funny thing is, I thought *I* was the only one who felt that way. Who just wanted out. But suddenly I notice that the linebacker with dreads is nodding. So is Paulson.

"I feel ya, Coulter," Paulson says. "I feel the same way a lot of the time."

I almost say something. Almost. But I don't trust anyone. Any of these guys could rat me out to the coaches. I'll let them feel sorry for themselves, dwell on shit they can't control. I need to keep pushing.

THE PLAYERS SHUFFLE THROUGH the practice field's iron gate, flanked on either side by, you guessed it, our logo. You probably heard that some teams practice at local colleges and other random locations during camp. Not us. We're staying at our complex in the heart of our big, messy all-American city. That's three and a half fields of the greenest, best-watered grass you've ever seen, all surrounded by thick evergreens and a twelve-foot-high chain-link fence to keep the pesky masses out and the highly paid prisoners in.

The sun is hot, the humidity is hotter, and the grime in the air has already left a nice little coat in my mouth. Today is helmets only, no pads, which sounds easy but just means I'll be playing across from a mean 340-pound D lineman with almost nothing to protect me.

I stand on the sidelines next to the rest of the scrubs waiting as the starters take their snaps. All I can do is watch. The first string gets twenty-four plays. The second string gets sixteen. We, the third string, get *eight* total plays. Four sets of two plays each.

That's eight plays to work out the rust from the off-season, eight plays to learn how to run a brand-new offense. Eight plays to do something so spectacular that even these coaches who don't give a shit about us will be forced to notice.

And we *suck*. Literally, by definition, the threes are the worst players on the team.

For some positions, that might not matter. But for the offensive line, it means everything. We actually *need* one another to be good. Our whole job is to work together, a moving, thinking, adapting wall that protects our quarterback and creates space for our running back to run. If there's a crack in that wall—if even one guy misses a block or goes in the wrong direction—then the whole thing comes tumbling down, and we all look bad.

Right now, standing on the sideline, I'm worried about our cornerstone. He's our center, a chubby-cheeked, 305-pound rookie named Wilton, and he looks absolutely shattered.

As our center, Wilton is supposed to be our leader on the field, the one in charge of reading the defense and telling the rest of us what to do. That means before every play, he's gotta look at the defense, analyze it to figure out exactly what they're gonna do and how we're gonna counter it, while also executing our own play at the exact same time. Then he has to tell all of us the plan in this loud, constantly changing environment, before he finally snaps the ball to the quarterback.

That's a lot of shit. And yes, it gets better. Jack is a fanatic when it comes to pace. Always wants us to move faster. So for *all* that shit—getting the play, reading the defense, shouting the plan, snapping the ball, all of it—Wilton's got exactly eighteen seconds. That's it. Eighteen seconds, every single play.

And Wilton currently looks absolutely terrified. He's standing off to the side, away from the group, shifting on his feet, kind of mumbling to himself. Our "leader" reeks of fear. And we're almost up. I sigh, put on my friendliest smile—hey, I can be friendly when necessary—and head over.

"Hey honey-p—"

And I can't even finish my disarming greeting, the guy just starts rambling.

"Man," he whispers. "Did you hear what they said to me? Did you? Fuck! Looks like my ship has sailed. Yep, my ship has most definitely sailed."

I have no clue what the fuck he's talking about.

"Relax, baby," I say. "Have fun. It's a game."

I punch him on the shoulder, and Wilton looks like he's gonna puke. For all I know, he already has.

But what the fuck can I do? I'm not the center, I'm the left guard. My job is to stand to his left and do what he says. Wilton leads, I follow.

The threes are finally up. We jog onto the field for our first two plays. Not only are the coaches there, Jack, Lopez, and the rest, but so is the general manager, Lowry, the guy who hired us all. Tall, thin, blond, and a total pompous asshole. I shit you not, he's standing on a raised platform at the edge of the field, overlooking us all like a god, pondering which one of us he'll kill off first.

That creates a shitload of pressure on everyone, players *and* coaches.

And you know what? For our first set, we're not horrible. So far we're all moving together, not exactly a unit, still a ton of kinks, but I give a little nudge to the tackle who's next to me to get him to go the right way, a small nod to Wilton to let him know he's doing an okay job, and we're getting through it. Not exactly a wall, more like a pretty strong net.

The first and second teams take their turn, then we're up again. Our second set of two plays. We line up. I can feel the eyes on us. Jack is sweating just as bad as we are, his pale face turning red in the sun.

The whistle blows and the clock starts, the seconds tick away—18, 17—

Wilton glances at the sideline—16—

The coordinator signals him the play—15, 14—

I'm scanning the defense—14, 13—seconds ticking—what direction's the rush coming from? What pass protection?—11, ticking, 10—A 3-2 dime look? A 3-3-5 nickel?—10, ticking, 9, ticking—something weird, something normal?—ticking, 8—something that looks normal but is really weird?—7, 6—and I see it, I make the read—

6—And it's *simple*! Let's *do* this! 5—

And Wilton shouts the call—4 ticking, 3 ticking—

"Ram 51!"

Wait—What??!—Fuck!

2—and Wilton snaps the ball—1—

And we all go in completely the wrong direction.

Right instead of left, *away* from the attacking defensive line. Well, all of us except Wilton, who goes left. It's not our fault, we did exactly what he told us. "Ram" is the signal for "right"; "Lion" is the signal for "left." Wilton fucked up. If we were playing in pads, our quarterback would've been crushed nose-deep in the turf.

The play's not even dead yet, guys still scrambling, but I grab Wilton by the jersey. All I'm thinking is *This is my line, this is my problem. This rookie needs my help.*

"Hey man, you wanna call 'Lion,' on that play, not 'Ram,' okay?" I say.

Wilton looks at me like I'm fucking crazy. "See, Lion's got an 'L' in it for left so—"

Suddenly I hear the whistle blow. Shit. *Now* the play is dead.

"Hey! *Hey!*"

I turn around. It's Jack. The coach.

"What the fuck was that? Back to the line! We got another play!"

"I was just telling him the right call," I say.

"What?"

"I was just telling him the right call on the play."

Jack is now also looking at me like I'm fucking crazy.

"You don't correct him, okay? I watch the tape later, and *I* correct him."

He starts to turn around. Probably any sane human being would know to shut up at this point. Hell, they probably would've never said a thing in the first place, especially with Lowry, the general manager, watching. Who knows? Maybe I am fucking crazy.

"But it screwed up the whole play!" I shout.

He stops, turns, stares right at me. Not through me. At me. Talks real slow, as if I don't understand basic English.

"I. Watch. The tape. Later. And I. Correct him. Got it?"

He walks away, but probably not fast enough to miss me rolling my eyes. Something I'm really good at. If I'm really lucky, maybe Lowry caught it too.

A big part of what makes me such a good offensive lineman is my intelligence. I'm smart, I pick shit up quick, I'm decisive. I'm always right and I know I'm always right and I love being always right. Well, that doesn't always go over so well with coaches. If they criticize you, you're supposed to take it. They want you subservient. "Yes, sir! Thank you, sir! You're welcome, sir! Fuck me over again, sir!"

Yeah, I'm not so good at that.

In the past, in college and high school, I was so important to my team that being a smart-ass didn't really matter. I could hit a coach with an amazingly witty comeback, and he just had to accept me for the lovable asshole I was. But the NFL is different. Why would coaches or GMs put up with a guy who's completely replaceable? They don't even know my name! Who the hell needs a nameless asshole? Even if he is a genius?

I head back to the line for the fifth of our eight total plays. I look over to get the call from the sideline, just in time to see Jack having a little chat with Lopez, the offensive-line coach. I see Lopez mouth two little words: "Johnny. Anonymous."

So I guess they know my name now.

"FUCK THIS," I SAY. "I am *this close* to packing my bags and going home."

I'm back at the hotel after the very long day, talking to Kate on the phone. After all these years, she's still blond, smart, petite, and calls me on my shit.

"All right," she says. "So why don't you?"

Oh, and she still wants me to quit football.

"What?" I ask, even though I already know.

"Why don't you just come home if it's really so bad?"

"I don't know."

The funny thing is, packing my stuff and leaving would really be pretty damn easy on a purely logistical level. Most of my shit—seriously, most of the stuff I own in the world—is packed in my Durango right now. Honestly, what's the point of unloading if I could get cut? Since I finished college my car's actually been the closest thing I've had to a permanent home. I take it with me wherever I go, wherever they send me, always ready to pack or unpack, always completely liquid. My Liquid Life.

"Think about it, Johnny," she says. "You don't even *like* football. You say it all the time. So what are you there for? What's the point?"

"Well, the money is pretty damn good," I say.

"So the money is good," she says. "Is that really even important?"

"Yes, I hate to break it to you, Kate, but money is actually pretty important in the world."

She sighs, exasperated. Man, I can be obnoxious sometimes, can't I? For some reason, she takes it, and I love her for it.

"But you can make money other ways," she says. "Do you know how lazy people are out here in the real world? If I'm tired one day, I just come in and Instagram for a few hours. You work, like, fifty times harder than any of us."

She works at a bank, which tells you something about banks. I laugh, relax a little. She always has a way of calming me down.

And honestly? I'm starting to wonder myself. Is all this garbage worth it, just to be the Best NFL Backup Ever™? This is the first time I've laughed all week. Because of my girlfriend.

"Yeah," I say. "Maybe you're right."

"So just do it!" she says, the excitement rising in her voice. "You'll be happier! You can stop dealing with all these idiots, and you can spend time with me. That would be pretty nice, wouldn't it?"

"Well," I say chuckling, "you can also be an idiot sometimes."

She laughs.

"Ha-ha. I knew the sincerity wouldn't last."

"Oh, come on!" I say. "You don't love me because I'm sincere!"

"Yeah?" she says. "Why do I love you again?"

"Because . . . I'm awesome?"

"Oh right!" she says. "How could I forget."

"Listen," I say, "I gotta go."

"Why?"

"Because my arm is getting tired."

"Shut up."

"It's true! You try holding up a phone with such a heavy arm! It's not easy!"

"Fine," she says. "Bye."

"Wait," I say. "I love you?"

She hesitates, but just for a second.

"I love you too."

THE NEXT MORNING I GO to breakfast at the cafeteria to load up. Jack is there again, sitting right by the door, just like yesterday. Except this time, he looks right at me.

I try to ignore him, try to stare ahead, push through to the counter to grab my fucking whole-grain pancakes, but it's no good. I can sense his eyes staring at me. He packs everything into them, all his anger, all his contempt. It's like he's boring into my soul, judging me, ripping me apart.

I turn my head, make eye contact with him for one split second, try to show him I don't give a fuck what he thinks—right before he looks away, down at that goddamn playbook. He even writes something down.

I grab my pancakes, fuck the syrup and brown sugar. I sigh, try to remember what Kate said, what I was thinking just last night, that I'm better than football, that I don't need it anyway. And I *know* this, or at least I should.

But it's no good, they got me. It's like I'm trapped, stuck, knee-deep in all the shit that's currently building up in my bowels.

I look around for a place to sit in the crowded cafeteria. The white guy table is all full, so I take the last seat at the black guy table. Swear to God, five minutes later they all get up and leave; most of them haven't even finished eating yet.

I eat the rest of my breakfast alone.

"HEY, SO THIS GIRL ON Tinder says her three favorite things are 'whiskey, beer, and burgers,' " says Antonne, our starting center. "What should I say my three favorite things are?"

It's the morning offensive-line meeting, which comes right after our offense meeting, which comes after the full team meeting. I swear, we have more damn meetings than most lawyers. This one is just the O linemen, about fifteen guys—Antonne, Jeb, Teddy, Paulson, everyone. We're waiting on our position coach, Lopez, so naturally we're discussing some profound philosophical issues.

"Your drunk ass?" says Williams, another starter, and someone who's had his own issues with alcohol. "They probably be like 'Courvoisier, Crown, and Hennessy.' "

"No, wait, wait, I got it!" Teddy shouts, a giant grin on his face. "Football, football, and football!"

As the leader of the line, Antonne takes his job very seriously, he even talks blocking technique over lunch. He's also what's commonly referred to as a "man whore." Like most of us, he's a long way from home. He lives by himself in an apartment he rents, and he doesn't have any real friends in the city, just work buddies, so he fills his time with drinking, fucking, and analyzing blitz packages.

"Fuck all y'all," Antonne says. "This is serious shit here!"

He starts typing.

"I'm putting 'ass, tits, and pussy.' "

The room busts out laughing.

"All I know is y'all better shut the hell up before I kill all you fuckers," Jeb the Old Vet growls from the back, where he's trying to nap. Antonne may be the line's leader, but Jeb is a multiyear Pro Bowler, so he can say whatever the fuck he wants.

The door swings open and Lopez finally walks in, his big belly swaying; he's chewing gum as always. Now Jack might be the head coach, but Lopez—or "Lo," as we all call him—is *our* coach, the guy directly responsible for the O line and who makes the cut. He's the gatekeeper's gatekeeper, so I figure it's time to make a good impression.

"Hey, Lo," I call out. "You ever try Tinder? Or you a match.com guy?"

Lopez stops chewing and glares at me.

"You always got something smart to say, don't you, Johnny?" he says. "Well, I don't have time for that shit. I'm here to work."

And I finally figure this guy out.

There are two kinds of coaches: the kind who actually played the game at the highest level, and the kind who really wish they had. The first kind of coach tends to be confident, comfortable in his own skin. He's succeeded on the field, so he doesn't have anything to prove to the guys he's coaching. The players know that deep down, he's one of them. So when he coaches, he doesn't tear guys down, he's positive, he builds them up and makes them better. That doesn't mean he's not tough; if anything, it's the exact opposite. He's tough enough to work with a bunch of big, alpha personalities, get his ideas across and not feel threatened.

Then you got the kind of coach who didn't make it to the NFL. Most of these guys played ball somewhere, high school, maybe even a small college, so they've got hands-on experience. But at a certain point, they couldn't hack it, so instead they got into coaching. Now don't get me wrong—just because they couldn't play doesn't mean they don't know football. Some of them are pretty smart guys. But they all got this chip on their shoulder, this insecurity, this need to show all the players—guys who frankly are more successful than they ever were—who's in charge. So they yell, they humiliate guys on the field. Instead of *being* tough, these guys *act* tough. And it's irritating as shit.

Lopez is *that* kind of coach.

And he's got more to prove than most. This is his first year in the NFL. Maybe he used to be a big deal coaching in college, but in the NFL, the only thing that matters is what you've done in the NFL. All it takes is one season not making the play-offs or failing to live up to expectations, and you're out of there. Hey, the general manager and head coach need *someone* to blame, and it's damn well not gonna be themselves. Tag, Mr. First-Year Assistant Coach. You're it.

Not only that, but a brand-new assistant's gotta work just as hard to impress *us*, the players. Hold up, you say. He's the coach! Don't the players have to do everything he says? Sure, if you're a second- or third-string guy like me and your job hangs in the balance. But the starters? Guys with multiyear contracts like Jeb and Antonne make twenty times more money than Lopez does. They'll all be around no matter what happens, and they all have their own ways of doing shit. Any new coach is gonna have to convince *them* that his way is better. If he doesn't, they simply won't work as hard for him. They'll almost never call the coach out to his face—don't want the general manager seeing that. But they'll undermine him in other ways: talking shit behind his back, turning the other players against him, slacking off during drills, or simply ignoring his orders altogether. I've seen players give a coach the silent treatment for weeks—the coach tries to pull the guy aside, the guy just walks right by like he doesn't even exist. So you tell me who's really in charge—the starters, or the first-year coach coming right out of college?

Somewhere down deep inside, Lopez knows that; he feels that power imbalance, and he needs to demonstrate his authority somehow, with someone. And after yesterday's practice, I gave him the perfect target.

"All right, Johnny," he says, pointing up at the giant projection screen. "What exactly is happening here."

Big fucking surprise—he's playing the series I got yelled at for yesterday. Now, watching tape of myself is never easy for me. I'm a perfectionist, so when I see proof that I'm not, it's just plain painful. But to get yelled at for this play? Something that wasn't even my fault, and in front of all these guys I barely even know? That's just bullshit.

"Well," I say, watching the action unfold on the screen, "that right there is me hearing the call, Ram 51, and going right, just like I was supposed to."

I look at the other guys on the third string—I mean, they went right too, all of them except Wilton, the center—but they don't want any part of this. It's just the third day of camp, for fuck's sake. They're all very mysteriously looking anywhere but at me.

Paulson, on the other hand—the left guard who's on the second string, the guy I gotta beat out for a spot—is on the other side of the room, staring right at me. The worse I do, the better it is for him.

"That's what you see, huh?" Lopez says.

"Yes. That is what I see."

"What about here?"

He uses the laser pointer to focus on the center, Wilton, going left. I glance over at the kid real quick—he's sitting right there with all of us—and yet again he looks terrified. I sigh.

"I don't know what happens there."

"Oh!" Lopez says, looking all surprised. "You don't know."

Lopez puzzles over this for a second, then—

"Wilton!"

Wilton's eyes open wide.

"Yeah?" Wilton says.

"What happened here?"

Wilton fumbles with his pen awkwardly. How did someone so constantly terrified even make it on his high school team?

"Um, I thought I said 'lion.' "

"*You said 'lion'!*" Lopez says, turning to me accusingly. "Johnny, he called '*lion*,' but you went *right*!"

Fuck, I should've known the punk would throw me under the bus.

"Look," I start to say. "Everyone else—"

"Johnny, you gotta be more attentive!"

Remember how I said before that I'm good at rolling my eyes? Actually, I'm the *master* of rolling my eyes. No one does it better than me. But the eye roll I give Lopez when he says this is a work of art, an eyeball Picasso, even for me.

"What?" I say. "Attentive??"

You don't care, I try to tell myself. *Remember? You don't care.* I mean, "attentive"? Who even uses that word!

Except I do care. And it sucks.

"You're not attentive enough!" Lopez is saying, shouting, now. "Shit moves fast! If you don't focus and pay attention to everything around you in a big game situation, the whole line is fucked."

"He said 'Ram'! I heard what he said! I did what he said!"

"In a big game situation, you have to be more attentive."

"Lo, *everyone* except him went right. Everyone!"

I look around, and "everyone" just stares directly at their shoes. You know that movie *Zoolander*? There's this part where everyone is acting so stupid, so absolutely dumb, that Will Ferrell is, like, "I feel like I'm taking crazy pills here!" Well, right now I'm taking crazy pills. And Lopez just keeps feeding them to me.

"Arguing won't get you anything," he says. "You just gotta be more attentive."

What can I do? Finally I just shrug and start laughing. All the other linemen are watching me—Paulson, Antonne, Jeb, Teddy, all the guys who have a job that could be mine. And I just laugh. But it doesn't feel good, this laugh. It doesn't feel right.

"Ho-kay!" I say. "You win. I will be more attentive."

Lopez looks at me for a second.

"Good," he says.

Practice comes right after the meeting. I'm hoping I'm past all this nonsense. I'm wrong.

Completely out of the blue, I'm not even playing yet, just waiting my turn for the one-on-one drills, Lopez walks over to me, his big gut sticking out as usual, and says, "Johnny, you gotta be more attentive."

I just laugh, pat him on the back, and walk away. It's all I can do.

AFTER PRACTICE, I HAVE my second offensive-line meeting. The last thing of the day. I get to the meeting room and all I'm thinking about are my bed and my Durango and how it's already packed and ready to go.

I've made up my mind. If I get cut—really *when* I get cut—I'm done. I'm going back to Ohio, back to my girlfriend and my family and my friends, and I'll find a sales job or something where I can just fuck around on the Internet all day if I want to, and I'm done with football, done with the NFL, once and for all.

Why should I keep trying? What do I really have to prove? That I'm "better" than a bunch of asshole coaches? That I can "beat" a mindless system that only cares about money? So what if I don't live up to their bullshit standards? It's a paycheck, a dumb game that takes over people's lives. *Other* people's lives, not mine.

It's kind of a relief, actually. Freeing, knowing I'm not gonna have to put up with this bullshit anymore. That I can just get on with the rest of my life. Fuck it.

I take a look around the meeting room. Coach Lopez isn't there yet, and some of the guys are still shuffling in. I'm not the only one who's tired. In the back corner I spot Paulson, my so-called competition at left guard who's basically already won. Yeah, he had the groin injury last year, but so far he's held up fine, and, besides, at this point the guy could be a paraplegic and the coaches would take him over me.

Up to this point, I've completely avoided him. It's easier to beat someone when you don't really know them. But I have met him before, back in college, when he was playing for our rivals and perennial douchebags, USC. He's a couple years older than me, and whenever I talked to him he seemed like a nice enough guy. If I'm gonna lose out to anyone, might as well be him, right?

I grab the seat next to him. He's reading something.

"What you got there, baby?"

The pet name doesn't phase him. He shows me the cover. Some paperback with aliens or some shit.

"*Typhon Pact: Plagues of Night,*" he says, like I should know what he's talking about. When he sees I don't: "It's a *Star Trek* book. You know, *Star Trek?*"

Oh yeah, I saw the movie. Based on the look of his book, I can tell he's read it a few million times. There's at least one Likable Nerd like Paulson on every team. Some of them are gamers, some of them are comic book geeks, some of them are Trekkies. A guy I know on the Chargers goes to the San Diego Comic-Con every year—and he's always joined by other NFL fanboys from all over the country, all there to celebrate their dorkhood together. Thank God it's during the off-season.

"Oh!" I say. "Well then! A fantasy guy, huh?"

"Sci-fi," he says. "Not fantasy. Big difference. I'm not into elves. That shit is stupid."

I crack up.

"Right, sorry, I should've known. Looks like you've read that one a bunch."

"Yeah," he says. "It's my favorite book. That and the Bible."

Funny enough, the Bible part doesn't surprise me. A ton of players are big-time into Christianity. Black guys like Paulson and born-again white guys, especially from the South. They all grew up with it; it's part of their identities. They pray together before games, they carry around Bible verses with them on little cards. Almost every team sponsors a Bible study the night before games, sometimes led by a player or coach, sometimes led by a preacher they bring in.

"*Star Trek* and Jesus have a lot to teach you," Paulson says, dead serious. "It's all about good and evil and life."

"All right," I say, trying as hard as I can to respect that. "I can respect that."

"What," he says, kind of defensive. "What do you do?"

"What do you mean, 'What do I do?' "

"You don't read," he says. "So what do you do?"

"I don't know," I say, thinking about it. "I guess I don't do anything."

There is something, actually. But I don't want to tell him about it. It's personal, my own thing. He starts laughing.

"Man, you are fucking weird!"

"I'm fucking weird?" I say, laughing. "You're reading *Star Trek*!"

You see how fucked up this business is? If I want any shot at making this team, I have to want this guy, this gigantic, Klingon-loving dork, to fail. I mean, gimme a fucking break.

Lopez walks in, the screen flickers on.

"Yo," Paulson whispers. "Don't let what Lo says bug you. He's just giving you shit. It's not a big deal. Fuck it."

Yeah, I think. *Exactly. Fuck it.*

OUR FIRST DAY OFF. FINALLY. Enough time, enough energy to do exactly what it was I was so hesitant to tell Paulson about. Take a trip to the mall.

Yes, the mall.

Look, football players are human, more or less, and humans need to let off steam. Everyone's got their thing. A ton of the guys play video games. My roommate at my last team? I'd leave our place on a weekend morning while he was playing *Grand Theft Auto,* come back after dinner, and he'd still be sitting there, playing the same game and stuck at the exact same level. He didn't even care about moving forward, he just liked killing people, over and over and over again.

Then a bunch of other guys, especially receivers and corners (yep, you politically correct bastards out there, I'm talking about the black guys), just go out clubbing. Every. Night. How they manage to practice and play the next day, I have no fucking clue. Some guys are just insanely physically gifted, and yeah, I'm a tiny bit jealous.

And some guys, honestly, all they ever—ever—do is think and talk about football. Breakfast, they're talking about block techniques. Lunch, they're talking about protection schemes. Dinner, they might get crazy and talk about block techniques *and* protection schemes.

Me? I go for walks in the mall.

My dad thinks it has to do with my mom. And yeah, he's probably right. But I could've done other things to remind me of her too. Hell, I could sit in my hotel room making flower arrangements if I really wanted. It'd be our little secret, just you and me.

Now that I'm older, there's just something about the mall. Something that kind of clears my mind. Just a whole bunch of regular, normal people going about their lives. No massive dudes smashing into you. No red-faced coaches screaming at you. No fans scraping and scrambling for your autograph. Just a whole lot of space for me to not care about football.

I really lucked out in finding this mall. Not only is it close to my hotel, it's actually right across the road. Just a short walk through the filthy city street to those polished, fake-marble floors. I head over in the middle of the afternoon. It's a weekday—they give us days off whenever the fuck they want—so the place isn't too crowded. All three levels almost to myself. Perfect.

I walk down one wing, then another, then another, hands in my pockets, looking at the stores but not really seeing any of them. I'm in jeans and a shirt, no team jersey, no cap, no nothing, as anonymously normal as a six-foot-three, 279-pound lineman can be. I check out some of the fancy stores. Ralph Lauren, Coach, Gucci. Fuck that. Way too expensive.

Finally I stop inside a J.Crew, interrupt some flirting teenage clerks, and buy three collared short-sleeve shirts and one pair of khaki shorts, the biggest size I can find. For fun I toss in a pair of slacks and a long-sleeved button-down. The ideal business casual uniform, just like if I had a normal job.

It's evening now, starting to get dark.

I stop in the middle of the mall, sit down on one of the benches, drop my bags of J.Crew at my feet, and stare at the last few stragglers as they pass by.

A mom pushing her crying kid in a stroller. A black dude wearing a fedora. A couple chicks in white tank tops, their thin arms covered in ink.

My mind is empty, not a single thought, no ideas, no memories, no judgments. It's heaven.

I close my eyes, and I'm gone. When I wake up, there's an old guy in a Hawaiian shirt sitting there, looking at me.

"Ten o'clock," he says. "Mall's closing."

I blink, take a deep breath, stand up and stretch. It's just me and him and a couple security guys locking up. I've been out for forty-five minutes. It felt like five.

"Yeah," I say. "Thanks."

I pick up my collared shirts and khaki shorts, and I walk back to my hotel room.

DAY FOUR OF CAMP STARTS with more of the same. Eating a ton of food in the cafeteria, getting the soul-sucking evil eye from Jack, and then more garbage from potbellied Lopez. This time the guy doesn't even wait till the offensive-line meeting. He finds me in the general team meeting, stops at my seat as he's walking up to the front, leans down, and says, "Johnny, you gotta be more attentive!"

I shit you not. It's been a whole day, and he still hasn't let it go. He doesn't even lower his voice—probably because he's worried I'm not being "attentive" enough—so everyone hears him, guys who aren't even on the offense! And I'll admit it, I kinda lost it. I stand up so I'm towering over him, and I talk real slow, landing hard on every single word so there's no mistaking anything I say.

"*I. Am. Attentive.* I can't help another player if he can't help himself."

That's what I say with my mouth. With my eyes, I'm saying, "Back. The. Fuck. Off."

Lopez looks at me a second, then turns and joins the other coaches at the front of the room. I sit back down, don't even blink an eye.

The first round of player cuts take place right after our first preseason game. That's eleven days from now. But now I'm figuring maybe I get real ambitious about this thing. Maybe I make them hate my guts so much they actually toss me *early*. Hell, I could set a new record for just how fast someone gets dumped from a team! And then it's an hour and twenty minutes later and we're in the middle of practice and Paulson goes ahead and reinjures his groin.

And everything changes. Just like that.

I'm standing there with the other bottom dwellers watching the twos play, then Paulson kind of shuffles off the field—maybe he looks a little stiff, I'm not even sure, he walks by me, doesn't say a word—then Lopez shouts, "Johnny, get in!" And the next thing I know, there I am, out in the field, playing with the second team.

And it feels good.

When Paulson got injured, the second string had just finished its third play of the day. That means I have thirteen reps left to somehow erase all the shit that's built up over the last three days. Just thirteen reps. On the third string, as you know, we get eight.

Thirteen is a gift.

There's no time to think, no time to process or analyze what just happened. All I can do right now is play. And for the very first time since I got here, I'm not thinking about not caring—I'm just not caring. I'm having fun. The guys I'm playing with aren't terrified rookies like Wilton, they're veterans like Teddy. Our leader, the second-string center, is solid, nothing special, but he doesn't have to be special. He could make the wrong call, and these guys would still go the right way. They've all been here before, they know what to expect, how to react, how to move, and we move together seamlessly.

Fuck forming a wall, we're a big, fat, beefy ballet.

Line up, Read the D, Get the Call, Go—

Line up, Read the D, Get the Call, Go—

It's so much fun I'm laughing. Not laughing because everyone's nuts, not even laughing at anything or anyone, just laughing because this feels easy, it feels right. Fuck being attentive, I'm just having fun.

Teddy is lined up to my left, and he's slumping. He's playing, but his mind isn't there, probably back in the islands with his kids. I just laugh.

"Hey, baby, lighten up!" I say. "Fuck it!"

He blinks, grins, and says, "Hell yeah."

Line up Read the D Get the Call Go—Line up Read the D Get the Call Go—and on and on and on and on.

And now that I don't have to worry about the little mistakes the other guys on my line might make, I can focus on my *own* game.

The three tech—the defensive lineman who comes directly at me—has never played against me before, and he's fucking huge, six foot four, 320 pounds. But they're all huge, and I've handled them my entire life.

I punch, I press, I angle my body to get leverage. I move my feet, he moves his, I get into position faster every time, I block him every time, I beat him every time. And if they blitz, Teddy is right there to pick it up.

"Fuck!" the guy says, huffing and puffing. "You too quick, you skinny shit! And you fuckin' strong!"

And I just laugh.

Even when I get in with my old gang the third team—because the coaches *have* to play me again, because there's no other backup left guard—I still dominate. It's all clicking, even with the rookies, even with Wilton, because I'm not caring; I finally got my head out of my own stopped-up ass, and the coaches out of my goddamn head.

Then, just like that, it's over.

I walk back to the sideline. Paulson isn't there anymore, already back at the building with the trainers getting checked out. He could be out for the season, he could be back tomorrow, I have no idea. But I got my shot, and I took it.

The energy has changed. Looser, lighter. Starters from the line like Jeb and Antonne are looking me in the eye now, patting me on the back, telling me good job.

Lopez is busy with his playbook, but even he knows things are different. I stare at him till I catch his eye, and I wink. He shakes his head, muttering, and gives me an eye roll that could almost compete with one of my own.

Nothing is locked, not by a long shot. They could still cut me at any minute.

But if I go out, I'll go out on my terms, laughing the whole way.

THE NEXT MORNING I HEAD to breakfast for my usual mound of whole-grain pancakes, and somehow my gut doesn't feel quite as bad, even though I'm pretty sure if I move too suddenly, I'll shit all over the floor.

I see Paulson on his way in too. This time he definitely looks kind of stiff.

"Hey," I say.

"Hey."

"How's the groin?"

"Tight." He shrugs. "Whatever."

"Shit, that sucks," I say.

"I'll sit out a day, maybe two. But I'll be fine. All part of God's plan, you know?"

It's a message to me that he's not going anywhere, he's still in this, but he sounds like he's trying to convince himself too.

"Yeah, God and *Star Trek*," I say. Then, more serious, "I'm sure you'll be back out there soon. Just gotta stay positive."

He smiles. I hate to admit this, but half of me hopes that's not true, that he won't be back out there this season, that he'll need surgery and spend the year rehabbing instead of competing with me. Honestly, it wouldn't be that bad of a deal—he wouldn't be on the team, but he'd earn worker's comp, settling with management for a lump sum to cover the work he'd miss. Probably less money than he'd make as an active player, but still a lot. And best of all, there'd be an open spot on the roster for me.

Of course he knows all this, knows what's going through my mind. That's the business.

"Cool," he says. "I'm gonna grab some eggs and stuff. I'll save you a seat."

"Yeah, okay. Sounds good."

We walk through the cafeteria door, and Paulson heads over to the eggs, right past Jack, the head coach, who's sitting at his own table, as always. Waiting.

I'm not sure what to expect when I walk by him, not sure if I should expect anything, really. And for once, those black eyes don't tell me a thing. No anger or disgust. No approval or congratulations. Definitely no Old Coach's Handshake or pat on the back. But you know what? He does say something.

"Hey, Johnny."

He says my name. And I smile.

"What's up, Coach."

And I keep on walking. Looks like I'll be a football player at least a couple more weeks.

Shit.

Chapter 4

THE REAPER

The most terrifying man in the NFL isn't the player who lines up across from you on the field. It's not the head coach, or the general manager, or even the owner of the team.

It's the Reaper.

The Reaper comes around twice during training camp—once after the third preseason game, and again after the fourth and final game, at the end of August. Every team has one. Usually he has no name at all, he's just "the guy" or "the GM's assistant." But on this team, they call him the Reaper.

The Reaper strikes quickly and quietly, without warning. He can grab you during a team meeting, in the middle of a workout, before practice, or just as you're sitting down to lunch. He generally isn't much to look at. The Reaper can be skinny or pudgy, maybe balding or with a bad comb-over, a pair of thick glasses on his face and a clipboard in his hand. More accountant than angel of death. But somehow his ordinariness just makes him more frightening. You can't argue with him or beg for mercy. He's a front-office guy, nothing but a courier, and he has a job to do.

He taps you on your shoulder, says in hushed tones, "Please come with me, the GM would like to see you," and he leads you out of the room to the boss's office. The general manager gives you the news, shakes your hand, and just like that, it's over. You've been officially cut from the team.

Today is the fifth day of camp, so that means there are three and a half weeks until the Reaper takes his first pass at the chaff, cutting us down from ninety players to seventy-five. Then just a week after that comes his final pass, leaving us with fifty-three.

It's funny. Now that I actually have a chance, now that Paulson's injury has given me a shot at making this team, I'm feeling more pressure than ever.

Even Dante—probably the biggest name on our team—feels it. During camp I caught him watching a rookie receiver during drills once, a guy not nearly as talented as him—but who's six years younger.

"Fuck, he sure is fast though," Dante said, shaking his head. "And I'm just getting older."

Sure, he'll probably be fine. But he knows that every young receiver beneath him is after his spot. All it takes is an injury or a horrible camp, and he could be gone. Guys like T.O. and Ochocinco were uncuttable once. Then all of a sudden, they weren't.

Do I fear the Reaper? Deep down, we all do.

TODAY IS THE FIRST PRACTICE of the year in full pads. Something every player dreads and loves at the same time. We get to hit, and hit hard.

A lot of guys don't just want to hit. They need to.

"*Man,* it's been too fuckin' long!" a second-string linebacker shouts as he paces back and forth. "I *need* this shit, I been pissed off for two months now. I just gotta fuckin' hit something!"

"It's fucking go time!" Antonne yells. "*It's go time!*"

Then you got me.

"Hey, Teddy, guess what?" I say, turning to the big Samoan, my voice dripping with fake excitement. "We're in full pads today! Woohoo!"

"I know," he says sarcastically. "I can't wait."

We awkwardly high-five and bust out laughing. Teddy doesn't seem to hate football, not like I do, but he's not drowning in the football Kool-Aid either. He just sips it every now and then.

The laughing does me good. I'm actually kind of nervous. It's been over half a year since I played in pads, and I wonder if I'll be able to tap into the rage I need to hang with these guys. There really is something about full contact that takes the game to another level. Hitting another human being at high speed taps into something primal that all NFL players have, I don't care what position you play. It's a natural aggression that's gotten us to the highest level of football, and it's been lying dormant in everyone for months over the off-season. Now it's ready to explode.

Will I still have it?

Then there's Paulson to worry about. He knows how well I did when I took over for him, so he's gonna try to play through the pain of his injury today. It's stupid to do that with a groin injury. He should stay out at least another week, probably even have surgery, and I'm not just saying that because it'd be good for me. Groin injuries are no joke. If he aggravates that thing, if he doesn't heal the right way, that's not just the end of his career, he could be stuck with a limp for the rest of his life.

But the way Paulson sees it, if he loses his spot on the team to me now, or if he gets a reputation in the League as being injury-prone, that could be it for his career. Who cares if he ends up walking a little funny?

We get out on the field, and Paulson doesn't make it past the opening one-on-one drills.

I see him limp over to Coach Lopez on the side. Paulson says something, shakes his head, and I can sense his shoulders slump even under those massive pads. He heads back to the locker room, done for the day.

Do I feel terrible for him? Yeah. But I'd be lying if I said I wasn't sort of happy, too. I know what this means for me and my dream. I just won the lottery off another man's pain. And I'm disgusted with myself. I hate what football does to me.

Lopez looks right at me. His gaze is blank, cold. He's got his best poker face on, but I know what he's thinking. He can't believe that his offensive line, his first season in the NFL could all depend on this skinny, know-it-all, completely *nonattentive* piece of shit. In other words, on me.

And what do I do? I smile at him. I'm pretty sure he noticed.

He rides my ass for the rest of the day. It starts when he yells at me after our center fucks up the count and Teddy moves early. How the hell could it possibly be my fault if I'm not the guy who moved? But whatever, I can take it.

Then two plays later he goes after my technique. And that's when I lose my shit.

Blocking technique is an offensive lineman's bread and butter, our most basic, fundamental skill. If you can't physically push your opponent out of the way, you're completely worthless. It doesn't matter how well you read a defense or how fast you run a play. Especially as a smaller guy, if my blocking technique isn't flawless, I'm fucked. I don't have the sheer mass to simply shove people around. I need skill.

Thankfully for me, I have it.

The ball snaps, and I move my guy out of the way, just like I'm supposed to. Rip my hands through his chest, trigger my leverage, and even though he's forty pounds heavier than me, I knock him the fuck over.

Before the play is even done, Lopez whistles it dead. For some stupid reason, I'm actually surprised he decides to single me out.

"Johnny!" he shouts. "Johnny!"

"Lopez!" I shout back. "Lopez!"

"Fucking lift the guy!" he yells. "Just fucking lift!"

Now look. I could give you a complete dissertation on what exactly that means. All you really need to know is that Lopez wants me to get my hands under my guy's breastplate, grab him, *lift* him up, and walk him back. Some bullshit about taking them out of their power angles. And he's absolutely wrong.

"Lo, I'm not gonna fucking lift," I say. "If I push, I get more leverage. I'm not some three-hundred-thirty-pound fat ass. I need the fucking leverage."

"Johnny, you're doing it wrong!" he says, like I never spoke a word. "I want you to fucking lift!"

"Lo!" I shout. "You saw what I did! It worked! *Just admit . . .*"

Okay. Let's take a quick break here. I know what you're thinking. Why can't I just shut up and let this shit go? Sure, my coach called me out in front of my peers, treating me like a fucking moron, but he's my *coach.* He holds the key to my future, to making hundreds of thousands of dollars for a year of not-work. Why can't I kiss his ass, just a little? Why can't I just say he's right? Is it really that hard?

Yes. Yes, it is.

Okay, let's continue.

"*. . . that it worked!*"

"I'm not admitting shit!" Lopez shouts. "You need to lift!"

"Un-fucking-believable!" I yell.

By now, this has become a scene.

"You guys are like some fucked-up old married couple!" Jeb the Old Vet shouts from the sideline. A few guys laugh and yell "Keith! Keeeith!" because it's become a big joke that the special teams coach got my name wrong the first day.

"Look, Lopez," I say. "I'll try it your way, okay? I will. I just want you to say, just *once,* that my way worked too."

He stands there, looks me in the eye, and folds his arms.

"You. Did. It. Wrong. You fucking need to lift!"

"Fuck!" I shout.

I give Lopez a look mean enough to melt the liver spots off his fat face. He turns around and stomps off, muttering to himself.

Later, at the end of practice, there's another fight, an actual fistfight, not involving me. Dante, our Diva receiver, goes after some second-string corner who was trying to impress the coaches by knocking Dante around a little. A bunch of guys start screaming, there are a few shoves, a couple punches, and everyone backs off pretty quick.

"You play like a bitch, TJ!" Dante yells at him.

"Dante, shut the fuck up!" Jeb says. And Dante shuts the fuck up.

The fight will make the news tomorrow, because it's Dante, and he's our big name so he always makes the news, but it's no big deal. He'll probably send out a tweet about how he "beat some ass" even though we all know he got bitched.

Scuffles like that break out at least three times a week at training camp. They never last longer than a punch or two, and they almost always come from sheer desperation. A second- or third-string guy is playing his ass off for the coaches, doing anything necessary to make the team—even if it means challenging a starter. The starter, of course, feels like he should never be challenged, and if he gets pushed too far he fights back, literally. But here's the best part: if the starter gets injured in the fight? The coaches won't give a shit who started it—the backup will be off the team the next day. That's why Dante can talk so much shit. He knows TJ could never kick his ass. It'd be career suicide.

The funny thing is I never get into fights like that. Never. I can't fathom wasting that much energy and *still* having to get through the rest of a practice. But if a coach tells me I'm wrong? It's fucking over. I cannot, will not, let it go.

At the end of the day, Antonne, the starting center, pays me a little visit at my locker. Before this moment, we've barely said a word to each other. I'm a third-string backup, and this guy has a contract for five years and $28 million. I know he likes to drink, and I know way more about his sex life than I'd ever want to, but beyond that? Starters like him don't have time for guys like me. They don't even know we exist. At least I thought they didn't.

He sits down next to me, looks me in the eye.

"Johnny," he says. "Be coachable, man."

"You see what Lo's doing to me!" I say. "He's fucking riding me, driving me crazy!"

"Yeah, he is," Antonne says. "But he does it because you good. You got potential, man. If you didn't, he wouldn't give a shit."

He pats me on the back and walks away. It feels good to exist.

THE NEXT MORNING ON my way into breakfast I see Paulson coming out the main building. He has his bag.

"Hey, baby," I say. "What's going on?"

"I'm having surgery," he says. "Tomorrow."

We stand there for a second, quiet. That's it. Paulson's year is over, and possibly his career. If this were a fake happily-ever-after Hollywood story, something fun and uplifting would happen, like the team would hire him as an inspirational reminder of how hard work always pays off. But that's not how this shit works. It's real life, and someone has to lose.

"Well, you'll get to spend the day high on painkillers," I say.

"Yeah," Paulson says, forcing a laugh. "That'll be fun."

"Look, this fucking sucks," I say. "I've been there, I know. I've had five surgeries myself. But I'm glad you're taking care of it. Heal up. Get it to a hundred percent. Ride out the money they give you. It's the smart thing to do."

"It'll all work out," he says. "It's all part of God's plan."

"Okay," I say. Hesitate, then, "Gimme a hug, you big bastard."

We hug. Two gigantic NFL linemen on the front walk of their team's headquarters. It feels good, forgetting about all the competition, all the bullshit. Even for just a second.

"Good luck, Johnny," Paulson says as he walks away, carrying his bag. I'll need it.

A FEW OF US ARE in the training room, soaking in the cold tub after practice. Cold tubs are exactly what they sound like—cold fucking tubs. Fifty degrees, filled with ice water, and made entirely of stainless steel for that second wave of "fuck you" when you sit down. We use them to help our muscles recover after a long day spent destroying them. And for some reason we have some of our most honest discussions here. Maybe we're just trying to keep our minds off how damn cold it is.

"Hey, Johnny," says a third-string lineman I like to call G.I. Joe. "What's a preseason game like anyway? Is it different from regular-season stuff?"

Our first preseason game is in three days, and the rookies are all freaked out. They should be. This is G.I. Joe's first training camp. He got that nickname because he had some connection to the military before he decided to give the NFL a try. He's the only player I've known in the League who doesn't just *like* the army but was actually in it. There are rumors that he bounced around Afghanistan, running down terrorists, but who knows, the story always changes. All I know is this crazy bastard is infatuated with death. He spends his nights in the hotel watching live leaked videos of extremists executing people. I dig the guy.

"Preseason's different," I say. "People talk the usual crap about how important it is to win the games. But no one really gives a shit about the score. Everyone's concerned with how they play. Worry about yourself now. After you make the team, we can all be brothers."

"Fuck," Joe says. "This whole thing is over on the twenty-eighth, can you believe it? Just a few more weeks. No more cuts, no more wondering. I can't wait."

Joe is a physical specimen, six foot ten, 330 pounds of Polish-American muscle. But he's horribly raw, not too skilled. The team will probably keep him on just for the publicity, at least on the practice squad. Coaches love pulling living metaphors from the armed forces. Some even show war films or clips of SEAL training, thinking it's going to motivate us.

With G.I. Joe, at least they'd have a real warrior now.

"You'll be great, Joe," I say. "Gotta figure the average NFL game is what, a little over fifty plays? In the first preseason game, the starters are only gonna get about ten of those plays. That gives guys like me and you a good thirty-five or forty plays to make an impression, right?"

"Yeah," he says, finally smiling. "Cool."

I don't mention he'll get a lot fewer plays than me because he's stuck on the third string, but why bring the guy down? Plus, as of yesterday, so was I.

THURSDAY MORNING WE FLY OUT for tomorrow's game against the Bengals. They fly the whole team, ninety players, all the coaches, the support staff, and crates and crates of gear. Not just helmets and footballs, but whiteboards, iPads, papers, food, and medical shit. We're like a traveling army. Hopefully Joe is happy.

We land in Ohio, and it feels really fucking weird. Not just because I'm about to play a game that could decide my future, but because this is home. Cincinnati is an hour's drive from my town. An hour from where I grew up, from where my mom died, from where I first put on pads and a uniform. Everything here feels right. It just clicks. And it's distracting as hell. I almost forgot what being home felt like, and it's only been a few weeks.

Kate is coming to stay with me tonight. I want to see her of course. I also want to get laid. Real, real bad. But I need to focus on what I'm really here for, My Glorious Backup Dream™.

I spend the afternoon at the hotel in team meetings. But tonight we're free. Unlike college, in which I would've been locked in all night before a game, my current team leaves a lot to the players' discretion, for better or worse, until curfew at ten.

"Hey, Johnny."

I hear Kate's voice in the lobby of the hotel and I see her standing there and she looks beautiful. Not beautiful in an airbrushed "NFL Cheerleader" way, but beautiful in a way that feels real. We kiss, and I realize how much I've missed not just being home but being with a person who wants to be with me.

It's the taste of a life I wish I could live, but can't.

We have dinner at a Ruth's Chris Steakhouse. The food is good but our waiter is slow, and he brings me french fries instead of rice for my side even though I very specifically, very clearly told him to bring me not one, not two, but *three* servings of rice, so I stiff him on the tip and Kate gets pissed at me and calls me a cheap ass.

It's perfect.

We get back to the hotel and head to her room. Wives and girlfriends are allowed to stay at the team's hotel, but we're supposed to stay in our own, separate rooms for the night.

"So are you happy to see me?" she says.

This is a very "girl" question to ask. We've just had sex, twice, we're lying on the bed, both naked, and she asks me if I'm happy to see her.

"What do you think?" I say.

"I don't know," she answers.

"Of course I'm happy," I say. "But I'm also miserable. Being with you just reminds me a thousand times that I need to leave."

She smiles. I knew she would like that one.

"Do you think about quitting a lot?" she asks.

"Pretty much every single second," I say. "But . . ."

"But what?"

"If I quit, I just don't know what I would do."

This is a very difficult thing for me to admit. She misses the emotion completely, focuses on it only as a practical matter. For her, that's all my situation amounts to.

"You could do anything," she says. "You'd find something. You might not make as much as you do in football, but you'd be fine. More than fine!"

"It's not about the money," I say, trying to explain. "It's . . . the fear of not knowing."

"You could always work with your dad."

She's right, I could. My dad is my best friend. We talk a couple times a week, text every day, and he's floated the idea of me joining him in real estate a few times. Would it make him happy if I achieved my dream of being the Best NFL Backup Ever™? Absolutely. But he also knows the League drives me fucking crazy. At this point, he hates all the politics and the bullshit as much as I do. I think part of him just wants football to be over with as much as I do.

Fuck. This is exactly the kind of distraction I don't need right now.

"It's late," I say. "I gotta get some sleep."

I get up, start putting my clothes back on. She looks hurt.

"Just stay!" she says. "Come on, no one's gonna know. It's just a pre-season game!"

Just a preseason game? She has no clue. No clue at all.

"Sorry," I say. "I can't. I'm really tired."

"Okay," she says. "I love you."

I take the elevator upstairs and fall asleep in my room, alone.

THE NEXT DAY, AFTER TWO and a half weeks of training, conditioning, and practice, we have our very first preseason game against the Cincinnati Bengals.

Before a *regular*-season game, the mood in the locker room is intense, focused, like you're getting ready for war. But today? The starters are relaxed, laughing. This game doesn't count against our regular-season record, and they've already made the team. They know they're not going to get cut. They're safe. So what the fuck do they have to play for? Pride? The pursuit of excellence? The love of the game? The fans?

Yeah, right.

Their biggest concern is what they're wearing. Dante, Antonne, Brody the quarterback, even Ollie the fucking kicker, all act like they're getting ready for a fashion show. Spending thirty minutes adjusting their uniforms and pads just right. Pulling out the special black tape instead of the generic white stuff because it looks cooler. And the things they do with the eye black, holy fuck. Some of them cover their whole faces in paint! They look like extras from KISS, though something tells me Dante has no idea who the hell Gene Simmons is.

Meanwhile, the backups are so overwhelmed they don't know what the fuck to do. Should they play it cool and try to joke around with the starters, or should they mentally prepare for one of the biggest days of their lives? The serious ones sit in front of their lockers with towels over their heads and headphones in their ears, rocking back and forth to the music, whispering to themselves, getting their minds right.

But some of the rookies—especially the threes, because God knows how long they'll last—just want to soak up the moment. They take selfies in front of their lockers along with their brand-new jerseys, texting the shots to their friends. "Look, Ma! I made the NFL!"

One ballsy bunch of rookies even goes up to Jeb the Old Vet—all six feet five inches, 335 pounds of him—to ask for a group photo. Jeb grits his teeth, nods, and takes the shot as the rookies pose, smiling their brightest and flashing some gang signs for good measure. After they're done, the ringleader, a defensive back who couldn't be older than twenty-two, takes a look at the pic. His smile drops.

"Uh, Jeb?" he says. "This one didn't turn out, like the focus is bad. Could you take another one, man?"

Jeb stares down at him as the other ones crack up laughing.

"Fine."

The next photo is flawless.

THE GAME FINALLY STARTS, and our first-team offense plays like absolute horseshit. In four series on the field, they turn the ball over once and go three-and-out three times, failing to pick up a single first down. What a fucking surprise.

But hey, it's all good by me. The worse they play, the better I look when I get on the field with the other twos.

There's just one problem. We play just as bad in our first series. We're out of rhythm. Teddy is hyperventilating, he's so nervous. We manage to pick up a total of 4 yards, giving up one tackle for a loss and a sack, which, in case you're wondering, does *not* reflect well on an offensive line.

Lopez is over on the sidelines going fucking *ballistic*. Every coach has his own sideline shtick during games, and offensive-line coaches are the craziest of the bunch. In college, my O-line coach got so tense he'd spend the whole game on the ground, on his hands and knees watching plays, in full-pounce mode. It was the only way he could focus.

I'd never seen Lopez in a game-time situation before. His shtick is apparently going full-on, foaming-at-the-mouth, straight-up batshit crazy. He's pacing back and forth, stalking the sidelines like some balding, potbellied jungle cat. The whole time he's chomping down on his pen, mashing it, just tearing it to shreds with his teeth and screaming his fucking head off—never at the starters, of course, can't afford to scream at them, but at any other sorry sucker who happens to be below his pay grade.

And the funny thing? I quickly realize that our real problem is that we actually *over*prepared—for the wrong defense. Lopez got us ready to play against Cinci based on *last year's* scouting reports. He had no other option since it's the first game of the year. During our walk-through on Wednesday, we went over every play, every coverage, every situation we could possibly face, over and over again.

Surprise! The Bengals said "fuck you" and hit us with something different.

It's not even that different. In football terms, they were shifting from an over-front to an under-front and dropping a linebacker to play the tight end. In a layperson's terms, "We moved a couple guys. BAM! Fuck you! Now everything is different."

On the sidelines after our first series, Lopez lays into me. I mean just destroys me.

"What the fuck are you doing out there!" he screams. "It's like you never put on a helmet in your goddamn life!"

Yelling at me, of course, makes no sense. I'm not playing center, it's not my job to direct the line, and I didn't fuck up any of my individual blocks. But because I stood up to him once, I'll be his main target forever. He wants to break me, show that right or wrong, win or lose, he has the power.

But this time, for once, I refuse to take the bait.

"Lopez," I say. "Slow down. Work through this with me, okay? You tell me what you're seeing, and I'll tell you what I'm seeing. Okay?"

Even at football's highest level, it's extremely difficult for coaches and players to make good midgame adjustments to their game plans. Shit out there moves fast. When you're in the thick of it, at eye level, it's all a blur, barely any time to react, much less think. Recognizing new patterns on the fly, shifts in the defense, isn't easy, even for the pros.

But it's not just a mental shift, it's psychological. Coaches don't *want* to adjust. They don't want to change. And they damn well don't want to listen to anyone else. As far as they're concerned, they shouldn't have to—they're the boss. They didn't get this far in life by changing; they got here by being right.

So next time you're watching your favorite team and you can't figure out why the fuck your coach isn't making a blatantly obvious change to his game plan that any idiot could see, there's a good chance it's not because he's stupid. He's just too damn arrogant.

Which is why what Lopez and I accomplish is a minor miracle.

By not screaming back at him, by not engaging with his irrational ego, and by not letting my own ego get the best of me, I actually manage to reason with the guy. We study photos of the last few downs—yes, live photos are taken of every play of every NFL game and immediately printed out for players and coaches to examine on the sidelines—and together, we agree on what's happening out there. Lopez communicates our conclusion to the offensive coordinator. I communicate it to our center, who communicates it to the rest of our line. People relax, Teddy starts breathing, and suddenly that lightning-fast game slows down.

On our next offensive series, we go 77 yards down the field for a touchdown. Half those yards are rushing yards, which is a good sign for an offensive line. It means we're pushing fuckers out of the way. We're making holes for people to run through.

When we jog back to the sideline, I feel someone hit my shoulder pad. I turn around. It's Lopez.

"Hey," he says. "Nice drive."

From then on, our offense owns Cincinnati. Every single series. We win the game, 27–10. Not that it matters. What matters is that I played well, and Lopez knows it.

TODAY IS FAN DAY AT practice. Yippee.

The team pulls out all the stops. Practice is in the stadium, not on the usual practice field. Music is blasting, media is everywhere, our skanky cheerleaders are prancing around on the sidelines—I swear our cheerleaders are the ugliest ones in the League—and they even have an announcer who describes each part of practice and what each drill is for.

They even add a "Support Our Troops" twist to the whole thing. The national anthem is sung by a high-ranking officer from the U.S. Marines, and almost two hundred military personnel get full access to the locker room, stadium tunnels, and time on the field. All while another veteran, our very own G.I. Joe, prays to God that he isn't going to get cut.

Look, I don't mind fans watching us practice. I definitely love supporting the troops. And some players really do thrive off the extra attention.

Dante gets stacks of fan mail every week. Does he read any of it? Absolutely not. But he loves letting it pile up outside his locker like a towering paper monument to his ego. Then the janitor throws it all away, and Dante starts a brand-new pile. Never opens a letter.

As for the fans, if you've got some kind of deep, personal connection to a team, I respect that. Old-timers with season tickets that've been passed down for generations. Middle-aged dudes with a passion for football because it reminds them of going to games with their dads when they were boys. Or little kids who've just started playing touch football in their backyard coming to their very first big game. That kind of stuff makes perfect sense to me. I have walking in the mall, they have football. I'm happy I can be a part of their special ritual.

But what I don't like, what I can't stand, is the business of it all. To a lot of fans, we're not human beings, we're commodities, entertainment. Their own private gladiators. They send us hate mail, they troll us on Twitter, sometimes they even applaud when a player from an opposing team gets injured. They feel entitled to it, just because they buy a ticket to a game or watch us play on TV. I know guys who homeschool their kids because they don't want their sons and daughters to face the abuse of their classmates after Daddy loses a game. The Players Association even offers us a discounted personal security package if we need to be guarded from the real psychos.

And the NFL higher-ups don't do anything to stop that mentality—if anything, they encourage it.

Before we head out to practice today, management tells us—*orders us*—to stay behind and sign every single autograph, take every single photo that anyone asks for. Why? The team wants to breed new fans, hook new junkies. Simple as that. And as much as I love supporting the military, I question the team's true motives. Are we really celebrating the troops, or are we exploiting them? Using them to make football and the NFL seem as patriotic, as all-American as the troops who actually fight and die for us? There's nothing I hate more than people comparing football to war. What we do is play a game. What the military does is safeguard our freedom. The two don't even compare.

When practice ends, we get mobbed. Absolutely mobbed. These people aren't senior citizens gently reliving their childhood memories or little kids named Timmy with twinkles in their eyes. These are rabid, foaming-at-the-mouth superfans, men, women, and children, who are honest to God *throwing stuff* at us. Shirts, programs, banners, everything. Literally hurling shit at players over the tops of the crowds and getting it passed back to them.

Thankfully, as a lineman—especially a backup—no one gives a shit about you. You can hide in the shadows of the star players. As they get killed, you can ease your way through the line, past the hordes of people, all while looking like you care.

But suddenly I get snagged. A ten-year-old kid grabs my jersey and tells—not asks, *tells*—me to sign an old team photo (never mind that I wasn't on the team then). I start to sign it, and he grabs my hand.

"Wait!" he says. "Make sure you sign here, in the margins! Don't mess up any of the photos!"

Dumbfounding. What happened to kids asking you to sign their Nerf football that looks like hell because it's been thrown around the cul-de-sac a thousand times? Did those golden days ever even exist or is it just all in my imagination?

But we do it. We sign it all, we take all the photos, we shake all the hands—because that's what we're supposed to do. And some guys really do enjoy it. But the same time we're trying to make all the fans happy, putting on these big bright smiles and trying to be the unstoppable heroes they all want us to be, deep down inside, we're terrified.

Because ten days from now, fifteen of us—almost 20 percent of the current roster—will get fired.

At breakfast, lifting weights, eating lunch, or soaking in the cold tub, the upcoming cut is all the backups talk about. Is my stock up? Is it down? Am I safe, on the bubble, or already out? Conspiracy theories fly everywhere, gossip about which coach said what about who to who else. Every conversation ends the exact same way, with the exact same words:

"You think you made it?"

"I just don't know."

AFTER OUR BREAKTHROUGH during the first game, it's like Lopez does a complete 180 on me. Or at least a 165.

During individual drills, I execute a combo block flawlessly—even more important, I do it exactly the way he told us to. Lopez grabs me.

"Johnny," he says in almost a whisper. "I really wanna praise you for using your hands on that block, but I just can't bring myself to compliment you."

He even starts trying to include me in his private jokes, as if I'm the smart one on the line who will actually be able to understand his sophisticated humor. In one of our line meetings, he starts bitching about our offensive coordinator.

"Yeah," Lopez says to everyone. "He can be a little laissez-faire with his calls, if you know what I mean."

Then he stops and gives me this look like he's waiting for my approval, like, *Hey, I just used a French economics term with football! Pretty impressive,* oui? The funny thing is, his southern accent was so thick I barely caught it.

Honestly, all the positivity starts to freak me out. A couple days later in practice, he starts congratulating me on yet another block, and finally I pop.

"Don't you compliment me!" I shout, only half kidding. "That's not your *thing!*"

"What?" Lopez says. "Hey, I don't like it either, but you're doing a good job out here!"

Antonne and Teddy are just bawling laughing, mocking me for not just doing things the right way—but the Lopez way.

"Oh shit," Antonne says. "Looks like Keith is finally drinking the Kool-Aid! He's the teacher's pet!"

I don't even think about how annoying it is that people are still calling me Keith. All I can think is, *Is it true? Am I drinking the Kool-Aid? The guy who always makes fun of everyone else for drinking the Kool-Aid?*

My answer to myself is simple: *No fucking way.*

"THE REAPER'S HERE!"

"The Reaper's out hunting."

"I saw him walking around, watch the fuck out."

The day of first cuts finally arrives. I gotta say that last night I was feeling pretty good about my chances. I played well in the first three games, there was no more competition from Paulson, and Lopez wasn't riding me as hard. What were they gonna do? Cut me and hire someone totally new who didn't even know the system? Camp was almost over! They *had* to take me.

And the guys who *did* get cut? I figured it'd happen so quick it'd be like they were never even here. On to the next game. No big deal. That's the business.

Then the Reaper shows up. And it hits all of us hard.

He can take someone anytime, anyplace. So it turns the whole day, the whole team, to shit. Twenty minutes into the morning workout, seven guys are already gone. I head into the offense meeting, and two seats that used to be filled right next to me are empty now. Guys I saw and talked to every day, gone.

The lunchroom is usually loud, filled with dudes laughing, joking. Today it's quiet. There are a few conversations, but they're smaller, hushed, like we're all at a funeral. In a way, we are. Death is random, and this feels the same way. It doesn't matter what you've done over the last few weeks, how hard you've worked, how much ass you've kissed, you can still be gone. Maybe you just weren't very good. Maybe you *were* good, but there are two other guys at your same position who are just as good, and one of them's a little more experienced, or one of them got along with the coach just a little bit better. Maybe one of them just happens to share an agent with an assistant coach. Who knows? Sometimes it's fair, sometimes it isn't. There's an old joke in the League among all the players—that NFL really stands for "Not For Long."

That's the business.

Finally, after lunch, the bloodletting is over. Someone from personnel walks in, announces that they've cut everyone they needed to cut, then leaves.

G.I. Joe doesn't make it. The guy's massive. The perfect media figure. But he was also really, really raw. Just didn't have the skill or experience they were looking for. So they cut the motherfucker.

I head to the lockers, and a few guys are still clearing their stuff out. One of them, a tight end, is shoveling his gear into a big gray garbage bag. Reminds me just how close a lot of us are to being flat broke.

I see Joe with his own bag about to head out.

"Hey, baby," I say, holding out my hand to shake. "It was good—"

He cuts me off.

"Don't do that," he says. "Don't do that. I'm not good at that shit."

He walks out. It's the last time I ever see him.

THE NEXT DAY THE OFFENSIVE LINE, or what's left of it, gets a visit from a special guest. He's a former player with the team, made the Pro Bowl a few times back in the day. He's fifty-two years old, but he looks about seventy-two, his eyes a little cloudy, his back crooked and stooped, his walk slow and deliberate, like he has to think before each step.

He talks to all of us about how proud we should be to be part of such an amazing organization. How much it means. How fortunate we are to have this opportunity. We listen attentively, a couple guys nodding at his words.

The old-timer shakes a few hands, shuffles out, and comes back five minutes later.

"Any a' you fellas seen my notebook?" he asks us.

We meet his question with blank stares.

"It's all right," he says. "I'm used to it. Y'all better get used to it too."

"Aw, man," Jeb says. "Don't tell us that. I don't even wanna know."

Jeb is in his midthirties—ancient for an offensive lineman—so he's probably thinking about the lifetime of postretirement pain he has to look forward to more than anyone else on the line. But it's in the backs of all our minds. Linemen, defensive and offensive, take by far the most physical abuse in football. What we do is just pure body-to-body, head-to-head human demolition. A good (and lucky) receiver or defensive back can last in the league till his forties. Not us. Too much wear and tear. Most of the guys I know don't make it past their early thirties, either retiring or getting cut. And the problem isn't just concussions—it's the toll on your entire body. I've met former linemen in their fifties who are almost completely immobile.

Even with all that, the attitude of most linemen I know is resignation to their fate. They're football players. They've been football players most of their lives, and they didn't start playing because they thought it was a peaceful game. They know they'll be fucked eventually, they know they've already failed themselves with years of hard hitting, so they figure they'll make as much money as they can while they can still play, then never have to work again.

The fact that they won't remember their grandkids' names just isn't a pressing matter right now.

For me, though, the terror is constant. I enjoy my mind, I don't want to lose it. But I tell myself that as a backup at least I'm not getting hit as much. That's gotta make it safer, right? At least a little?

Later that night, at 5 A.M., I wake up sweating and breathing heavy after a bad dream. I don't want to forget it, so I grab my notebook off the bedside table and scribble it down.

Here's what I write:

> *Walking around the mall or some sort of lobby w/*
> *escalators escorted by some sort of staff member.*

Introduced to 2 old players walking w/ the (team) owner.
Owner holding a trophy, glad-handing these 2 older
players. 1 player w/ a crazy attitude with bloodstains on
his shirt as if he were bleeding through his nose. Shaking
erratically. "Y'all will be really successful here. You have
a great support staff." Then takes off. Obvious concussion
trauma.

(Suddenly my mom is with me.) My mom: "Did he come
off as superior to you?"

Another parent now w/ a younger kid: "Yes." Feeling no
remorse.

We walk away quickly, my mom getting mad.

I put my pen and pad down and fall back asleep.

AFTER MAKING IT THROUGH the first round of cuts, I figure all
I gotta do is keep my head down, ride out these last few days of camp, get
through our last preseason game, and I'll be golden. On my way to being
the Best NFL Backup Ever™.

It should've been the perfect plan.

Then on Tuesday afternoon, just three days before the final cuts, I'm
lifting by myself in the weight room, and I see the team's general manager, Lowry. Tall, thin, and pale, God and the devil himself, all wrapped
into one. The Reaper's boss.

Lowry is—just what *is* that, anyway? Is that supposed to be *boxing*?
He's with a trainer, working a punching bag. His hands all taped up, got
the boxing gloves on, the shorts, all the trappings of a real fighter.

And he punches like a total fucking pussy.

He's got no strength, no technique. No understanding of leverage,
no idea how to use his body to get behind a punch. I witness an attempt
at a punch—he literally steps back and punches the air. Fucking comical.

The trainer, of course, is gripping that gigantic bag like Lowry could
knock it off its chain any second. He's shouting, "Yeah! There you go! Hit

him with that cross!" like he's fucking working out Manny Pacquiao. Why? Because Lowry is the boss.

And it hits me. This asshole who controls all of us, this douchebag who judges us, who buys, trades, sells, and slaughters us like we're a bunch of fucking cattle, he's *nothing*. If you put him on the field with G.I. Joe, an actual warrior whose dreams he just destroyed, Lowry wouldn't last a second.

Lowry finishes his "fight," goes to grab a drink from his water bottle.

I walk over. He looks at me, kind of surprised. I smile the friendliest smile I can possibly manage.

"Hey, Lowry, let me give you a little advice. If you're ever in a situation where you're in a real fight . . . call me, call anyone. You're gonna get your ass kicked."

I pat him on the back, just as nice as can be. His eyes narrow, he gets this weird little smirk.

"Fuck you, Johnny."

He walks out of the weight room. I think that may just have been the end of my NFL career. And you know what? It was 100 percent worth it.

THE NEXT DAY I GET a call from Bernie, my agent.

He's in his sixties, he's been doing this forever, and he's just about had enough of everything. Including, right now, me.

"I talked to Lowry yesterday," Bernie says. "We discussed a few different guys, but he brought you up."

"Yeah? What did he have to say?"

"He says you talk too much."

"Okay," I respond, trying to play it cool. "What did you say?"

"I said, 'Of course he does, everyone knows that. But he's been playing really well.' "

"And?"

"He said, 'I know.' "

"Okay," I say impatiently. "So what do you think? Am I safe?"

There's a pause.

"Yeah," he says. "I think you're safe. If they cut you, it's bullshit."

"Okay," I say. "Good. Thanks, Bernie."

"But Johnny?" he says.

"Yeah?"

"You gotta shut the fuck up."

AUGUST 28, FRIDAY, THE BIG DAY, the final round of cuts, comes and goes. I don't hear a thing.

On the one hand, that's good, because I haven't been cut. On the other hand, no one's told me I *made* the team either.

This small detail is weighing on my shoulders like five thousand pounds of shit.

"Don't worry," Teddy says. "The final roster isn't really set till Monday. They'll just tell you then."

"Yeah, but they told *you* today."

Teddy looks at me kind of puzzled, shrugs, and says something that sounds like "Mmmuh." Somehow it fails to convince me.

Teddy and I have already decided to share an apartment during the regular season. The complex we chose has some kind of deal with the team, and we're just picking up the lease from a couple of other players. They'll even furnish the place for an extra $1,050 a month. Gotta love that Liquid Life. But I'm worried. Maybe signing the lease jinxed me? You know, that and basically telling our general manager he's a pussy to his face.

The hallways are quiet at the end of the day as I head back to the hotel. I pass by the personnel offices, and the HR ladies are still speaking in hushed tones. The stink of the latest round of firings hasn't quite left the air.

By the main door I see a receiver walking in. He's on the second team with me, the only receiver I can actually tolerate.

"See you later, baby," I say.

"What are you talking about?" he says. "I got cut."

He walks away before I can say anything.

Fuck. That guy? He wasn't supposed to be on the bubble. He's been in the League for four years, playing on this team two of them, in the prime of his career. At least he was.

I drive back to my hotel. I pack my bags for the move I'm supposed to make to my new apartment. It doesn't take long. I think about going to the mall to walk off the nerves but I'm too exhausted. I remind myself that I'm not nervous at all, because I don't care about any of this.

I steel myself for a very long, very fucking terrible weekend of waiting.

Twenty minutes later I get a call. It's Lopez.

"Hello?" I say.

"Yeah, hey Johnny, it's Lo. I just wanted to call to, you know, ease your mind. I respect your game, how you play. Didn't want you to feel on edge all weekend. So yeah, everything's good, you made the cut, and I'll see you on Monday."

Lopez hangs up. He was talking fast. He never even let me speak, didn't give me a chance to say a single goddamn word. And for once, I have absolutely no problem with that.

My dream is alive!

Chapter 5

MY GLORIOUS
BACKUP DREAM™

The first day of the new season. The first day of living my dream.

I get to the facility, and it's a pleasure weighing in. I only hit 281 pounds, but who gives a fuck if I'm a few pounds light? I made the fucking team.

The shit I take afterward is the greatest dump I've taken all year. With that one massive crap, it's like I shed all the exhaustion, all the stress, all the uncertainty I had built up over camp. It was like cramming a full season into five goddamn weeks. But who the hell cares? I made the fucking team.

I get to the locker room, and the whole place feels like one big party. All the other backups are just giddy, absolutely bursting with joy and pure unadulterated relief. Grown men acting like a bunch of teenage girls who just received official invitations to sit at the popular kids' lunch table. I spot a rookie nose tackle who was on the bubble, standing at the end of the locker room.

"*Heyyyyy!*" I scream.

"We both made it!" he says, running toward me, his arms outstretched.

We grab each other and hug right there in the middle of the fucking room, laughing. We probably look about as straight as Michael Sam on a Grindr date. But who gives a shit? We made the fucking team.

Over the weekend I called up Kate and my dad, gave them the news. Kate pretended to be happy for me, but I could hear the disappointment in her voice. She had hoped that I'd be done with football forever so she could have me all for herself. Yeah, I kind of need a little break from Kate.

Even my dad hadn't sounded incredibly thrilled.

"It's good that you made the team," he says. "But it kind of sucks, doesn't it? You'll get paid, but you'll have to put up with all the NFL's bullshit."

And he was right. I was this close to ending my abusive relationship with football forever. Maybe not on my own terms, but still—it would've been over, I would've been forced to move on. Now I'm in it for at least another year.

But honestly? Deep down under all the aches and bruises, under the reams of athletic tape and the haze of the pain pills, in ways I didn't even want to admit to my own father, I was ecstatic.

Over the next four months, I'd get paid thirty thousand dollars a game to stand on the sidelines, watch all the action, keep a close eye on the guy that I was backing up, and think *please don't get hurt please don't get hurt please don't get hurt please don't get hurt* over and over and over again.

"Oh my God!" Dante yells back in the locker room. "Is that *Keith*? *Keith Nunn* made the team?! You gotta be fucking kidding me!"

Dante laughs. He means it as a joke, a way to welcome me, but damn, I am sick of that joke.

"Ha-ha," I say. "Congrats to you too, baby."

Now that the final roster has been set, most of the divisions between the starters and the benchers have fallen away. Preseason it was every man for himself, guys were just worried about keeping their jobs, and they'd do anything to keep themselves on top. But now? We're all on the same side, and we're all we really have. If we can't figure out how to work together, we're fucked.

"Congrats, Johnny," Jeb says to me, patting me on the back. "You get to put up with Lo's shit for the rest of the year."

"You in it for the long haul now, Johnny," Antonne says.

"Holy fuck," I say. "It's gonna be miserable!"

But I'm smiling. They both called me "Johnny." I made the fucking team.

LOPEZ LOOKS OUT OVER ALL his linemen, quietly scanning the room from his desk at the front, his large, flabby, almost perfectly spherical body looming over us all. He likes to do this at the beginning of O-line meetings. Build the suspense, heighten the anticipation, drive into our brains just how important, just how *critical* whatever he's about to say is to the future of our team, to the future of motherfucking humanity itself.

This, people, is the NFL regular season.

No more of that preseason pussy shit, where guys pretend to care about the outcome of the games but no one really does. This is the real deal. Where every snap, every series, every game, and every win—or loss—counts.

For the next four months, from September through the end of December, we will play sixteen games. Our only goal will be to win them all. And after that, in the all-important play-offs, to win some more. Life will be good if we win. If we lose, life will cease to have meaning until we win again.

This is what we're taught, this is what we must believe—starters and backups alike.

I hate how much the NFL focuses on winning. Drives me nuts. The League markets winning as a matter of pride and honor. Like there's a morality behind it, and if we win, that somehow means we're good human beings, and if we lose, we're scum. That's all garbage. It's simple economics. If we lose, fans won't like us. If fans don't like us, they don't buy our shit. If they don't buy our shit, we're all out of fucking jobs.

You know what guys like Dante say when they make a great catch in practice? Even multimillionaires like him? The thing I hear them say most often isn't "Fuck yeah" or some generic cheer. It's "Feed your family."

That's what each catch is to them. Not glory, or honor, or even arrogance. It's food.

That's a fucked-up reality. I respect anyone who does a job and does it well, but let's keep our priorities straight here. Winning a football game should be fun, and losing should be a mild annoyance. It should not be a matter of life or death, or someone's personal religion. This is football, not World War III.

Lopez looks out over his linemen, but he doesn't fix his gaze on a starter like Antonne or a star like Jeb. He turns his focus to another new guy, a backup. A dude who, by all rights, is a complete and absolute nobody on this team. Just like me.

"Hey, Grossman," Lopez says. "Who did you play for again last year?"

Lopez, of course, knows exactly who Grossman played for last year. He played for the team we're going to face on Sunday. Which is exactly what Grossman tells him.

"Oh yeah!" Lopez says, not making any real effort to act surprised. "Yeah, yeah. Right. And you were probably on their scout team, yeah?"

Another question Lopez—and everyone else—already knows the answer to. One of backups' main roles is to play on their team's "scout team." That's the squad that plays against the starters in practices during the week, helps get them ready for the upcoming game. So anyone on a scout team's offense would have very, very thorough knowledge of his team's defense.

"Yeah," Grossman says. "I was on the scout team all the time, sure."

Which means one thing: assuming Grossman's former team hasn't changed much about their scheme from last year, Lopez has got himself the perfect spy.

"Oh okay, yeah," Lopez says, still trying to act vaguely uninterested. "And they were running a 4-3 under, right?"

After that, whatever was left of the extremely thin curtain falls down. Lopez spends the rest of that meeting *and* the next offensive-line meeting ignoring the rest of us and flat-out grilling Grossman about his former team's defense. Every one of their plays, every one of their calls, every one of their habits, from where they liked to position their safety to who lets the meanest farts—he gets it all.

That Sunday, we win the game. Is it cheating? Absolutely. And it happens on every team in the League.

Coaches interrogate players from every position—quarterback, defensive back, kicker, whatever—to get info on their former teams. And not just their habits, but their actual *calls,* essentially allowing them to intercept their opponent's communications during a game. Teams even pick guys up just to use them as spies. On my last team, management cut a guy during camp who was so old he had no business going anywhere near a football field anymore. The next day, he got signed by our biggest rival in the League. Not just to their practice squad—which would've allowed us to poach him back—but to their active roster. He didn't play all year, but he knew our offense front and back. Dude had a better scam going than I do. They fucking beat us too.

Then my team cut me, and I got my own taste of just how dirty everyone is. The first team I interviewed with was scheduled to face my former team in their season opener. Someone made sure I didn't leave town without having a nice little sit-down with their defensive coordinator, who grilled me about my former team's game plan.

I told them everything I knew. And I felt guilty as hell afterward. I obviously didn't give a shit about my former coaches, but some of the players I had left behind were buddies of mine. So what did I do? I texted my former team's starting center and told *him* the *other* team's game plan.

I became a football double agent.

That's why I always laugh whenever people act so outraged about the Patriots and whatever their latest "scandal" is. The Pats are no different than anyone else in the NFL. They worship winning so much they'll do anything for it. The only mistake they make is that they get caught.

THE RAY RICE VIDEO HIT the Internet yesterday. Today, it's all anyone can talk about. Teddy and I walk in, see the receptionist, and instead of saying "hi" the first thing out of her mouth is "Did you see it? Did you see the video?"

Yeah, I saw it.

The guy knocks his fiancée out like it's nothing, then drags her across the floor like she's a broken mannequin. It's fucking disgusting, there's no other way to put it. But honestly it's not very surprising, either.

My line of work *rewards* guys for being hyperaggressive maniacs. Not condones, rewards. The guy who's most aggressive, who's most vicious, who's most relentlessly psychotic on the field will succeed. I learned a long time ago, when I first started out, how to cordon off that anger, how to unleash it only at very specific, very special moments while I'm playing.

The rest of the time? I'm the nicest, joking-est, fun-loving-est guy you'll ever meet. I'm even that way most of the time on the field. Relaxed, having fun—it's when I'm at my best. It's only when that ball snaps that I really turn the aggression on.

But many players don't know how to create that separation. They come from a background—whether it's the hood or the trailer park— where violence is a way of life. Crime, gangs, drugs, you name it. Football hasn't just given them an outlet for their aggression on the field, it's also given their lives structure and discipline. They literally get told what time to wake up, when to eat, when to sleep, even what to wear. But take that team structure away for an off-season or even a bye week, and their aggression finds ways other than football to express itself—sometimes through the same violence they grew up with.

Don't get me wrong—a lot of guys learn how to control themselves, leave the past behind, and never look back. But for some of them, if it wasn't for the NFL, they wouldn't be playing football, they'd be in prison. Then you got your lucky few like Aaron Hernandez or Michael Vick who just happen to get both.

How does the League deal with this violent streak? By treating us to more fucking seminars, of course. Meetings! The answer to all life's problems.

The second week of training camp, the NFL had one of its security officers come in to give the whole team our annual "crime talk."

They blasted us with a shitload of statistics about all the trouble players get into. From 2010 to 2013, there were 89 DUIs, 47 charges for drug possession, 39 traffic violations, and 31 domestic violence charges. These are all the NFL's *own numbers*. It's no secret that we fuck up, not even to the League.

They showed us diagrams and charts, quizzed us about driving drunk, told us we couldn't gamble, showed us cautionary videos about guys like Tank Johnson, who got arrested for six unregistered guns, and ended with a quote from Roger Goodell himself, telling us "the highest standards must be met by NFL representatives because it is a privilege to be in the NFL, not a right."

That's what he said, but the overall takeaway was "Please, please, don't fuck up, because then we'll all look really, really bad." They talked a little about domestic violence, but honestly, not much. It was, after all, only the fourth-biggest problem over the last few years.

Then a few weeks after the seminar, the Ray Rice scandal hits like a giant pile of my morning shit. Looks like the NFL's approach worked out pretty well, right?

Teddy and I get to the locker room, and it's mayhem. Opinions, conspiracy theories, and excessive amounts of profanity flying back and forth.

"That *motherfucker*! If I ever—*ever*—caught another man laying a hand on a woman like that, I'd fucking kill that *fucker*! Ray Rice better stay *the fuck* away from me!"

A helmet rifles through the air and smashes against the wall at full force. I turn to see who this zealous defender of women's rights happens to be, and I'm completely floored. It's none other than Dante our Diva receiver. The same guy who owns multiple cell phones to keep all his mistresses straight.

"Fuck," I whisper to Teddy. "I wonder how Dante's girlfriends feel about his position on domestic violence?"

"I don't know," Teddy says, legitimately puzzled. "I guess they like it?"

The locker room is full of gossip about Rice. Like I said before, the NFL can be a lot like high school. There are only two thousand of us in the entire League, so everyone knows a little bit about everyone else, but no one knows the whole story. Word is that before this huge fuckup, Ray Rice was already a cancer on his own team—someone who tears a team apart because instead of being a leader, he's a selfish, arrogant prick. Is it accurate? Who knows, it's gossip, could all be bullshit. But when Rice does finally get the ax—Baltimore fires him after the video's released—everyone believes he got exactly what he deserved.

But the biggest talk by far has nothing to do with Ray Rice, it's all about the NFL. What did top executives know and when. See, the incident itself is old news. The media's known about it since summer. It's the graphic video that's new.

Shockingly, NFL officials claim they had absolutely *no* knowledge of the video before it got released to the press. If they had seen this horrible video, then *of course* they would've given Ray Rice more than the slap on the wrist they initially gave him. Of course!

"Bull-fucking-shit," Jovan the Preacher says, up on his soapbox. "NFL knew it all from the beginning, they just covering their ass now, that all it is."

"Come on," one of the rookies says. "You saying there ain't even a chance they didn't know? I mean just a *chance*?"

"No way they didn't know," the Preacher says. "No fucking way."

"The League fucking knows everything about us," Jeb says. "Everything. They're plugged in. Those fuckers got connections everywhere."

"Absolutely," I say. "When I got interviewed at the combine three years ago, they fucking asked me about a speeding ticket I got in high school. A fucking speeding ticket!"

It's true. The combine isn't just a big series of physical tests the League puts prospects through before the draft, it's also a chance for teams to vet everything about you. I had to take three personality tests for three different teams. One of my buddies had to take seven. They were basic

multiple-choice questions with what seemed to me like ridiculously obvious answers. Stuff along the lines of "If you see a person you know on
the street, do you (a) say hello and shake their hand? Or (b) punch them
in the face?"

I wonder how Ray answered that one.

"Hey," Teddy says to me, watching the video on his phone for the
fourth time. "Think I should tweet something like 'What about that left
hook, though'?"

"Yeah," I say. "Probably not a good idea."

Who knows? Maybe next year they'll add a seminar on public relations, too.

ANOTHER LONG, HOT DAY. It's the beginning of practice, getting in
our drills, basic stuff, blocking technique, whatever. Stuff we've all done
a million times before.

And Lopez just can't help himself.

"Jeb! Jeb!" he shouts. "No, no, no. Let me show you something here—"

Lopez grabs Jeb in the middle of his drill—physically touches our star
lineman—probably to correct Jeb's blocking technique. I can't tell you,
because Lopez never got that far.

"Who the fuck you think you are, man?" Jeb shouts at Lopez. "I know
what the fuck I'm doing! This is pros, not college! Back the fuck off and
let me play!"

And what does his "boss" say back? Nothing. What can he say? Lo's
a first-year coach. Jeb is a franchise player. He banks almost $900,000 a
week. *A week.*

Is Jeb a little bit of a diva? Absolutely. Not all stars act like him, and
some work even harder than the benchers. But the guy knows how valu-
able he is, and he takes advantage of it. Shows up at O-line meetings
late, skips workouts, and takes naps in the players' lounge instead. That's
right, naps. Dims the lights, turns off the flat-screen TVs, pushes a couple
couches together, lies down, and falls asleep.

But none of us, none of the players, even faults him for it. The schedule is a grind, especially for a starter, and Jeb isn't young anymore. Rest for him isn't a luxury, it's a necessity, something his body needs to keep performing at his top level, week in and week out. If we could, we'd do the exact same thing.

Part of coaching in the pros is understanding this fact. Lopez doesn't yet, but he'd better figure it the fuck out. If the team really wanted to, it could find another Lopez—another fifty Lopezes—in a heartbeat. It can't find another Jeb.

TWICE A DAY, MORNING AND AFTERNOON, we have our miserable, tedious offensive-line meetings with Lopez. But once a week we have another kind of meeting—the only meeting I actually enjoy. It's players only, just our position, and no coaches allowed.

Of course, we're supposed to use the meetings for work. And at first, that's exactly what we did. They were 100 percent football, 100 percent work. As offensive linemen, we like to consider ourselves the brains of the team. But now, after a few meetings, work is down to maybe 5 percent.

Today, for the other 95 percent of the time, Teddy gives us a better "cultural awareness seminar" than the team could possibly come up with.

The meeting starts out normally enough. Antonne is talking about blocking technique, because Antonne can—and does—talk about blocking technique all fucking day. Until Teddy interrupts it with a belch so powerful that it stinks up the whole room.

"There goes Teddy's incest breath," Jeb says.

Jeb is a gigantic country boy from the South. So obviously a lengthy debate is immediately sparked over who has the most incest, the islands or the South? (As far as I'm concerned, it's the South by a long shot.)

"Come on, man!" Teddy argues, grinning. "We don't do all that shit. You guys got all this, like, mistaken ideas about us and stuff. We got, like, culture!"

"My ass," Jeb says. "What culture you island fuckers got?"

"Well, like the haka."

The group collectively "ooooohs." There are so many Samoans in football that all of us have seen a traditional tribal haka dance before, at least on TV. But none of us has ever done one.

Pretty soon, everyone is pushing the chairs to the edge of the room.

"*Hahhhhhhhhhhhhhh!*" Teddy growls from the center of the room. His eyes are open wide, his tongue is sticking straight out of his mouth, he's crouched like a warrior, hands on his knees, ready to pounce. I had no idea this guy could look so terrifying.

"*Hahhhhhhhhhhhhhhhhhhhh!*" we all repeat after him.

I look around me. We're all together. The scrub benchers like me and all the starters, Antonne, Jeb, Coulter, Marcus, Williams—professionals who make millions upon millions of dollars—all of us with our tongues jutting out, our eyeballs round and bloodshot, making the craziest, most ridiculous faces we can make, slapping our thighs and snarling like animals, all like it was the most natural thing in the world.

Fuck. I love these guys.

THERE'S NO WAY TO REALLY, like, lead into this, so I'm just gonna cut to the chase.

During our away game today, one of the rookies, a guy named Perry, shits his pants. This isn't, like, a metaphor. No, in the middle of the first quarter, Perry honest-to-God, flat-out shits his pants.

Perry's a second-string corner, and when one of the starters gets tweaked, the coaches send him in. It was his first time ever playing in a real, regular-season NFL game. He plays a few downs. He comes back out. He's got a massive brown spot streaked all over his ass.

In case you're wondering, there's no mud in artificial turf.

News gets passed along the sideline faster than a naked pic of Kim Kardashian.

"Perry shit his pants!"

"You see that?"

"Dude didn't even get hit that hard!"

And of course, "Hey, shit happens."

Guys are laughing, walking up to him, making subtle comments like "Hey, Perry, you got some, uh, business you need to attend to?" And then laughing some more.

Look. We play a physical game. People get nervous, even "warriors" like us. Plus, you know that stereotypical football code about fighting through all the pain and discomfort? Yeah, well, for some guys that applies to losing control of your bodily functions too.

I'm serious. I played with a guy in college who would piss himself in practice at least once a week. Part of it was because he was so terrified of our O-line coach he didn't want to ask for a bathroom break. But the other part was that he thought it was badass. Like "Hell yeah, I pissed myself. I was too focused on the play to care!"

He was the fucking Billy Madison of college football.

For some guys, linemen especially, pissing your pants is actually a thing, a sign that you're so into the game, so much of a fighter, that you won't even take a piss break. You'd rather let it spill out all over your legs. People who believe this are, obviously, fucking idiots.

Then again, even they aren't into shitting their pants. That's pretty damn rare.

At halftime, Perry finally gets the chance to change his pants. But minutes into the third quarter, they're already streaked again.

"He shit his pants again!?" I ask Antonne.

"Naw," he says. "Motherfucker just didn't wipe his ass."

Oh yeah, we obliterated the other team. Led the entire game. When you're winning, everything is funny. Everything is right. Even a guy shitting his pants. Twice.

WE'RE IN THE OFFENSIVE-LINE MEETING of the week, about to start prepping for our next opponent. Lopez looks out over everyone, as usual, building the suspense.

Suddenly a change in the routine. Teddy raises his hand.

"Hey, Lopez," he says. "You see their roster? G.I. Joe is on there."

You remember him, right? G.I. Joe, the real American hero our team cut during training camp? Turns out the guy managed to get on the practice squad of another team after we dropped him. Specifically, the team we're about to play—a team that just happens to be one of our biggest rivals. Purely coincidence, I'm sure.

"I know," Lopez says. "I already texted him not to share any of our shit with them."

"Seriously?" Antonne says.

"Of course," Lopez says, with no hint of irony. "Told him it'd be unethical."

THIS AFTERNOON I HEAD INTO the cafeteria to grab some lunch. As usual, players are sitting at two separate tables—one white, one black. As usual, I take my heaping mound of chicken and rice and head straight to the white table. No big deal. It's just how it is.

But for some weird reason, Jovan the Preacher decides to say something.

"Yo, Johnny!" he yells. "Why the fuck you sit over there with them? We got plenty of seats over here! You guys be having a Klan meeting or some shit?"

Everyone looks up. For a split second, the entire cafeteria goes silent.

Now if the politically correct mainstream media got their hands on tape of just that moment, they'd probably start screaming about racism and the fault lines running through our team and all the strife in our society or whatever.

My response? I laugh.

"Hey, baby," I say. "I'm just terrified of that Black Panther party you got over there."

Tension gone. Everyone cracks up.

"You plottin' to take over the team and shit, ain't you?" Antonne yells.

"Yeah," a white player says, "we gotta save ourselves from all you militant motherfuckers!"

Racism does exist in the NFL. This is America; that shit is everywhere. I hear players from the Deep South call people coons and all sorts of fucked-up shit when no black guys are around to listen. And frankly, I hear black guys call each other far worse every day.

During camp, we had the usual meeting with NFL refs where they go over all the rules. There was one black ref. At the end of the meeting, he cleared his throat.

"Now, I want to address the elephant in the room," he said. "I don't care if you're just joking around, talking to your friends or what—if I or any ref hears you use the n-word, I will throw a flag."

A black guy raised his hand.

"Does it matter if it's the '-er' kind versus the '-ah' kind?" he asked.

(It doesn't, in case you're wondering.)

Black players call the white players crackers and honkies all the time— usually to their face, because they're black and they can get away with it. And I'll be honest. If I'm sitting next to two black dudes on the bench, I can't even understand what they're saying to each other 60 percent of the time. Last time that happened, Antonne walked by, looked at me, and said, "Don't worry. I can't understand what the hell they saying either."

You got some white guys who grew up in the inner city and are more "culturally black." You even got a couple of black players—these upper-middle-class dudes from the suburbs—who "act white" around white teammates, then switch to pure Ebonics around the black guys. You got Americanized Mexicans like Lopez and Samoans like Tommy. You got a whole shitload of different people from different backgrounds.

Are there misunderstandings sometimes? Sure.

But we're a team. We're working toward a common goal, fighting against the same adversity, putting up with the same bullshit. That bond matters, even in a league as money hungry and "me centered" as the NFL. And it creates a kind of safe zone, where guys can be themselves. Where barriers can fall and political correctness doesn't apply.

So most of the time we just laugh like hell at how ridiculously human we all are. And when the bad shit happens, we talk it out and move on. We don't just bury it—like everyone else in this nation—where no one can find it. We bring it out in the open, we mock it, we fuck with it, we laugh about it until it's not a threat, until we strip it of all its power. We don't act all high and mighty when someone doesn't conform to a single, boring PC standard.

So yeah, we got racism in the NFL. We just handle it better than everyone else, that's all.

"Fuck it," I say to Jovan and Antonne. "Tomorrow I'm sitting at my own table, by myself, and watching TV."

"Awww, now you being antisocial," Jovan says, laughing. "Can I watch with you?"

"Sure, baby," I say. "Welcome to the Klan."

THE TIME IS RUNNING OUT on our third game. We're going to lose for the first time this season. And everything, all the positive energy, all the laughing and haka dances and the hanging out with the special teams guys, it's all about to change.

The score's not even close. We're down by seventeen.

Our offense is fucked. Now that we've played a couple games—and won them both—other teams have had a chance to scout us, analyze our new plays. When you're on a tear in the NFL, other teams' defensive coordinators will call up their buddies who've already played you and ask for tips, tendencies, calls that were overheard, anything to get an advantage. Anything to win.

As of this game, we've officially been figured out.

Antonne sits on the bench by himself, a towel over his head, slouched over, reliving his mistakes over and over again. Our center, the leader of the line, and he looks absolutely defeated. I notice the other linemen watching him too—benchers like me, starters like Jeb and Coulter and Marcus. They're watching him, following his cues, and I can see them slumping, drawing off Antonne's horrible vibe.

Antonne's been going out a lot, almost every night, drinking a fucking ton. That kind of lifestyle is fine—as long as you're winning. For him, this job is all he has. Not because of the money, but because he has no life. When he loses, he feels like he loses everything—and he risks taking everyone else with him.

Finally I walk over. I lean over and whisper.

"Hey, pick your head up. People are watching you."

Antonne does nothing, doesn't move until the clock finally ticks down to zero.

During the postgame speech, Jack does an impressive job blaming the players for all the fuckups and taking none of the responsibility himself. I've noticed over the last few weeks that whenever anything goes wrong it's always "*you* did this" or "*you* did that." It's always the players. But whenever anything good happens, it's always "us." *We* did it, together. Thank God for me, your head coach.

On the flight home, everyone puts on what I like to call their "shit face." Stony, serious, staring straight ahead. Brody the quarterback, Dante the receiver, Jeb the Old Vet, even Teddy. Antonne keeps muttering to himself; I pick up scattered phrases like "I should've been there . . . I fucked shit up . . ."

Last week, after we won, our plane ride home was fucking awesome. Antonne going on about all his latest Tinder dates and Ollie the kicker and the other special teams guys doing their best to convince him to try eating a chick's ass, because, you know, he *should.* Laughing and talking and playing cards and just making a big old mess out of things because we were winners, and life was grand.

Tonight there's nothing. Only dead quiet.

I look around at all the shit faces. I wonder how many of the guys actually feel bad, honestly depressed, because we lost a stupid football game. It's ridiculous, when you think about it. That a game would ever seem so important to someone.

That, I guess, is why they're starters, and I'm not.

I sit on the plane in my forced silence and close my eyes. I feel so lucky to be a backup right now. Did I ever care this much about winning games? Maybe a long time ago. But it seems impossible now.

Pretty soon I'm fast asleep.

OUR FIRST DAY BACK AT WORK, and it's still hanging in the air. The stench of losing.

"Fuck," Teddy says as we walk through the doors. "How you think Jack's gonna be?"

"Does this look serious enough?" I say, doing the best "Jack shit face" I can possibly manage. It's pretty close to my haka dance snarl.

We both crack up. The laughing feels good.

It amazes me how little it can take for a team to fall apart, to turn against itself, look for people to blame. It's so easy to have fun, to feel like friends and brothers, when you're all winning. You almost start to believe it's real.

But lose a game, and if you don't have strong leadership from a core of players or a well-respected coach, that sense of unity and purpose goes to shit. We're 2-1. That's a solid start to the season. Still on track with plenty of time to make the play-offs. But today, in the locker room, none of that matters.

"Man," Jeb says, "if Bobby was back, he'd fix everything."

Bobby was the offensive-line coach last year, before Lopez. He'd been with the team for six seasons, a lifetime in the NFL. But last season they got knocked out of the play-offs in the first round. Jack had to blame someone, so Bobby was gone. Now that Bobby is gone, the starters are naturally going after the new guy. Lopez.

"Yeah," Coulter says. "I heard that Jack shit all over Lo after the game."

"So what?" Jeb says. "You know Lo is throwing all of us under the bus every fucking chance he gets!"

"*No doubt,*" Marcus says. "Lo always says he's a positive coach. Like he's here for *us*. But he ain't positive at all, he's negative all the time."

"Fuck yeah!" Jeb says. "It's like Lo's got this mentality like 'Did you practice that play? Good, so it's not my fault if you fuck it up.' Mother-fucking Mexican shouldn't be coaching, he should be cutting grass."

"Or at least making us margaritas," Coulter says, laughing.

Lopez, of course, was born in America, as were his parents. He has a southern accent and probably makes a horrible margarita. But he could've been named Bob Smith and they would've found a way to tear him apart.

Later that day, we all shuffle in for the offensive-line meeting. All of us except Jeb. Jeb's been showing up later and later for meetings over the last few weeks. Lopez, of course, hasn't been able to do a damn thing about it. He just doesn't have the fucking clout. He's tried playing all Jeb's tape first, you know, to entice the guy to arrive on time, but even when that has worked—maybe about half the time—Jeb just left early. It was actually kind of funny—when we were winning.

But today is different. Or at least it should be.

Lopez cues up the game tape right to Jeb's film, presses play—and realizes Jeb isn't there. He angrily hits fast-forward.

"One of these days," he growls, "that motherfucker—"

"Yo, Lopez! Why you skip that play?"

It's a voice from the back. Jeb's voice. He's sitting on the floor with his back to the wall, where no one can see him.

Lopez physically gets hot. His face turns bright red, sweat beading up on his forehead.

"Oh," he says. "Uh, nothing, Jeb."

Everyone laughs, all except Lopez.

LATER THAT WEEK, I GO in early to work out by myself in the weight room. Lopez walks in. First time I've seen him do anything even *close* to exercising. He immediately starts benching, doesn't even warm up, which is absolutely horrible for you.

And he's struggling.

Barely any weight, not even 150 pounds. But he's so fat and out of shape he'd have a hard time lifting the bar alone. Plus, his form is all wrong. You could be the strongest guy in the world, and if you have bad form, forget about it. You won't be able to lift shit.

"You know what, motherfucker?" I say. "I'm gonna spot your sorry ass."

He looks up with a start, probably didn't even notice I was there.

"What?" he says. "I'm fine! Hey, let go of the fucking bar!"

"Here," I say, positioning the bar over his chest. "It should be right over your nipples, wherever the fuck those are, and don't tell me because I don't want to know. And your wrists should be rigid, not angled. You can get more force that way."

Slowly, his muscles shaking, Lopez does ten reps. I grip the bar loosely the entire time, probably carrying half the weight myself. But he still does them, all ten.

"You can't tell me you're this fucking weak," I say, getting up. "You better get your shit together."

I reach out my hand, practically pull him up off the bench until he's standing.

"Fuck you, Johnny," he says.

It's a much different "fuck you" than the last one I got in the weight room, from our pompous general manager. This one somehow feels appreciative. Like he's grateful there's a player he can curse out without worrying about losing his job.

"Admit it, Lopez," I say. "You like me."

He looks at me and grins.

"Don't tell anyone, asshole."

MY DAY OFF. I DECIDE to go for a walk in the mall. I haven't been here in a while, and it feels like therapy. All the stores, all the regular people. All the total lack of football.

I follow my usual ritual. Head right past the expensive stores. Make a quick stop at Teavana where I take advantage of each and every one of their free samples. The guy behind the counter tries to fill the sample cups themselves, but I insist on doing the pouring. Fill those babies all the way to the brim. Nothing like the taste of free.

Then I head to Macy's to check to see if there's a sale.

Half off on sheets, you say? Don't mind if I do.

For the first few weeks of the season, I didn't have a bed because of a fuckup by the rental company. I slept on a goddamn air mattress. Every night it deflated and I had to wake up at 4 A.M. to pump it up again. Supposedly it was top of the line.

Yesterday my bed was finally delivered. It's brand-new, king-size, and absolutely gorgeous. A bed like that deserves new sheets, especially if they're on sale.

I get the good stuff. We're talking Egyptian cotton, one thousand thread count here. I don't skimp when it comes to my sleep.

I go to pay for the sheets, and the cashier lady tells me they're on clearance. So not just fifty percent off. *Seventy-five percent off.* Let me repeat that:

"Seventy-five percent off!" I say to the woman, in case she didn't hear me the first three times. "You gotta be kidding me!"

"No," she says, smiling. "I'm not kidding. Seventy-five percent."

I allow this amazing fact to wash over me.

"You're beautiful," I say. "Absolutely beautiful. This is the best thing that's happened to me all week."

"Really?" she says.

In case you hadn't noticed, I'm very friendly when I save money.

Kate is flying in tomorrow to visit for the weekend, and I'm feeling good.

She's coming to watch our game on Sunday. A game where I'll do absolutely nothing. We win? Great. We lose? Fine by me. Sure, maybe people get a little grumpy, but what do I care? I'm a backup, I'm still getting paid, and I just saved $225 on sheets.

Everything is going exactly according to plan.

Chapter 6
FUCK

Kate's gonna sit with Teddy's fiancée, Andrea, during today's game. Andrea is small and blond, just like Kate. Teddy, of course, is massive. I don't know what it is about linemen. Somehow we always end up with these tiny chicks, usually blond.

The girls take a half-pint of whiskey with them to the stadium.

"Go for it," I tell Kate. "Drink up. There's no way I'll be playing."

There's no real need for me to tell her this. It's my third year in the NFL, and I've still never really played in a regular-season game. Sure, I've gone in for a couple snaps here and there, some garbage time. But I haven't *really* played. So she already knows I'm not getting in. But still, I feel kind of guilty. She flew here for this, for me, and I know she wants to see me play, but I'm not gonna play, and even if I could, I wouldn't fucking want to. So I tell her, just to make it extra clear, "Honestly, there's no way I'm getting in."

And there isn't. Until the middle of the second quarter, when the entire world goes motherfucking crazy.

First Marcus goes down, the right tackle. He goes for a cut block and catches the ground awkwardly, and the next thing I know he's down, grabbing his knee, clawing at the turf, dragging himself across the ground as he shrieks in pain. From the sidelines I'm guessing it's an MCL tear, an injury I suffered in college, something that doesn't actually hurt that much but will scare the shit out of you.

All I can think is *There's no way I'm getting in.*

Teddy takes Marcus's place on the field. Two plays later, Antonne goes down. He's holding his back. He most likely pulled something, probably be out for a play or two, no big deal. Then I remember that Antonne was just complaining about an old back injury a few days ago, and I think, *Fuck, this is serious. He's out for the game.*

That and *There's* no fuckin' way *I'm getting in.*

Parkman, the backup center/right guard, goes in for Antonne. And one play later, another lineman goes down with a pop. Parkman. It's gotta be the Achilles. That's it for Parkman.

But still. There's no way I'm—wait, I'm the only backup left. Fuck.

"Johnny! Johnny!"

It's Lopez, even more panicked than usual. The pen he's chewing flies out of his mouth as he screams with all his might.

"Johnny!"

We need a center out there, and both our centers, Antonne and Parkman, are out. But I'm a fucking guard! Technically I'm *supposed* to be able to play center—all backups are *supposed* to be dual purpose—but I haven't practiced at center all season! The last time I snapped a ball in a game was in college!

And *now,* not only do they want me to go into the game, practically my first real game in the NFL, but they want me to be the center—the guy in charge of reading the defense, who makes the calls and leads the entire fucking offensive line?

I guess they do. There's no other option.

The next thing I know a bunch of players, dudes I barely ever talk to, guys I hardly even know, starters and backups, are walking up to me and patting me on the back. "You'll do good, Johnny." "You got this, man." "It's all you out there." And I nod my head and say thanks but what I'm really thinking is *Why the fuck are they encouraging me so much? Do I really look that lost right now? They must think I suck!*

Lopez pushes past all of them. He has this resigned look on his face.

I realize he's in even more shock than I am, and for one brief moment that makes me feel better.

"Johnny," he says. "You're in."

And then, the closest thing Lopez will ever give to an honest-to-God moving motivational speech: "Get pumped!"

Fuck. I'm going in.

I JOG ONTO THE FIELD. There's a loud, pulsing vibration all around me that I assume is the fans but to me is nothing but static, background noise. All my energy is focused on the zillion totally new things I need to figure out on every single play. My breathing is even, my hands are steady, my will is determined.

And I play like absolute *horseshit*.

I'm trapped inside my own head, seeing only what's right in front of me, too panicked to look around, to breathe, to take control.

The easy part is reading the defense. I do that all the time as a guard anyway, and Lopez loves to quiz me on my reads just to fuck with me. Except *now* I don't just have to worry about myself, I have to worry about the entire rest of the line *and* the quarterback.

They're all used to following Antonne. They're used to his timing, the rhythm of his count, the way he snaps the ball, even the cadence of his voice. They've got a finely calibrated chemistry. And now they've gotta switch to me, to someone completely new, without any warning.

On my very first play, we false start. That's not good. And it happens precisely because we're not in sync, and one of the linemen flinches before I snap the ball.

Next play, I get the snap off, but I snap the ball too high, almost over Brody the QB's head, and he has to land on the ball just to prevent a turnover. Not good.

Lopez is screaming something incoherent on the sidelines, pacing back and forth like a maniac, his normally cold eyes on fire. Teddy is hyperventilating like we're all about to run out of oxygen, and Jeb glares at me as we line up a third time.

"Hey, man, relax!" he says.

I snap the ball. I get it off, but I'm so worried about not fucking it up that I read the defense wrong.

Their nose tackle straight-up bull-rushes me. There's no technique, no move, no swim or club, just two big hands to my chest and he fucking drives me straight back to Brody. I figured I'd block the same way I do as a guard—how much different can it be, right? Turns out, very.

He looks down at me and grunts.

"Gonna be a long day, 61."

Sixty-one, that's my number. He's no poet, but I hear the message loud and clear. Our offense goes three-and-out. End of series.

At the end of the half, we're down 14–6. Our fans boo us as we jog off the field. Thanks, guys. Fuck you too.

WE GET INTO THE LOCKER ROOM, and something happens. I can't really explain it. It's not one single thing, and it all happens really fast, crushed together, a big messy blur.

Jack and our offensive coordinator realize the other team has one of our trademark plays called "32" figured out, and they make adjustments. Lopez comes over and gives me some advice for my center technique. Jeb grabs me and tells me to get out of my shell, and even Dante shouts something profound that sounds like "let your swag hang!," which somehow makes me both roll my eyes and smile at the same time. Teddy stops hyperventilating, catches me giving him a stupid look, and we both start cracking up for no good reason at all.

Shit, I almost forgot to take a piss!

Somehow, it all adds up to one amazing result: I realize that Antonne and Parkman aren't coming back into this game. I'm in this, win or lose, no matter what, so honestly, who gives a shit? I get the fuck out of my own skull, and I get the fuck out of my own way.

I finally start having fun.

"Get pumped!" Lopez says to me again as we head back out to the field. Teddy and I execute a perfectly ridiculous chest bump.

"We're pumped!" we shout mockingly.

On the field I stop trying to do a bad impersonation of Antonne's style. He's intense, hard-core, lots of snarling and screaming. Way too serious for me. My style is the exact opposite. I like being cool and relaxed; I like to laugh and have a good time. I'm a breath of motherfucking fresh air. That's who I am, that's what I do. And I own it.

We drive 43 yards on our first six plays. On our seventh play, we bait the defense into thinking we're gonna run 32 again, but we throw an iso play at them instead. Our running back picks up 7 yards, and I knock that douchebag nose tackle 15 yards down the field, take him completely out of the action.

If I were Antonne, I'd be talking shit right now. Instead, I crack up and smile.

"I hope we just run the ball all game!"

The guy looks confused, then actually laughs with me.

"Yeah!" He laughs like a total moron.

His rage is gone, and I proceed to own him for the next twenty minutes.

It's actually pretty simple. As a guard, you have time. There's this short, comforting window when you can react to the defender's move, see where he's going to put his hands and how he's going to counter your technique. At center, you don't have any of that. The guy lined up across from you is so close you can smell what he ate before the game. Contact is instantaneous. It's aggressive. It's a car collision on every snap. All you can do is try to survive the Buick to your forehead and create movement.

I forget about being a guard and adjust. That's it.

Once I get into a rhythm on the field, nothing else matters at all. It's just me and the game. I forgot how much I missed this, actually playing. I forgot what it was like, the energy, the emotion, the fun of it all. This isn't practice. This isn't preseason. This is a real game, on the world's biggest stage. This is a big fucking deal.

By the beginning of the fourth quarter, the nose tackle who started out so cocky gets yanked from the game by his own team. They replace him with someone even worse.

Our next series, we score. Then we score again—a field goal, but it's enough. We win the game, 16–14. Now, look. I'm not gonna claim we played some kind of offensive masterpiece here. I mean, we scored 10 points in the second half. If anything, it was a defensive win.

But still, we won. That's what matters in this League.

And I have to admit, it feels pretty fucking good.

BACK IN THE LOCKER ROOM after the victory, I suddenly belong to a club I never even knew existed.

I check my cell and I've got a hundred text messages from people I forgot I knew, or maybe they had just forgotten me. The best one, though, came from my dad, right after I went into the game. "What the hell are you doing out there? Letting you play center? Let's show them! Love you, proud of you."

From him, those couple lines mean everything.

A pack of media mobs me, suffocating me with questions. Me, a guy they've never even noticed before. They're stupid questions mostly—it is the media, after all—but who cares? It's like all of a sudden I exist. Johnny Anonymous has his own fucking name.

Even Lowry, the general manager, comes up and shakes my hand. That's right, the same guy I basically called a pussy a little over a month ago! And this motherfucker smiles at me, shakes my hand, and says, "Nice job out there."

I'm stunned. And before I can even recover from that shock, I feel this tap on my shoulder and it's the owner! The owner! Let me repeat, *the owner*!

He's in fucking penny loafers and a jersey, looks like a jackass, but he's worth a billion bucks so he can wear whatever the fuck he wants. This toothy, wrinkled old country club fuck has passed me in the halls a million times, never even said hello, and now he's chatting me up like we're best buddies, talking about the tactical differences between being a center and a guard or some shit, although I get the sneaking suspicion that he still doesn't know what my name is. Whatever. From him, I'll take it.

Jack, the head coach, doesn't say shit to me, probably because he's even more socially awkward than most head coaches. But Lopez is the coach whose opinion matters most to me—I hate to admit it, but it's true—and I catch him glancing at me out of the corner of his eye while I'm talking to the owner. Lo's got this look on his face. It's not pride or happiness or anything like that. It's more a look of understanding, of revelation. Like *Oh. Johnny can do this. He can really play.*

After the postgame circus ends, Teddy and I head out and meet up with Kate and Andrea. By this point, Kate is totally trashed.

"Congratulations, Johnny!" she says, giving me a kiss. I smell the booze on her breath. "Don't let this go too much to your head!"

She laughs awkwardly.

"Uh-huh," I say.

Whenever I've done well in football, in anything really, Kate always freaks out, gets paranoid that I'm gonna dump her, give in to all the temptations that come with playing high-level football. Which do exist, especially for the guys who seek them out, going to clubs and showing off their money and status. There's plenty of women who'll use you for exactly that. But that's not me—I'm no Antonne, right-swiping on Tinder five hundred times a day.

"I love you, you know that, right?" she says, slurring her words. "You know I love you, right?"

"Yep."

We all head to this restaurant near the stadium called Big Chaz. It's a total dive. Ribs, pizza, cheap beer. Flickering neon sign, duct tape patches on the seat cushions, the whole deal. But it's also the unofficial team restaurant. Players, coaches, everyone eats for free. There's even this special secret door in the back so none of us ever has to wait in line. It's like we're a bunch of wiseguys or something.

Teddy, the ladies, and I walk through this exclusive entrance. Inside it's dark and noisy, people are laughing and bullshitting, and the air is thick with the smell of barbecue and grease: every TV airing our postgame show. Literally the entire team is here. We're talking assistant coaches, trainers, even a goddamn intern showing off for this girl he brought for a first date. I hope he gets laid tonight.

I see the offensive coordinator with what looks like his entire extended family. Kids, cousins, grandparents, aunts, second uncles twice removed by marriage. They're taking up three full tables. He looks at me, his mouth stuffed with ribs.

"What? Free food!!"

The four of us grab a table by the wall and the waitress comes over to take our order. I've heard her say what she's about to say to every other table, even the one with the intern.

"Hey," she says. "Good game tonight."

But somehow, for some reason, this one feels like it's meant just for me. I look at her and grin.

"You know what?" I say. "I completely agree."

THE AFTERGLOW LASTS AS LONG as our day off. Then it's back to work, and back to reality.

Lopez doesn't waste any time and grabs me right before the first meeting of the day.

"Johnny, you, uh, did pretty good the other day," he says. "But we gotta make sure you're the best option for us to be successful."

Translation: They want to find someone else to be center.

"Yeah, I get it," I tell him. "I'm too small, blah blah blah. The story of my career. Whatever, it's your grave."

I should've known this was coming. Antonne and Parkman are both out of commission. Antonne's back rehab will take at least six weeks, maybe more. And Parkman, Antonne's backup? Torn Achilles. He's done for the year. But I just don't have a ton of experience at center, no matter how well I played the other day. They just don't trust me to get it done.

Centers can actually be a little smaller than the rest of the line. But this is the NFL; the teams in this league want the mold, the prototype. It's one thing to have an undersized backup. But an undersized starter?

It's like that spare tire you got in your trunk. It's fine when you get a flat and you just need to make it to that gas station down the road. But there's no way you wanna drive on that doughnut every day on the highway.

Fine, I think. *They're not paying me enough to put my ass on the line for these douchebags every Sunday. Fuck the coaches and their bullshit.*

I find out management has already picked up a free agent to be the new center. Hired him yesterday. Hell, the GM was probably making calls to agents at halftime, an hour before he congratulated me on a good game.

The new guy is some old-timer who's bounced around the League for years. He looks the part. He's bigger than me, slower than me, and a lot more expensive than me.

There's just one problem. When he shows up, he sucks.

It's a pretty significant problem.

It's clear in his very first practice. He's not objectively a bad player, but it's hard to learn a brand-new offense in the middle of the season. There's also that chemistry thing. True, I haven't really played center with our guys, but at least I've played with them. The new guy doesn't even know their names.

But the best part for me, the guy who's always "too small," is that this guy is actually *too big.* Fuck, I love irony. See, the old-timer would be great at an old-school offense where you spend half your time standing around in a huddle, but the game moves fast these days. He's a dinosaur, too large, too slow, too out of shape.

"You'll be able to play this weekend, right?" Lopez asks him nervously between plays. "You'll be ready, you think?"

All the old dude can do is nod and huff and puff. He's too tired to talk, and we've barely even done anything.

Jack motions Lopez over to the sidelines and they have a talk. Meaning Jack talks, and Lopez listens and agrees. I can tell Lopez isn't happy. And I know I've won.

That night on my drive home I call my dad.

"So?" he says. "What happened?"

"Well," I say, trying to play it cool, because after all, I really don't care about any of this. "Looks like I'll be starting this weekend as center."

My dad, on the other hand, has never been into playing things cool.

"You're goddamn right you are."

THE NEXT DAY, BERNIE the agent calls.

"Johnny," he says, "this is the chance you've been waiting for."

That's right, agents actually say shit like that. As you may have guessed, I've never told Bernie how I really feel about football.

"But," he says, "that means now you gotta play all those political games you hate so much."

Okay, so some things are impossible for me to hide.

"Bernie," I say. "I can't. I am physically, genetically unable to kiss ass."

"I know," he says before he hangs up. "Do it anyway."

The way Bernie sees it—hell, the way *I* saw it until I decided to chase My Glorious Backup Dream™—the whole point of being a backup is to try to become a starter. Not because we should always strive to be "better men" or some shit like that, but because contract starters get paid a ton more money than the ones riding the pine. I'm talking at least $1.5 million a year. *At least.* The right opportunity, and I could get all the way up to $7 million as a center.

To get me (and him) that starter money, Bernie needs to get me a new contract with a new team next season. To get me that new contract, Bernie needs to show other teams that I can play. He needs game tape.

For the last two years, he hasn't had it. I mean, I've been a backup for fuck's sake—the whole purpose of my existence was *not* to play. Now I finally got my shot. I'm gonna start, I'm gonna play, I'm gonna get more game tape than I know what to do with. And if I play well, if I rack up enough highlights, if I prove that I'm capable of doing everything I know I can do . . . Fuck. I could become a permanent starter. I could end up playing in the League for another five or ten years, making big-time money.

Forget about being the Best NFL Backup Ever™. I could be the Fucking Man™.

Shit, until just a month ago, there was a good chance I was never gonna pick up a football again. Never watch another game for the rest of my life! Now all of a sudden . . . this?

I feel like Al Pacino in *The Godfather 3*. Just when I thought I was out, they pull me back in! Except without the ridiculous overacting. But potentially with a hell of a lot more long-term brain damage.

IF I WANT TO WORK out any major life decisions, it'll have to wait till after the game this weekend. It would've been nice if my first time starting was against some cream puff, but the team we're facing is legit. An away game on the other side of the country, dealing with a complex blitz scheme, one of the League's best. I look up the stats of the nose guard I'll be going against, realize it's actually someone I used to play against back in college who's a solid forty-five pounds heavier than me.

But the biggest joke of all is my own weight they got listed in the media guide: 290 pounds. Yeah, right. Maybe if I don't take a dump for four straight days.

I can already feel my nerves creeping back, the darkness, the paralysis, the tendency to get trapped in my own thoughts. And I'm not the only one who's worried. Even Jack is stressed about how our—my—line is gonna play. He tells the media he's concerned about how we'll respond and that the pressure is on all of us. He says it in a goddamn press conference, for the whole world to hear. It's like he's throwing us under the bus before the damn thing's even turned the corner. Thanks for the inspiration, Coach!

But what's really fucked up is that he's right. Not only am I taking over for our center, but Marcus, the starting right tackle, is also out for the season, which means Teddy will be playing the whole game too. So two of our five starters will be career backups. If anything goes wrong, who do you think they're gonna blame? It damn well won't be the veterans.

Best of all, I have a cold, some kind of virus, my sinuses filled with mucus, snot constantly dripping down my throat. I'm a fucking loogie machine. My adrenaline keeps me going during practices, but the minute they're over I collapse. Probably all that crap food I ate at Big Chaz. No wonder it's free.

And Lopez, the one guy I hoped might possibly keep his cool, doesn't. I make a huge effort to be more coachable. I even start admitting when I'm wrong! (It does happen occasionally.) I'm not kissing his ass—Bernie knew that was ridiculous—but still, I'm working at it.

Does the guy care? Not at all. If anything, this week he fucks with me more than ever.

During our afternoon walk-through on Wednesday, we review our blitz pickups, and I apparently don't call things *quite* the way Lopez expected.

"Stop! Stop! Stop!" Lopez screams. "What the fuck are you doing?"

"I was—"

"You can't 'Ricky' that!" he says, referring to a play.

"I know, I—"

"Motherfucker, we've gone over this twenty times!"

"Goddammit, Lo!" I fire back. "I thought we were past all this bull-shit!"

"What?" he says. Dude looks totally mystified.

"Lo," I say, "why don't you just stop and ask me *why* I was doing what I was doing?"

"I don't know!" he barks. "What the fuck? You want us to like kiss and make up now?"

"*Yes!*" I say, grabbing him and hoisting him off the ground in a massive bear hug. "*We're making up right now!*"

Lopez grins, but I can tell he's pissed at me. For what? Like it's my fault the old guy they signed sucked balls and I got stuck playing center? My fault Lo's very first season coaching in the NFL is coming down to two professional benchers, one who's too small and another who can't remember how many sides a stop sign has? It's like we're suddenly back where we started, like all the positive shit we accomplished in the last game means absolutely nothing. I've had coaches like this before—guys who take the game so seriously that even the tiniest setback will send them on a rampage; football coaches are notoriously volatile personalities—but Lopez is on the far end of the spectrum. And his insanity has been rubbing off on me. All it takes is a shitty comment from him, a shift in the tone of his voice, to fucking ruin my day.

Well, to hell with that. I'm gonna make my own success.

I work my ass off all week to get ready for the game. Now that I'm gonna be starting, no one works harder than me. No one.

Every free minute, at breakfast, at lunch, back at the apartment, I spend watching film on my iPad. Twice a day in our O-line meetings, Lopez quizzes us on defensive coverages and the right calls, flashing formations on an overhead projector and cold-calling all the guys to make sure we're all paying attention. Like the week before the bar in an Ivy League law school, the entire room is dead silent with tension. He calls on me about 75 percent of the time. If I hesitate in answering for even a split second, I fail.

"Hurry up, motherfucker! Hurry up, Johnny!"

"Okay, okay, I—"

"BAM, you're dead!" he screams, his face red, flecks of spit flying from his mouth. "You just got our quarterback killed. What the *fuck* is wrong with you!"

Honestly, it scares the shit out of me.

At the beginning of the week, Lopez gives me some amazing advice about how I should lead the line.

"As center," he tells me, "you gotta be hard, you gotta be completely serious, and completely in charge. You can't show any weakness."

It's advice I completely ignore.

My leadership style is the same off the field as it is on the field: intense when it needs to be, but fun and loose the rest of the time—and it works. It helps that Teddy is starting with me—not just a guy I've played football with, but a guy I actually live with, a guy I *know*. I know the names of his parents. I know all he ever eats is Chic-fil-A. I know he could spend the rest of his life playing *Gears of War 4* and literally never bat an eye. Seriously, shit like that translates to the field.

Then I got Jeb. He's a guy who takes himself seriously, like he's a big fucking deal, so I gently take him down a peg.

"What's Jeb short for, anyway?" I say. "Jebediah or some shit? Does anyone actually call you that?"

"Just my mom, man."

"Perfect, Jebediah," I say, laughing. "Whatever you say, Jebediah."

Sensing all the pressure I'm under, Jeb takes me under his massive, pale, Celtic-tattooed wing, just like an Old Vet should. He's an intimidating motherfucker—he even intimidates the coaches—but underneath it all he has a soft spot, especially for young guys like me. After Lopez bitches me out in practice on Wednesday, Jeb comes up to me in the locker room and jabs me in the chest, his sign that he wants to talk.

"It's not just you out there during the games," he says. "We got your back too. Antonne, he messes up calls all the time. But we all know what to do, we'll kind of look at each other after a huddle and say, 'Hey, you got this guy covered, I got that guy.' So fucking relax."

"Thanks," I say. "Really. Jebediah."

He grins. I appreciate it more than he can know. Especially because developing "chemistry" with our starting QB, Brody, is going to be a pain in the ass.

Starting quarterbacks are dull as rocks, completely humorless and absolutely unrelenting. The exact opposite of my style. And Brody is no exception. He never jokes, never laughs, never even swears. If he screws something up in practice—which is rare—the closest thing he comes to dropping an F bomb is "What the *freak*, Brody! Freakin' *heck*!"

And yes, he talks about himself in the third person.

Football is his life. His dad was a coach, and probably his dad's dad too. He's smart as hell, he's been in the NFL for what seems like forever, and he understands the game better than anyone you'll ever meet. Yet he's never made it to a Super Bowl, and you kind of know he never will.

He seems to know it too. Now it seems like he's just biding his time till his retirement, probably trying to figure out just what the hell he'll do without football in his life.

Every single day we practice our snap, getting our timing down. Every single day I try to talk to the guy about something, anything other than football. Every single day I fail.

"Good work!" he says robotically. "Mind over matter! Preparation is everything!"

Chemistry will never happen here.

THERE'S NO ONE I CAN really talk to about just how fucking nervous I am. I can't really open up to Kate and my dad. They're both supportive and encouraging, just like they should be, but nothing they can say will actually change the reality or make it any better.

Fuck, I'm not even sure what the problem really is. I've started in college games a million times before, including bowl games when there was a ton on the line. And I just played a great game last week. Sure, I didn't actually start, but is there really any difference when it comes down to it? A couple extra minutes of playing time, that's all.

So why the hell can't I fucking let go and relax?

The closest thing I get to any real help comes from the most unexpected place of all: the media. They eat my story up. I'm the poster child for the whole underdog-makes-good thing. Going from almost getting cut one week to starting for the first time at a completely new position a few weeks later. I know they're just using me for their stories, but for the few moments when I talk to the sports reporters, I actually feel like I'm in control. They like me, they laugh at my jokes, hang on every word I say, pat me on the arm and say, "Jesus, I wish all the players were as much fun to interview as you."

Who knows, maybe they see me for who I really am—a normal, anxious guy who somehow finds himself about to start in his very first NFL game.

IT'S FRIDAY EVENING. We don't fly out for the game until tomorrow afternoon.

We finish off the workday with another offensive-line meeting, and even more quizzes from Lopez. We've had about a million of them this week, and right now it feels like there'll be a million more before Sunday's game. It doesn't matter. I nail them all.

He flashes a diagram of a defense up on the overhead, surveys the room grimly, then without warning he belts out our play.

> *Lopez:* Johnny, scat right!
> *Me:* Lion 56.
> *Lopez:* Why?
> *Me:* Safety inverted weak, it's gonna be an edge pressure.

New diagram. New play. My name.

> *Lopez:* Johnny, key left!
> *Me:* Ram 51.
> *Lopez:* Why?
> *Me:* Linebackers are at different levels, expect middle cross dog.
> *Lopez:* What if 56 comes first?
> *Me:* Gotta take him, always take the penetrator.
> *Lopez:* Then who the fuck is gonna get the other guy, are you just gonna let him go and kill the quarterback?
> *Me:* Running back will pick him up.
> *Lopez:* [*stands and uses his fat finger to gesture to the screen*] What if they bring the safety down right here in middle?
> *Me:* Then I call "Ricky."

I show no hesitation, no second thoughts, no errors. Lopez is furious. He collapses in his seat, shaking his head, stupefied. God, I love this.

"Goddammit!" he shouts, furious. "Someone else answer these goddamn questions! Johnny is fucking pissing me off!"

Everyone is silent. I just laugh, loud and hard.

"There goes Johnny," Coulter, one of the starters, says. "Stealing Lo's thunder by laughing in his face."

In reality, I'm stressed as fuck. As soon as I get back to my apartment I collapse, exhausted. I can't even manage a trip to the mall.

SATURDAY EVENING OUR TEAM arrives at the hotel.

Some of the players go out to dinner together, spend their traveling per diems at another Ruth's Chris Steakhouse. I swear they got one in every city, and a bunch of us go there every single time.

Not me, though. Not tonight. The rest of the O linemen and I order in and spend the whole night cooped up in a hotel conference room with Lopez, going over the same damn plays, arguing about the same damn calls, over and over. Lopez and I stand at a dry-erase board, talking over each other, scribbling over each other's writing, crossing shit out, and erasing and rewriting all over again as everyone else watches and sighs.

"All right," Lopez finally says, "we'll do it that way."

He points at my writing on the board. He won't even say my name.

It's 10:15 P.M. We've been here for more than three hours.

I stop in the hotel lobby on the way up to my room, trying to clear my mind. By this point, anyone who went out for dinner is back for curfew. Almost everyone is up in their rooms, but a few guys are down here—Dante, a backup running back, some defensive players—all huddled around the hotel's shiny, spotless grand piano as Danny, the same pimply assistant trainer who weighs us and makes our ice packs, tickles the ivory.

The kid is playing "Your Kiss" by Hall and Oates, and the guys jump in and sing along when they know the words, which is pretty much just the chorus.

"Because your kiss, your kiss is on my lips . . ."

They all look at each other confused, no idea where to go next, then start all over again at the beginning. Repeat. Danny has a big wad of chew in his mouth. He stops every few minutes to spit in a Styrofoam cup. He finally looks up the lyrics to the country song "Chicken Fried" on his cell, but that doesn't go over too well with the black guys. Then he tries a couple rap songs, which somehow they make work on a classical piano.

Everyone's laughing and having fun, not a care in the world, and I feel good for Danny because usually he's just stuck doing scrub work, refilling containers of cotton balls and packing Band-Aids. I wish I could join them.

There's an image people have of the "NFL Lifestyle"—that it's filled with glamour and excitement, expensive cars and gorgeous women. But during the season, we honestly live more like traveling salesmen, going from city to city, hotel to hotel, chain restaurant to chain restaurant. Hell, in some ways, the salesmen got it better than us—at least they make their own hours and can get wasted every night. We gotta be at our hotels by 10 P.M. and we drink more protein shakes than alcohol. The night before games most players just chill in their rooms by themselves, texting with friends, watching TV, or playing video games. It's a lonely existence.

I get back to my room and sleep like shit, which is strange for me. My night is a mix of weird dreams, fitful turning, and draining my clogged sinuses. I finally give up at 5:30 A.M., switch the light on, and check my phone. I think about texting Kate, but I know she's asleep.

Then, out of the blue, Kate's mom texts me. I've known her since high school too, of course. Somehow she seems like the right person to talk to right now.

"How you feeling?" she texts.

"Actually kinda nervous," I write back. It's the first time I've admitted this to anyone.

"You wouldn't be human if you weren't nervous," she replies.

"It's been a long time since I played. I can't even remember what I used to do to deal with it."

"You've been here a million times before," she writes. "It'll go away as soon as the game starts."

I look at the time. I'll find out in seven hours.

Chapter 7
CENTER OF ATTENTION

I walk out to the field by myself. The game clock hasn't turned on yet, it's too early.

It's the second time I've been to this stadium. The turf is already crowded with people. Not working, just shooting the shit. Ball boys, trainers, managers, tossing around footballs. Coaches and assistant coaches from the two teams, asking after wives and kids. Reporters in their cheap suits, clustered in the end zone, trying to fit in. Friends of the owners, taking photos and asking for autographs. And of course the players. Thirty or forty of them, hanging out together by the benches, bumping fists and laughing, eyeing me warily as I walk to the end of the field alone.

For me, this moment, by myself, all alone before the game, this is more important than anything I'll do today. It doesn't look tough, it doesn't look badass. It's just what I do.

This is my pregame ritual.

I started doing it in college. I've done it dozens of times now, the exact same way, at every single game. But this time is different. Because in an hour and a half, I'm gonna be a starter in the NFL for the very first time.

Here's how my ritual goes. I start in the far corner of the end zone. I walk down the sideline to the 50-yard line, then I turn ninety degrees and walk to the middle of the field, the center of it all, right into the heart of whatever glaring, ugly logo is there. And the whole time I'm walking, I'm looking. At everything. I'm looking up at the rafters. I'm looking at the lights. I'm looking at the TV cameras getting into position. I'm looking at the ads plastered everywhere and on everything, for Pepsi, Visa, Papa John's, and Campbell's Soup. I'm looking at the fans, the craziest of the crazies, drenched in their team colors as they file in over an hour early. I look at the goalposts, the tubs of Gatorade, and the fresh hash marks on the turf. The groundskeeper must've painted everything last night. It's still wet, it covers the toes of my cleats with white.

I look at it all, and I remember. I soak it up. I breathe it in. So in the middle of the game, when I get up after driving a defensive lineman who's forty pounds heavier than me into the ground, I can look around and feel like all of it, every single inch, is mine. Like this entire place, this stadium I hardly know, is my home. Like I'm fifteen again, and there are no stands, no fans, no cameras, no commercials. Just me, playing a game with some friends.

Sounds pretty good, right? Pretty confident, yeah?

Well, I fucking hope so. Because right now, I am scared shitless.

"HEY, JOHNNY!" I TURN MY HEAD. It's a D lineman from the other team; a few of them are straggling onto the field now. I played against him back in college. He's a starter in the League, usually wouldn't even look in my direction.

"Good luck!" he shouts as he passes me by. "You still suck!"

I laugh to myself, start to relax, just a tiny bit. I spot a few of our assistant coaches hanging out in our end zone and jog over to my favorite, Eddie.

"Hey, sexy," I call over. "Hold the bag for me, will ya?"

Eddie nods. He picks up the bag, a small hand shield, the size of his chest. He braces himself behind it, angling his body to take the impact. I crouch down like I'm at the line of scrimmage, wait for his call, tensed.

"Ready!" he yells. "Go!"

I smash into the pad, not full power, gotta save it for the game.

"Ready! Go!"

Practice my technique, inside zone right, inside zone left, outside zone right, outside zone left. Gotta be perfect, get into a groove, gotta feel *right*.

"Ready! Go!"

Eddie's not nearly as big as the D linemen I'll be going against during the game.

"Go!"

But this feels good. I feel every fiber of my muscles loosening, the sweat running down my back, the shudder of my bones with every crack against the pad. I'm almost starting to forget myself. Almost.

An hour to go till kickoff. I turn to jog back to the locker room.

The next fifty minutes are a blur of helmets, sports tape, pain pills, and Jack's lame motivational speech. Jeb says something encouraging to me, I think Teddy does too, but I can't really remember. I spot Coulter, another starter on the line, hunched in front of his locker, staring at his iPhone, watching videos of his two little boys playing in the park. It's how he gets mentally prepared for games.

All of it is just kind of flying by me, around me, not touching me, like I'm there but I'm not really there.

And now I'm walking out onto the field and thousands and thousands of people are booing us. My senses are heightened. I'm not just looking; I'm sensing, I'm tasting, tingling, pulling everything in, the smoke that's still in the air from the fireworks, the charred meat of the hot dogs in the stands, the salt in the sweat that's trickling down my face. And there, in the middle of it all, is Lopez. He grabs me by the back of my jersey.

"When they run split-mug and they drop the safety to the weak side, they could run Thunder X so you have to have a good set-line!"

"Lo," I say, "let's just try to have some fun today, all right?"

And he looks at me like *I'm* the one who's crazy.

"I've got enough to deal with!" he screams. "I don't need you fucking with me now, Johnny!"

The next thing I know we're all lined up in a row on the sideline, every single player and coach standing at attention as some country music singer with massive bleached blond hair walks into the middle of the field and starts singing. The stadium goes quiet. All except for her voice.

> *Oh say can you see, by the dawn's early light . . .*
> *What so proudly we hailed, at the twilight's last*
> *   gleaming?*
> *Whose broad stripes and bright stars, through the*
> *   perilous fight . . .*
> *O'er the ramparts we watched, were so gallantly*
> *   streaming?*
> *And the rocket's red glare, the bombs bursting in air . . .*

And right there, right after that line, I think of my mom. Just like I always do during the national anthem, before every single game. I think of her, my best friend, lying in the hospice bed, moments before she died. And I know she's still out there, somewhere, watching over me.

A chill runs through my body. My eyes water, just a little.

Then she's gone.

The song ends, and I'm not nervous anymore. I'm finally free. I'm ready to play.

IT'S THE FOURTH QUARTER, there are seven minutes left in the game. We're down by four, and our defense feels like it's been on the field forever. And we've been playing like crap.

You know all the preparing we did? All the arguing, debating, tweaking, and testing? Yeah, well, the other team went ahead and decided to throw a completely new defense at us—whole new scheme, nothing like their other games this season—so that was pretty much all for nothing.

On the sidelines, Lopez is doing his usual dance, pacing and chewing, pacing and chewing. Jack, as always, is quiet, blank, an island of arrogance in an ocean of upheaval. And the offensive line, my offensive line, is in revolt.

However we make it seem in press conferences after games, players disagree with their hallowed, sacred coaches all the time on the sideline—basically as soon as a team starts losing. Usually it's just general bitching to other players about the play calling. If they get really frustrated, they go complain to their position coach. And if it gets *really* bad, if they're getting utterly embarrassed on the field and the calls make no fucking sense whatsoever—then, and only then, a star player who's virtually untouchable will go argue with the head coach himself. At that point, it's a full-on football rebellion.

We're right on the brink of exactly that. For the last quarter and a half, all of us—me, Jeb, Coulter, Williams, even fucking Teddy—have been going up to Lopez and pleading with him to change the play calls, adjust our offense so we can handle the new defense. And all he keeps saying is no. No, no, no, no. Like his brain is stuck in repeat.

"Lopez," I say, summoning the most soothing, reasonable voice I can possibly manage. "Let's change this up, okay?"

"Back off!" he roars. "I got enough problems right now!"

Which is kind of funny because obviously the biggest problem Lopez should be facing is winning the game, right? Except I know that's not the case. His biggest issue right now is politics. He's not in charge of play calling. On this team, not even our offensive coordinator is in charge of play calling. Jack, the head coach, is.

When it's all said and done, Lopez is just a first-year assistant coach, and in a sense he's got about as much pull on this team as I do.

Finally it reaches the breaking point. Jeb—who makes more money than Jack himself—goes and bitches to Jack himself. And it results in exactly nothing. Jack stands there, arms folded, staring out at the field, and simply shakes his head. That's it, just one shake of the head, and it's over, case closed, we stick with the original plan. Even a multiyear Pro Bowler like Jeb only has so much sway. Jack is stuck, or maybe he's kind of stupid, I'm not entirely sure anymore. And our offense keeps playing like shit.

But you know what makes this all really weird? Not the arguing or the politics or the horrible play calling—that's just a normal NFL Sunday.

No, what makes it weird is how much I'm loving it.

We're getting beat, everyone is miserable, and I'm having the time of my life. I mean, fuck! I just started my first NFL game! Me! Johnny Anonymous! And not only did I start, not only am I playing, but I'm doing pretty damn good too. Sure, I miss a call or two, get bulled back once or twice. But that's football. I'm giving as good as I'm getting, sometimes even better. They push me, I push back. They rush me, I block their ass. I'm one of the guys. I'm a player in the NFL.

It's the stuff that happens between the plays that I love the most. The stuff that most people in the stands or watching at home never see or wouldn't really care about anyway. The banter, the camaraderie, the jokes in the huddle, the playful insults muttered under our breath.

On one play, the noseguard keeps shoving me after the action is whistled dead. "Okay, that's enough," I say like a preschool teacher scolding a child, and he immediately backs off with a sigh. On another play, I flatten an old-timer, an eleven-year vet. I reach down to help him up and he slaps my hand away. "Oh, come on," I say. "You're old as dirt, let me give you a hand." And he smiles and reaches for my hand.

A little later, a ref calls me for what he claims is a hold—it's *blatantly* not a hold—and I roll my eyes good and hard and it gets picked up right on national TV. Imagine that! My eye roll finally gets its close-up! We're famous!

It's good to be back, to feel like I matter on a team. It's something I haven't really felt since college. But it'll feel a lot better if we win.

Our defense stops them on third and two, and we finally get the ball back. We're still down 4 points. All we need is a touchdown, that's it. But over the last hour, that 4 points has become a physical and psychological wall we just can't get across.

We take the ball over at midfield, at our own 44-yard line. About five and a half minutes left now in the game, and we have to drive 56 yards for the touchdown we need. If we don't score, there's a chance we could get the ball back after this series, but there's just as good a chance we won't. This is our shot to win the game, and we all know it.

Usually Antonne would be the one rallying the linemen before the big drive. But he's gone, and I'm me, so Jeb, the star, the rugged vet who's been through it all, takes over and gives the big speech.

I've heard it all before. He goes hyperaggressive, all fire and brimstone. *We shall rain death upon our enemies, despair upon their friends and tragedy upon their loved ones! Plus at least mild discomfort for any pets they might own! Let's kill! Let's dismember! Let's defend the honor of our virginal daughters and our slightly sluttier wives! By scoring a touchdown!*

You know. Classic football stuff.

But just as we're about to line up, the commercial break almost over, I figure, what the fuck. I'm gonna get excited my own way.

"Hey!" I shout. "This is what it's all about, this is why we do this! If you don't have fun right now, something's wrong with you! Let's have a good fucking time!"

The guys on the line smile. Jeb pats me on the back, and everyone loosens up.

And just like that, we proceed to very calmly, very steadily march the ball right down the field. Completing one play after another, Brody relaxed, unhurried, and throwing darts; Dante hauling them in; our offense moving with a rhythm and precision it hasn't shown since the first five minutes of the game. It's like magic.

Okay, so it probably also helps that Jack's *finally* started calling the plays we've been badgering him about for the entire game. But I'm sure my little impassioned speech had something to do with it.

We make it all the way down to their 4-yard line flawlessly, without so much as a misplaced fart from Teddy. We're right on the verge of scoring, just a single well-executed run away from a touchdown and the lead.

And what does Jack decide to do? He decides to call one pass play after another. From 4 yards away.* Sure, Brody's been passing well this series, but we're talking 4 fucking yards here! He could literally fall forward

* Sound familiar, Seattle fans? Sorry, it's just so much fun to fuck with you.

four times in a row and that would be enough to get us into the end zone. The guy is fucking six foot five! It would be that easy!

But no.

First down. Pass play. Brody can't find an open man, so he throws the ball out of bounds on purpose.

Second down. Pass play. Dante drops one he should've had. Now all us linemen are eyeing each other, confused, grumbling: *Jack's gonna call a run, right? We're 4 yards away! We fucking got this!*

Third down. Pass play. They blitz. Brody tries to roll out before the throw, actually trips on his own feet, never gets the pass off. Now we're all looking at him—not because he tripped, but because he's the only one who can change the play at the line of scrimmage, no matter what Jack calls. *Come on, man! Call a run! Fucking do it!* He refuses.

Fourth down. We go for it. Pass play. By this point, the other team's realized there's no way Jack's gonna run, so they're guarding almost exclusively against the pass. Brody's throw is intercepted in the end zone.

Series over. Their ball.

"*They don't trust us!*" Jeb shouts on the sideline, tearing his helmet off and spiking it into the turf.

He's right, they don't. Our offense ends up getting another chance to score, but by that point it doesn't matter. We're pinned deep near our own end zone, and we go nowhere. We've been beaten by our own coaches.

Game over. We lose.

THE MOOD IN THE LOCKER room is darker than after our other losses. That's how it feels to me anyway. But it's probably just because losing sucks a lot more when you actually want to win.

Fuck. I forgot that part. How much it sucks to lose when you care.

Just like we knew he would, Jack completely throws the O line under the bus in his press conference. Says we have to play better, the injuries are no excuse, we need to start opening up holes for our run game to work. This from the same guy who refused to take his own line's advice about how to fix his broken scheme until the end of the game, on the only drive that worked. Who wouldn't even let us power the ball into the end zone when we were just 4 yards away from the winning touchdown.

Shit, he didn't just throw us under the bus, he *drove* the fucking thing himself and charged us for tickets afterward.

But that might be better than Lopez, who takes the exact opposite approach. He says nothing. Literally. The only lineman he speaks to is Teddy, just enough to ask him about a minor ankle injury he got during the game. When the rest of us try to talk to him, he won't even look us in the eye.

"Hey, Coach," I say on my way to the showers. I don't even have a question for the guy, just want to see what he'll do. The fucker walks right by me like I don't exist.

The media gathers around me again, my old buddies from the week before, but this time they're not quite as cheerful. They want me to explain Jack's calls, ask me why he wouldn't let us run the ball just yards away from the end zone, probably hoping I'll say something against him and ignite a controversy. But the truth is I have no answer. I really don't. I just say I trust my coach to do the right thing. Which we all know is a complete lie. But it's the only thing I can say if I want to keep my job.

MONDAY'S OUR DAY OFF. A lot of guys will go in for extra treatment from the trainers on any nicks and scrapes from the game. I could use some myself since I tore a tendon in one of my fingers for about the fourth time this year, but I stay away from work. I need space. I need a breath from all this bullshit.

No such luck. I get caught in a shitstorm from the very people who are supposed to be supporting me.

First, an angry text from Kate.

"I want to talk about all the stuff you've been saying," my loving girlfriend writes.

"What, you mean to the press?"

"Yes. You sound like a big shot. Like an arrogant football player."

"Are you serious???"

Then Bernie calls. I'm hoping he'll give me some insight into how I played. Fuck, maybe even some encouragement. Instead, I find out that the League is gonna *fine me* for a supposedly illegal block I made during the game. Officials found it after the game during their review of the film. Bernie tried to appeal—after all, this is one of my first games as a center, I'm not even used to some of these techniques—but he got rejected. There goes ten grand down the toilet.

Or, as he delicately puts it, "You're fucked."

My dad texts me next, furious about the fine. I text him back, also furious about the fine. We're all furious about something. But deep down, I know we're all just mad that I lost.

I think about going to the mall, but I can't do it. I feel too shitty. It'd ruin the experience. So I decide to go to the bank to deposit a check in my account. If anything will make me feel better, this will. It's even better than a clearance sale on sheets.

I pull into the bank's parking lot, get out of my car. I walk over to the ATM on the side of the building. I take my wallet out of my pocket, reach in for my ATM card. Suddenly a pickup truck drives into view. It's coming right for me. Faster, faster, until it finally brakes just a few feet from the sidewalk.

The guy who's driving sticks half his body out the window, looks right at me.

"*You fucking idiot!*" he screams.

Then he drives away before I can say a word.

Is he a crazy football fan? Did he recognize me from the game? Or is he just a generic insane dude?

I have no idea. But right about now, I kind of agree.

NOW THAT THE COACHES HAVE had a chance to go over the game tape, they've realized that Teddy and I—the two career backups—actually played a pretty good game.

"Teddy!" Lopez gushes in the O-line meeting. "You just had a fantastic performance. See the man you're blocking here? He's a fucking Pro Bowler! You really had his number. Just fantastic!"

Then he turns to me.

"Oh, Johnny. Yeah, you made the right call too."

Wow. I'm so flattered.

The guy who missed the most blocks, who always seemed a few steps behind, was Williams, a three-year starter. But somehow that doesn't stop the coaches from pinning most of the blame for the loss on me. That secret starters club, the one I never wanted to join? Yeah, well, now I'm wishing I'd never even been invited.

In the meeting for the entire offense, our offensive coordinator puts up tape from last week's practice and pauses it just in time to catch me walking back to the line of scrimmage after a play.

"What the fuck is that?" he says to me in front of everyone. He decides to answer it for me. "What, you're too good to *run* back after a play like everyone else on this fucking team?"

At this point I've learned a little about talking back to coaches, so I decide not to point out that no less than four guys right next to me are also walking back on the tape. They just happen to have higher pay grades than me.

Williams waits till they've moved on and nudges me.

"Thank God they got pissed at you and not me," he whispers. "Is there anyone you know who *doesn't* fuck with you?"

"No," I say. "Welcome to my life."

And the fun just keeps on coming. Now that he's got his ammo, Lopez tears into me in the next O-line meeting.

"Johnny, I was gonna have a private meeting with you, but fuck it. I'm gonna say it here and now. I never wanna see you walk in practice again. You're lazy, all right? I don't think you get it—this isn't a hobby, this is your job. Shit isn't fair, all right? Life *isn't* fair."

Even I can't laugh myself out of this awkward moment. The whole room is silent. Players just stare at their desks like they're back in kinder-garten, because that's what it feels like. At the end of the meeting, I pass Antonne. He's still injured, of course, rehabbing his back. And I can't help but wonder if he kind of enjoys seeing how fast everything falls apart with him gone.

But even he has a shell-shocked look on his face.

"Johnny," he says. "Lo's lost it."

The next day I see Jack walking through the hallway. I stop him and tell him I'll never, ever walk in practice again.

IT'S ALL OVER THE MEDIA. The idea that something is wrong with the offense because something is wrong with the line because something is wrong with me.

Can you believe it? Me, a backup, the center of a genuine media storm. I text my agent, Bernie, about it, and I literally pause because I can't believe I'm talking about myself. But it's true. Fox Sports, ESPN, everyone's printing the same thing, that Antonne is some football god, and Johnny Anonymous is fucking everything up.

Bernie is pissed as all hell. Both because he knows I'm getting a raw deal, and because he knows that if this story sticks, I've got no career left in the NFL. Fuck getting starter money next year, I could be done as a backup. Bernie even starts texting all the media guys—I mean, he knows them all, they all go to each other's kids' bar mitzvahs—telling them to quit talking shit about me, to just try *watching the fucking tape* and they'll see how wrong they are, but it does no good.

Fuck, I almost can't blame people, you know? Antonne's a starter, I'm a backup. Therefore he's good and I'm bad. Now he's gone and I'm playing. What else could the explanation possibly be?

THURSDAY NIGHT. THE OFFENSIVE LINE goes out to a fancy dinner. Just players, no coaches.

Antonne finds the place. It's French, posh. Which is the last place I'd expect a black dude with dreads to choose, but it turns out it's his favorite place. The waiters and busboys all know him, they even have a goddamn drink named after him. The "L'Antonne."

So I clearly don't know shit.

We're all sitting there at this nice, fancy table with this nice, fancy linen tablecloth, trying to partake in this team bonding ritual, and the waiter comes up just gushing about how they can't wait till Antonne is playing again, how horrible it was watching the last game without their guy Antonne on the field.

"Yeah," Coulter says. "Everything'll be better once you get back, man."

Coulter says this right in front of me. And look, I get it—he and Antonne are friends, they've been playing together awhile. But does he not know I'm here? Is he stupid, or does he just not care?

"Don't worry," I say. "I'm trying to get out of everyone's way as soon as I can."

It's like no one even hears me.

SATURDAY NIGHT. The night before my second game as an NFL starter. I lie in bed on my discounted sheets staring at the ceiling. And a single thought goes through my mind over and over and over again.

How can I get everyone to forget about Antonne?

WE LOSE THE GAME.

I play pretty well personally, but it doesn't really matter. Jack still refuses to adjust the play calling, continues to use the same tricks he used all last season, even though everyone's figured them out and every defense seems to know what we're gonna do before we do.

They load up against our run, put a ton of pressure on Brody, dare him to make passes to relatively open receivers that he hasn't made all season long, and watch as he doesn't make them. It comes as no surprise to anyone except, apparently, Jack.

Hell, it doesn't even surprise Brody. During the game he throws one of a few interceptions, and as soon as the ball leaves his hand I hear him shout "Nooooooooo!"

The guy isn't in a good place. None of us are.

As the clock is running down at the end of the game, one of the other team's defensive ends sprints past after the play is called dead and just flattens Brody. *Lays him out.* Dude's just writhing on the ground. An incredibly scary moment for everyone on the field.

So Jeb does the natural thing and clocks the defensive end. You don't let someone fuck with your quarterback like that, you just don't. Jeb winds up, helmet be damned, and absolutely nails the fucker, just drops him like he's nothing. And I'm right there, right next to all of it, and I can honestly say that it's completely fucking terrifying.

Have I mentioned how big Jeb is? I mean, I know I told you his stats—six foot seven, 345 pounds—but have you actually taken the time to seriously contemplate just how *huge* that really is? I mean, really? Here's a little homework assignment for you. Put the book down, go out and find something, an actual physical object, that's exactly that big, and stand next to it. Then imagine it with a large, pale, tattooed fist, and imagine that fist flying through the air at light speed and smashing into someone's face.

It is not pleasant.

Jeb gets tossed from the game. Brody gets up, slowly, shakily. Probably just got the wind knocked out of him. The game ends, and we all lose anyway. Yippee.

BACK IN THE LOCKER ROOM, I can barely move, can't even take off my uniform. I sit slumped over in front of my locker, staring ahead of me, in a daze.

Before the game I took three Toradols, the NFL player's current pain pill of choice. Doctors recommend that you only take one, but my trainers tell me three. Legal? Sure. Good for me? Highly unlikely. I'm counting down the minutes before the pills wear off and I can feel again. I'm not looking forward to it.

Until about 2011 and the signing of the new collective bargaining agreement, trainers on NFL teams used to pass out prescription painkillers like they were candy. We're talking Vicodin, Percocet, OxyContin, and whatever the trendy muscle relaxer happened to be. It was as simple as asking. Of course I wasn't playing back then, but old vets like Jeb refer to those days as the "Old NFL." These days, they call us the "Soft NFL." Since the CBA, all your prescription pain medication has to come from your doctor, and even then the team makes you sign a waiver saying you're taking them "at your own discretion."

Toradol's *supposed* to be safer than the other stuff, but just like with anything there are potential side effects, especially with long-term use, and some of them sound pretty scary. But what the fuck am I supposed to do? Ever sprained a finger, hyperextended an elbow, or even just gotten a plain old Charlie horse? It's painful as fuck. Now imagine getting all those sequentially, every couple plays, for almost four hours straight.

It's impossible unless your body is almost completely numb.

During the game I got hit and knocked to the ground, not *too* hard, but I landed on my hip at an angle that was just a little bit off. I could feel something in my lower back shift out of place. And given that that something was inside my body, well, it was probably kind of important. Now that the drugs are starting to wear off I feel it. It's just about the only thing I can feel. Pure hurt.

Sitting in front of my locker, I slowly, carefully tilt up my head, check the wall clock. I've been sitting here for over seven minutes.

Brody spots me from a few lockers away. Dude almost looks as bad as me, which for a pretty-boy quarterback is actually saying a lot.

"You tired?" he says.

The answer to this question is pretty apparent. But from Brody, the most Uninteresting Man in the World, I'll take it.

"I am fucking destroyed," I say.

"Yeah," he says. "Me too."

I take a deep breath, let it out nice and slow.

"I'm just gonna sit here and do nothing for another ten minutes, okay?"

"Yeah," he says. "Me too."

And that's what he does. He sits down across from me, and we just rest for ten minutes of pure, unadulterated nothingness.

It's the best time I have all day.

IN A WEIRD WAY, THAT same sheer agony gets me through the rest of the week.

It's amazing how much more damaged I am now that I'm starting. I know it seems like the difference should be obvious. Starters play, starters work, and backups practice and stand on the sidelines. *Of course* I'm more damaged. Half the reason I only wanted to be a backup was to avoid this kind of deterioration, the damage that I knew would follow me long after my football career ended. But even I didn't really understand how bad it is until I actually experienced it.

Every inch of me hurts. Every muscle aches. Every ligament feels like it's hanging by a thread. Some of them literally are, since my fingers are all taped to each other to give my busted, swollen joints added support.

I'm powered by the simple knowledge that if I stop moving, for even a minute, I'll break down, and I won't be able to move again. I just keep thinking the same thing over and over again: *Make it through this week, and collect my paycheck.* If I make it through this week, then maybe I can make it through next week. If I make it through next week, then maybe I'll make it through the season. If I make it through the season, I can sign a new contract somewhere else and get an even bigger paycheck.

As for next season? Fuck you. I'll worry about that later.

I also finally understand why Jeb takes naps instead of working out. The guy's not lazy. He just fucking needs to rest. God, I wish I could.

No such luck this week. If I thought I was running my ass off before, I didn't know shit. Jack has *finally* adjusted the offense by adding some plays that actually take advantage of my unusual speed as a lineman. Which is great for me and great for our offense, because it'll finally give us a chance to win some games, but it also means that when I say I'm running my ass off, I'm literally running my ass off. I sweat out twelve pounds in every single practice, no exaggeration. And since I still have my weekly weigh-ins for the team, that means that whenever I'm not practicing, running and sweating, I'm eating, guzzling water, and eating some more, all to keep the coaches from figuring out just how much I'm shrinking.

The media and the fans continue their Johnny Anonymous crapfest, praying that Antonne the Football Jesus will somehow miraculously rise again to save us all this weekend. Bernie's driving me crazy with all his worrying about how much this is hurting what's left of my career. And of course there's Lopez, who keeps riding me so fucking hard that on Wednesday *he* says something about it—in the middle of an offensive-line meeting.

"You know, I just want to apologize to Johnny," he says, standing by the dry-erase board, looking very studiously at the marker he's holding. "Yesterday I said a few things, uh . . ."

He just kind of trails off, then loudly clears his throat.

"Okay!" he says, clapping his hands together. "So the first play we got up . . ."

The insult he's referring to happened yesterday, when he announced to all the other linemen that his game planning is limited because he can't leave me alone to block the noseguard one-on-one.

Doesn't sound like much, I know. But even if it were true, which it isn't—I handled the noseguards in our last two games just fine, and one of them is a Pro Bowler—calling someone out like that in front of other players crossed a major line. You can argue with someone over a coverage, you can even crop dust the entire room with a massive fart—hell, Teddy just did it two weeks ago. But what Lopez did was personal. I'm supposed to be the leader of the line, and in front of everyone he announced that I suck so bad he has no confidence in me. Why the hell would they have any confidence in me either?

The guys just sat there and shook their heads.

But you know what? It didn't even bother me. And Lopez's half-assed apology doesn't mean shit to me either. I'm reaching that point where shit is so bad, it's actually good. I'm so sick of everything—the media, the fans, the coaches, other players, Kate, whatever—that I just don't give a fuck anymore. I stop worrying about making everyone else forget about Antonne, and *I* forget about the guy. I decide to just have fun being myself.

That's when I'm at my best. As a person and a player.

WEDNESDAY NIGHT. I ARRIVE AT my apartment and collapse, absolutely exhausted. My legs and back hurt so much I can barely even sit up straight on our rented sofa to watch Teddy play his video games.

I prop myself up on my elbow so I can start guzzling the gallons of water I need to make weight tomorrow morning, and my cell rings.

I look at the caller ID, and I can't believe it. It's my sister.

I've talked a lot about my dad, my girlfriend, and of course my mom. But I haven't said much about my sister. We're not very close, clearly. After my mom died, my dad and I figured out our own ways to cope. My dad poured his energy into work and raising us, I poured my energy into football. But my sister sort of floated along, unattached. In a weird way, although I was my mom's favorite, her death may have affected my sister the most. To this day, she's never quite figured out how to handle it.

I answer the phone.

"Hey, Johnny," she says.

"Hey," I say, still kind of confused. "How's it going?"

"Good," she says. "Hey listen, I, uh, I just wanted to tell you . . ."

"Yeah?"

"Well, a few guys I know at work, they follow football, you know. And they came up to me the other day, and they were, like, 'Hey! Is that your brother on TV, playing in the NFL?' "

"Seriously?"

"Yeah!" she says. "So I was, like, 'Yeah, that's him all right. He's starting.' "

"Wow," I say. "Really?"

"Yeah! Absolutely! Anyway," she says. "I just wanted you to know. It was cool."

"Wow," I say. "Thanks."

I hang up the phone. You may have noticed that I was a little less verbose than usual. That just shows you how shocked I was. She's never told me anything like that before. I couldn't think of anything to say. But I decide that from here on out, if I'm gonna listen to anyone, it's gonna be to people like her. The people in my life who really matter.

IN THE NEXT GAME, I decide to finally change the story.

We all head out to the field through the tunnel, fireworks going off, music blasting, smoke in the air—it's amazing, we haven't even scored yet, haven't played a single down, and we're already celebrating!—and I spot Lopez jogging along as fast as his chubby legs will take him. I move toward him, ready to hatch my little plan.

Before each of the last three games, I've grabbed him and said the exact same thing: "Hey, Lopez, let's have some fun today!" Always trying to make it about us, always trying to get him to relax too, not just me. And you know what? It didn't do a fucking thing.

I didn't want to admit that it had an effect on me, but it did. He got in my head, and I played worse because of it. Shit, at the very least I wasn't having as much fun, and these fuckers aren't paying me enough to not have fun. I'm league minimum.

Well, I'm through with that. I'm gonna think of me today.

"Hey, Lopez!" I shout as we get to the sideline. "Let ME have some fun today, okay?"

I know, it seems like a small difference, right? But it has exactly the effect I hoped for.

"Yeah!" he says. Then he pauses, looks kind of confused. "I always let you have fun, don't I?"

He's not bullshitting me. He really doesn't know.

"No, Lopez. No, you don't. I just need you to let me have fun, okay?"

He nods his head, his jowls shaking, almost excited by this new revelation that's slowly hammering through his hard skull.

"Yeah, Johnny. Yeah, sure!"

And guess what? The motherfucker actually does it. He stops riding my ass, stops pestering me about every little mistake, and lets me play. Does that mean *he's* able to loosen up? Absolutely not. He just spends all day going after Coulter instead. Right before half, Lopez lights into him about some stupid block that wasn't executed exactly the way he wanted—like he's really gonna change a five-year veteran's playing style in the middle of the game—and Coulter looks over at me and Teddy, furious.

"What the fuck did you do, Johnny?" he says.

Teddy and I bust out laughing.

"Look," I say. "I'm just thrilled he isn't using *me* as a punching bag for once."

For the first time since I've been a starter, everything comes together. Jack's new game plan completely baffles the other team, which just figured we'd do the same damn thing we'd been doing. Instead, we take advantage of the speed of our smaller line—meaning the speed of our smaller center, me—and force their defensive line to run all over the field to keep up with us. They can't.

Now all the giant bastards lined up across from me understand a tiny bit of the physical pain I've had to endure running around the past week, and it feels great.

When I do screw up, miss a call or a coverage, Lopez doesn't chew into me like he's been doing. He's got Coulter for that, thank God. Instead, Lo and I have cool, calm discussions about what just happened and what we can do to fix it. That's right! Cool and calm. We haven't worked together this well since the preseason.

Even the media gets back on board. After the game I find out from my dad that Troy Aikman specifically goes out of his way to say on Fox that I'm having a great game. Now do I really give a shit what Troy Aikman thinks about me or anything else? Of course not. But if Troy Aikman says I'm playing well on national TV, then everyone else will say it too. That's just how it works. Thanks, Troy.

We win the game. Fuck, we don't just win the game, we beat the shit out of them, winning by 21 points. Brody has his best outing in weeks, throwing for three touchdowns, and our running back rushes for 137 yards, which is even more important for me and the rest of the line, because the running game is how we're really judged.

Best of all, it's a rivalry game. You'll be *shocked* to learn that this doesn't mean anything to me. College football rivalries are one thing. Almost all the players are with the team for four or five years, so there's a sense of continuity and tradition. At my school, we heard about our in-state rivals from the moment we stepped on campus, from everyone from coaches to players to random students walking to class. We even had signs up in the locker room—*permanent* signs—that screamed at us to beat those fuckers, day and night.

But the pros? Sure, the coach will emphasize a rivalry game more because he knows it's important to the owners and it'll help us make the play-offs. And some old vets might reminisce about their classic games from the past. But for a lot of us the feeling just isn't there. We tell the media that we can't *wait* to beat our rivals, because that's what they want to hear—but we don't give a shit. This is our *job*—a job we could get fired from at any moment. A career bencher, even a star, can find himself on a new team after a single year. Year after year. And you're telling me I suddenly have to hate some random team's guts because it's in our same division? Or because it's located in some city I've barely ever been to before? Or because in 1972 there was some hard-fought game over a trophy that doesn't exist anymore? Yeah, right.

But it still means a ton to the owners and the fans, so after our big win, people are thrilled. Right now, that's more than enough for me. We're 4-3, which doesn't sound great, but our division sucks, and if we put together a good winning streak, we'll have a real shot at making the play-offs. It finally feels like we're coming around.

After the game, for the first time ever, Lopez himself walks up to me, shakes my hand, and honest-to-God congratulates me.

"Hey, Johnny," he says. "You did a good job."

I can barely believe it. The fucker still won't look me in the eye, but hell, I'm not expecting miracles here.

Even our ancient owner decides it's time to say hello again. The guy's somehow managed to avoid me ever since we started losing—just a coincidence, I'm sure—but now he makes his way over like life is nothing but roses.

"Good game, Johnny," he says.

"Thanks."

He starts to turn away, and I can't help myself. I just can't.

"Hey, before I was starting games, you didn't even know my name, did you?"

He halts midturn. His jaw drops so far I'm surprised his dentures don't fall out.

"What? Of course! I know all fifty-three players' names! All of them!"

I grin good-naturedly. Don't want to go too hard on the guy.

"Yeah, okay. Whatever you say."

I pat him on his frail little back and he sighs.

"All right," he says. "At the beginning of the year, I didn't know your name."

"Well," I say, smiling. "I snuck in under the radar."

He chuckles. Now it's his turn to pat me on the back.

"Yep," he says. "But you're coming on now."

Chapter 8

CELEBRITY HOMECOMING

Thursday morning we take the fastest team photo ever. It's our bye week. Time off. Not much time—we all gotta be back at work first thing Monday morning—but we'll take every minute we can get.

So we stand in a giant pack, row by row by row, one set of massive shoulders next to another, with bright, smiling faces, and behind each and every single grin, there's just one thought going through our minds: *Get us the fuck out of here.*

After that photo, we also have to take pictures and mingle pleasantly with all these rich old-timers, friends of the owner, friends of the team, soft, musty, wrinkled people who shell out lots of dollar bills to the organization so they can be a part of special team moments just like this one. "Nice to meet you, ma'am." "Thank you for your support, sir." "I bet you really could throw a ball back in your day! Ha! Ha! Ha!" *Get us the fuck out of here.*

Then just when we're about to explode, in come the fans, the media, the execs. That means more glad-handing. More smiles. More autographs. More pictures.

Get. Us. The fuck. Out of here.

When this is through, some of us might go to Vegas, a couple others may spend the entire time drinking their asses off, but honestly they're the exception. Most of us just want to go home. We want to see our parents, hang out with our buddies, sleep next to our girlfriends. Don't forget—almost none of us live here. We rent apartments for part of the year, or if we're really lucky, maybe we own a second house. But our team's city isn't our home, and we're stuck here for six or seven months out of the year. When we're not here, we're on the road, traveling to even more places we have no personal connection to.

Imagine if your job separated you from all your friends and family for half a year at a time, during which you did almost nothing but work. How would you feel? You'd want to get the fuck out too.

Finally, after two hours that feel like two centuries, we're allowed to leave. If you could take the drive, speed, and motivation of that gigantic mob of fifty-three men as we headed for the front gate, bottle it, and save it for game days, I guarantee you we'd be 7 and 0 right now.

"HEY, SO, I THINK I'M pretty much just gonna take it easy tonight," I say into the phone.

"Huh?" Kate says. "So, like, you don't wanna go out? Just wanna stay in and watch a movie together? That's totally fine!"

"Uhhh . . ."

I'm in the Uber on my way to the airport for the flight back to Ohio. This long weekend is exactly what I need. Time away from football, time to be normal. I'm just not sure how much of that time should include Kate.

"What?" she says. "What's wrong?"

"Nothing's wrong," I say. "I'm just exhausted. After the last game and everything. The last few weeks. I think I just want to kind of veg out at home, do nothing. You know, by myself."

"Oh. Okay."

"But you know what that means, right?" I say, excited.

"What?"

"You don't have to pick me up from the airport!"

"Wow," she says, somehow sounding less than thrilled. "Yeah. What a treat for me."

"I know, right? So yeah, I'll text you tomorrow. We'll figure something out."

"Okay," she says. "Love you."

"Love you too!" I say a little too enthusiastically.

I hang up the phone. I make eye contact with the Uber driver—I think he's Indian or something—and we both kind of shrug, like *Women, what are you gonna do?*

"Hey, can I have one of these little waters here, please?" I ask him.

"Sure," he says.

I crush the water in one gulp. Man, I love Uber. I just love it when things work *well,* you know?

"Thanks," I say. "I have to drink about twenty gallons a day."

He looks me over.

"You a really big guy," he says. "What are you, some kinda bodybuilder?"

"Nah," I say. "I'm in construction. Consulting."

"Oh," he says, nodding. It's a line I use whenever I don't want to talk about football.

Kate was clearly kind of pissed about not hanging out tonight, but, I mean, if I were her I'd be thrilled I didn't have to pick someone up from the airport. There's nothing worse than that. Plus, she's still been worrying about me finding some other girl now that I'm supposedly some football big shot, texting me twenty times a day, nagging me about checking my ego and staying away from all the "temptation" out there—me, a guy who barely has time to breathe, much less socialize. It's fucking annoying.

I mean, look, do some football players go out to clubs and fuck anything with a vagina? Sure, they're dudes—they're fucking disgusting. But a lot of us are just normal, dorky guys. Some of us are even sappy romantics.

The quarterback on my last team was a big name, the kind of guy who if I told you who he was you'd be, like, "Whoa, you played with *him*??" For my whole second season, this man—this star—was obsessed with a cute girl who worked at a sushi restaurant. He'd come up to me on our plane rides home and say, "Johnny, what do you think I should say to her this week? I don't know what to do, I'm so nervous!"

I'd just shake my head. The guy was worth $60 million, and he was nervous about picking up a chick at a sushi place. When he finally did ask her out, she said no—she already had a boyfriend.

Even Antonne, now that he has so much time on his hands because of the injury, is using Tinder less to get laid and more to actually meet someone. At lunch last week I saw him and Coulter huddled over his phone, all excited because his "ideal woman" right-swiped him, giggling like a couple teenage girls with a crush.

Kate and I have been together a long time. We've been through a lot. And that's important to me. But deep down I think both of us know we're not exactly a perfect match. It's easy to say that the long-distance thing is what's kept us from progressing in our relationship. (I don't even like to say the word *married*. It makes me roll my eyes automatically.) But there's more to it than that. Something just isn't quite right.

As you can see, football drives me crazy. Dealing with all the politics, all the egos, all the uncertainty—it's constant work. Nothing is ever easy.

I don't need that in my relationship. I want something that's fun, that helps me escape from all the bullshit in my life. Honestly, that doesn't always happen with Kate.

I unlock my cell with a flick of my finger and start to text.

"Hey, Dad, huge favor. Would you mind picking me up from the airport?"

THE PLAY CLOCK IS TICKING. I can't see it, but I know it's there, looming over me, over all of us, over the whole stadium, counting down . . . 5 . . . 4 . . . *Ram 51!* I shout . . . 3 . . . 2 . . . Snap the ball . . . Nose tackle comes right at me . . . not a moment to think . . . helmet down . . . angle my body . . . cleats dig into the turf . . . legs explode, power me forward . . . brace myself for impact . . . helmet to helmet shoulder to shoulder torso to torso a hundred miles an hour . . .

CRACK!

"Ahhh!" comes a high-pitched scream from right next to me.

What the fuck is a woman doing in a football game?

I open my eyes. I'm not *in* a football game. I'm on a plane, heading back to Ohio. Southwest Airlines, so it's a regular-sized seat, damn well not first class—not that I'd ever pay for first class myself, even if it was offered—and right next to me isn't Jeb in a three-point stance but a terrified chick who's very small, very cute, and very blond.

Okay, I think. *That's interesting.*

And I immediately fall back asleep.

I wake up thirty minutes, maybe an hour later, who knows—and she's looking at me with big blue eyes. God, I love big blue eyes on small pretty blond chicks, preferably with big tits. She's got those too. Fuck, I wish I didn't have a type. So fucking predictable.

"Sorry about that," I say. "You know, earlier."

"It's okay," she says. "Nightmare?"

"You could say that. My name's Johnny, by the way."

"Sarah," she says. "Nice to meet you. You know, awake."

She smiles. A sense of humor. *Not bad,* I think.

"Are you from Ohio?" I ask, really hoping she says no and she's from my team's city.

"No," she says. "Just flying in for work. I'm in sales, travel a lot. I'm from the city."

Yes! Jackpot.

"Nice," I say. "I *absolutely* love that city. *Beautiful* city. *Gorgeous.*"

"No, it's not," she says. "It's awful. I hate it."

"Good, so do I," I say. "It's *absolutely* disgusting."

"Well, I'm glad we agree," she says, laughing. "But I'm from there, I have an excuse. Why are you there?"

"I work there," I say, making sure to add: "But just a few months out of the year."

"Really?" she says. "What kind of work is just a few months out of the year?"

"Oh," I toss out all casually, "I play football."

"Oh!" she says. "Cool! You know, my dad is a huge fan of your rivals."

The team we just beat. Of course he is.

"Uh-oh," I say slyly. "We're in trouble then, aren't we?"

Kate wouldn't mind this at all, I think. I'm just having a friendly little chat with a person on the plane who just happens to be an attractive blonde. Totally innocent!

An hour later the attractive blonde and I are standing next to the baggage claim. We collected our bags thirty minutes ago. We're still talking.

"We should hang out sometime back in the city," I say. "After my break. I still barely even know anyone."

"Yeah!" she says, flicking her hair in a very cute, blond way. "That sounds great! Let me give you my number and you can text me."

"Great," I say. Assertive. I like that.

I pull out my cell, see the time.

"Fuck."

"What?" she says.

"Nothing," I say. "What's that number again?"

I completely forgot about my dad waiting outside.

MY DAD AND I PULL up outside his house.

It's the same house I grew up in. Whenever I walk past my dad's office, which is now just a generic office, I remember when it was my mom's hospice room. I remember the bed on wheels, the sheets covering the windows to keep out the harsh daylight, the silk flowers heaped everywhere, and my mother's thin, frail form lying under a heap of blankets.

This is where I come whenever I'm not playing football. I've got my own little pad above the garage, a single studio with its own entrance, bathroom, and even a miniature kitchen. If I were still in high school, I'd be the coolest fucking kid in class.

When I joined the NFL, I considered buying a place of my own, but it didn't seem worth it. I'd be gone six months out of the year, and I knew that for as much money as I made, I had less job security than a kid working the fries at McDonald's.

Besides, there's something nice about coming back to this place, to my old life.

My dad and I walk in the front door. He's finally getting over how I made him wait thirty fucking minutes at the airport. He lightened up when I told him it was for a blond chick with big tits.

"Well, you know what I like to say," he tells me as he hangs up his coat, the Ohio winter already close at hand. "Women are like a bag of M&Ms . . ."

"I know, I know. Gotta try 'em all."

"Exactly," he says.

My dad isn't much for sayings, but when he finds one, he really sticks with it. He likes Kate well enough, but just like me he's never been completely convinced that she's the one. He thinks I might be able to do just a bit better, maybe just a bit taller. *Johnny, you don't want to have short kids . . .*

He should know. The guy is an Internet dating machine. Absolutely *owns* eHarmony. Been engaged more times than I can count, married only a few times less than that. As far as stability with women goes, it all kind of went to pot once my mom died. Thankfully for me and my sanity he's between relationships right now.

"Well, well, look who's here! Johnny!"

My granddad gets up from the sofa, where he's in the middle of an episode of *Wheel of Fortune*. He watches it every night, followed by the news.

"Vanna," he says, gesturing at the toothy, ageless blonde on TV. "Lady's still got it."

"Absolutely," I say. "Hey, Grandpa. How are you?"

He gives me a hug, pats me on the shoulder like he's testing how solid I am. He's eighty-four but still tall and thin like my dad, only shrinking a little with age. His build is close to what mine would be if I didn't put my body through hell for football.

"Oh, I'm hanging in there," he says. "Just excited to see you! It's not every day we get an NFL starter in the family, you know!"

"Aw, it's no big deal," I say, secretly loving the compliment.

"Hey," he says, sitting back down. "You know I used to play football back in high school myself, right?"

"Yeah!" I say, cracking open the beer my dad hands me. "Receiver, right?"

This, of course, is a story I've heard an infinite number of times, but which my granddad retells every time he sees me like it's hot off the printing press of his mind.

"Oh, well, you know, back then we did a little bit of everything—receiver, corner, defensive end, you name it. I was really good, too! First couple years anyway."

"But you got injured, right?" I say. "Your knee?"

I know perfectly well it was his shoulder, but he loves a little nudge.

"Shoulder, actually!" he says, sipping a beer of his own. "Shoulder. Busted it up real good. Really could've had a future in football too. Well, not a starting professional like yourself. But something! Maybe college ball. Who knows?"

At a Christmas party two years ago, Grandpa had two or three more beers than usual and finally confessed that, although he'd technically been a member of his high school football team for a year or two, he'd actually ridden the bench the entire time. He never played in a single game. I like the current version a lot better.

"Yeah," I say. "I knew I got it from somewhere."

He motions me closer to him, lowers his voice to a confidential tone.

"Hey, Johnny," he says.

"Yeah, Grandpa?" I say, leaning in.

"I wish my brothers were around, your father's uncles. I would love to just sit back and brag about you. Goddammit, they'd be proud of you."

Now that's one I haven't heard before. I look over at my dad. He's beaming. I clear my throat. I pride myself on being a cynical bastard, but I can feel myself choking up. It's kind of embarrassing.

"Thanks, Grandpa," I say with a cough. "That, uh, that means a lot to me."

He nods his head, slowly.

"One more thing, Johnny," he says.

"Yeah?"

"Never, ever have sex the night before a game. You lose all your *drive*. Got me?"

He winks and turns back to *Wheel of Fortune* without skipping a beat.

"Come on! Buy a vowel, goddammit!"

I HAVE NO IDEA WHY the fuck I'm doing this with my Friday night. I mean, I get a measly four days off from football—four!—and I decide to do *what*? Go to a high school football game? I've obviously taken one too many hits to the head.

"Heyyyyyy! Johnny!"

Waiting for me in the school parking lot is the only reason I came. Roger Parker, one of my old coaches. He stands there grinning, five feet seven inches and 325 pounds of lard-ass, wearing an old team sweatshirt that barely fits, an XXXL that he can't even zip up, and already holding a couple hot dogs in each hand, probably all for him. He looks like a bowling ball with tiny feet. He's also the first guy who taught me anything about football, the first guy other than my dad to actually believe I could make it. God, I love this guy.

"Come here, you big, fat bastard!" I shout, gathering him in for a bear hug, or at least as much of one as I can manage. "Shit! Have you put on weight?"

"What, me?" he says, biting into a dog. "I'm solid as a rock."

I flick his massive tits. They jiggle like tubs of Jell-O.

"Oh yeah," I say. "You bet you are. I wish my girlfriend had a rack like that."

"Fuck off, Johnny," he says, laughing. "Come on, let's go."

We walk through the parking lot, past the school and toward the football field. Not much has changed. When you think about it, I've only been gone eight years. The place is just as tiny as when I went here, can't be more than five hundred students in the whole school. But nothing looks old or ratty. It might be small, but there's a lot of pride, especially in our sports.

The football stands are new, the bleachers shiny white vinyl, none of those faded splintered wooden benches here. The field is lush and green, all the yards marked with perfect precision. There's even a little broadcast booth where our local radio station calls the game. Ohio loves its fucking football.

As we head into the stadium, Roger and I pass by students, parents, families, aging sports junkies. It's embarrassing to say it, but if this were *Anchorman,* I'd be at a pool party saying "I'm kind of a big deal." People are staring at me, gawking. I notice a few whispers, some points. I think back to what it would've been like if an NFL player-alumnus had come to one of *my* games when *I* was back in school and realize I would've been just as starstruck. Hopefully, I would've hid it better.

A little kid totters up with a piece of paper and a pen.

"Excuse me, uh, could I—"

His dad rushes up behind him and starts tugging him away, looking up at me apologetically.

"Sorry about that, sir—"

"No problem," I say, taking the paper and pen and signing it. "Relax. And don't call me 'sir.' "

I might be an asshole, but even *I'm* not that much of an asshole.

By the bleachers Roger and I pass by a long, concrete wall, our "Wall of Honor." Hung behind glass are framed photos of all our school's star athletes from over the years. Basketball, baseball, track, wrestling, and of course football. A few of the photos are in black and white, most of them faded by the sun.

Roger's photo is up there, one of the only black guys among a bunch of white faces. He graduated in 1987 and went on to play on the defensive line for a small college in Pennsylvania. He's one of the few defensive linemen I've ever known with a brain. For the last fourteen years he's been the high school's defensive coordinator, its D-line coach, its safeties coach, its strength coach, which is how he worked with me, and its God-only-knows-what-else. My high school team has a staff slightly smaller than an NFL team's.

"Roger," I say, "now you know I don't care about this shit, but how the hell is it that I'm literally the only football player who's ever graduated from this school to go on to play for a major college program *and* the NFL, and I *still* don't have my goddamn picture on that wall?"

"Yeah, I don't know," he says earnestly. "You just gotta know the right people, you know?"

Fuck. Even in high school I can't escape the politics.

"Hey, everybody!" he shouts. "Look who we got here! Straight off the boat from the NFL! Johnny Anonymous!"

We're on the sidelines now, surrounded by the team.

"I took a plane, you old fart," I say. I clean up my language for the youngsters.

They look at me, all these kids, sweaty and pimply, wide-eyed and stupid, awed yet somehow also dismissive, and most of all, just really, really small.

All I can think is *Did I ever look this hopeless?*

"You, uh, you guys look great!" I say, completely unconvincingly. "Let's kick some fucking ass!"

So much for the clean language.

The game starts. I'm on the sidelines with the coaches for the whole thing.

At first I stand apart from everyone, honestly, out of sheer disgust at what I'm watching. Even though we're technically winning the game, we look *awful*. No more so than most high school programs, but it's still jarring. There's a huge talent difference when you go from college to the NFL, everyone knows that. But the difference from high school to college is ten times that.

The technique their offensive line is using . . . I can't actually talk about it, because it doesn't exist. All they've been taught to do is run fast and hit hard and try to knock fuckers over. How to use their hands? How to punch? How to gain leverage? Completely foreign concepts. The only thing they understand is harder, faster, bigger, stronger. That's all they've been taught, nothing but pushing that sled, every single day.

I know, because they have the exact same O-line coach I had when I was in school. He fucking sucks. Makes Lopez look like a football genius.

Finally I can't take it anymore.

"Hey, guys," I say to a few of the linemen when the defense is on the field. "Come on over here."

They look at each other hesitantly and then at the head coach, who also handles the O line. He shrugs. Roger isn't quite as reserved.

"Go on over there, motherfuckers!" he shouts. "Listen to what the man got to say! He's in the fucking League!"

The kids gather around me, and I look them each in the eye, making sure I have their attention, a lot like when I'm talking to the rest of my own line in a huddle. They look terrified.

"Now look," I say. "You guys are hitting hard, and that's great, okay? You're really good at it. You're strong, you're fast, you're huge. You're really impressive. I'm being honest here, okay?"

Of course, I'm not being honest at all, but I see a few smiles now. They're opening up, relaxing, ready to listen.

"Now that you got that down, now that you know how to be physical, you can add some technique to that, okay? When you run a run play, don't just try to open up a hole by slamming your face into the guy, right? Because if you do that, there's a chance he could spin, or you could hit him at an off angle and he'll bounce right off. Use your hands, okay? Like . . . Come on over here."

I pull one of the little goobers over to demonstrate. Now they're completely rapt. Hanging on every word. Perfect.

"Okay, so as you move to attack the other guy, which you're doing well, you have to do more than just headbutt the dude. Take your hands and shoot them right into his chest, like this."

I grab the kid's chest plate, he feels like a wet piece of paper just floating in his pads.

"Once you catch hold of him, grip down and press. Watch their D-line crumble."

The next offensive series I watch them intently. On the first run play, none of them get it right, but they all try. The next play, a couple of them get it to work, more or less. The following play, one of them completely misses, but another guy executes perfectly, using his hands to knock over his D lineman, creating a nice, big hole for their running back to dart through. Gain of 7 yards.

Now on the next play, for all I know, the same guy might fuck it up completely and get flattened back into his own man. But still. It's progress. They'll get it right, eventually.

I smile. There's something oddly appealing about all this. Dammit.

"YOU SEE THAT CHICK OVER THERE?" Roger asks me.

I'm on my fifth beer. He's on his ninth. For a guy his size who drinks as much as he does, that means approximately nothing, but I figure he's gotta have a slight buzz going by now.

"Yeah, Roger, I see her."

The game ended two hours ago. We won, 24–7. We're at a new bar in town. Excuse me, not a bar—a "brewery." Some attempt to do something trendy in a small Ohio town, with big, fancy copper pipes and kettles in a glassed-off room next to the restaurant. I think Roger wanted to show off. Not show off the bar, but show off *me,* his NFL buddy. All I wanted was a Pabst.

"Yeah, well, I could totally fuck her," he says.

"Sure you could, buddy."

Forget about the fact that at his weight, I'm not even sure if Roger is capable of fucking anyone, including his wife, who he's been married to for seventeen years. The woman he's currently talking about isn't gorgeous, but very, very far from hideous. And therefore totally out of Roger's league.

"What, you don't believe me, motherfucker?" he says. "Just say the word, I'll go over there right now, me and her be banging later tonight, no question!"

"Let's not and say you did, okay, baby?"

"All right, fine," he says, pouting. "But I could if I wanted, no question."

Claiming he could fuck any woman in the bar is pretty much standard Roger, kind of like my granddad telling me he used to be great at football, but a lot grosser. I motion over our waitress.

"Another round, please?"

"Sure thing," she says, then hesitates. "Um, so the bartender just told me you're famous. Are you?"

"Not really," I say, smiling. "Just hometown famous, I guess."

"Fuck that!" Roger says. "This motherfucker's *totally* famous! He plays for the NFL!"

"Really?" she says, her eyes opening wide. "Um, do you mind if I get your autograph?"

"Okay," I say. "I think I'd also like to order some food, if you don't mind."

"Oh! Sure! Hold on a sec, um, I'll be right back with some paper and pen. And a menu!"

I roll my eyes as she scampers off, both because I actually had to tell her to do her job, and because Roger was blatantly staring at her ass.

"Johnny," Roger says. "What you thinking about doing after you hang it up? You know, after you done with the League. You ever think about moving back? Setting up shop here?"

"I don't know," I say, finishing off my beer, the closest thing they had to Pabst, but five times more expensive and not nearly as good. "I try not to think about it at all."

"You were good with the kids tonight," he says. "Real good, man. They respected you, you know? They listened. You ever think about coaching?"

"No fucking way," I say. "Coaching is you, man."

"But why?" he says. "You good at it!"

The funny thing is, he's right. I am. The kids gave me the game ball after it was over, whatever that means for a normal regular-season game with no implications. I'll probably leave it at my dad's house when I fly out on Sunday, but it was nice of them.

"I don't know," I say. "No offense, man, what you do is important. Coaching, I mean. You played a really big role in my life when I was in school. I just want to do something different. Something more."

"All right," he says. "All right. I get it."

He doesn't really get it, though, because I can't be completely honest with him. Even though I do appreciate everything he's done for me, him and a couple other coaches, I still can't get past the feeling that at the end of the day it's still just . . . football. Not significant. A stupid fucking game.

Even now that I'm starting in the NFL, the idea that I could possibly spend the rest of my life working in football just depresses me. Especially because I could do it *so fucking easily*.

I could move back here, coach for the same high school where I played, just like Roger. Go trolling for chicks at townie bars, just like Roger. Hope someone will recognize me and ask me for my autograph, just like Roger.

I look at him, his eyes starting to fog over from the tenth beer he just slammed, leering at one woman after another, mumbling to himself about how he could fuck them all. I like Roger. But I do not want to *be* Roger.

"Hey! *Hey!* Why don't you keep your eyes to yourself, man!"

I look up. A dude is standing over our table, a guy who's apparently with one of the women Roger's been ogling. The guy isn't small, maybe about six-one, 200 pounds, but I'm not worried. Problem is, I kind of wish Roger was.

"You know who the fuck you're talking to, bro?" Roger says, getting to his feet. "No, seriously, do you *know*?"

"Fuck," I mutter to myself, covering my eyes with my hand. A few people in the bar are looking over. I do not want to get involved here.

"I'll *tell* you who you talking to," Roger says, hands in his jacket pockets, fumbling for something. "I'll *show* you."

Finally he pulls it out. It's a ring. An old championship ring.

"What the fuck is that?" the other dude says.

"That's a 1990 Division Three Regional Football Championship ring, motherfucker. You're looking at a starting lineman for the fucking 1990 Addison Cougars."

The dude looks at me like *Seriously*? I just shrug.

"Whatever, man," he says, shaking his head and walking back to his table. "Whatever."

"Yeah, that's right!" Roger says. "Walk back to your girl! Your dick couldn't even fill out this motherfucking ring! Fucker!"

Laughing to himself, quite pleased, Roger sits back down, grabs his beer, and swigs.

"That was fucking sick, man," he says.

I sigh. Like I said. I do not want to be Roger.

ON SATURDAY, I FINALLY SPEND the day with Kate. We drive to nearby Columbus—well, I drive her car, because I can't stand it when she drives—to look at condos.

That's right, I've finally decided to buy a place of my own. As much as I like coming back to my dad's house—the memories, the convenience, the total lack of rent—I want something more stable, more permanent, more rooted than my Dodge Durango. I know I could always get released after this season, but I'm finally starting to gain a little confidence. Who knows? If I play well in a few more starts, maybe I really can negotiate a bigger contract, just like my agent says. With my own home and a job that lasts longer than a single year, I could actually be on my way to being, you know, normal.

"Just one more address on the list," Kate says.

"Thank God!" I groan. "I'm fucking sick of this shit!"

Well, maybe not quite normal.

The place is fine. Close enough to Ohio State's campus to make it cool and a good investment, while far enough away so I won't have to deal with a bunch of drunken college bullshit. But what freaks me out is Kate's reaction. She puts everything she sees in terms of "us."

"Johnny, this closet will totally be big enough for *our* stuff."

"Oh, can you just imagine *us* having breakfast on the balcony?"

"Let's get married right here in the master bathroom! Look it even has two sinks! And travertine!"

Okay, so she doesn't exactly say we should get married, but still. I'm trying to focus on light fixtures and market value, and all I keep hearing from her is an echo of "us us us together together together forever forever forever forever."

I don't say much. Back in the car, she asks me what I think.

"I don't know," I say. "I'm not sure if it's right for *me*."

"Oh," she says.

I think for a second. Then decide to take the plunge.

"Kate," I say. "Do you feel like anything about our relationship still excites you?"

"Huh?" she says, her voice tense. "What's that supposed to mean?"

"I don't know. I was just remembering what it was like when we first started going out, you know? Everything just seemed so . . . *exciting*."

"And you don't feel that way now?"

"I gotta be honest," I say. "Not really."

She gives me this look like *I knew this football shit would go to your head. I knew it!*

But I refuse to engage on that level. I've felt this way about us for a while. And I think, deep down, underneath all her insecurity, she has too. Football has absolutely nothing to do with it. At least that's what I tell myself.

"What," I say. "Are you saying you get excited about our relationship the same way you used to?"

"No," she says. "But how am I supposed to be excited when we live, like, hundreds of miles apart?"

"Kate, that's not going to change. Not anytime soon anyway. Besides, it's more than that. It's not just the long-distance thing. I love you. I care about you. You know I do. But something's not working."

"Well, so, what do you want to do?" she says. "Are you saying you want to break up?"

"No," I say. "No, that's not what I'm saying. Not at all."

Look, it's like I said before. She and I have been together so long, through so much. I really do care about her. Besides, she and her whole family already bought plane tickets to come and watch me play in two weeks. Breaking up with her right now would be a real dick move.

"Well, what then?" she asks.

"Don't worry," I say. "We'll figure it out."

I WAKE UP LATE SUNDAY MORNING, knowing that on this, the NFL's Weekly Holy Day, I won't be doing a damn thing with a football. Not watching film on my iPad, not watching games on TV, not even checking any scores.

Although, come to think of it, I'm not sure how I'd check scores if I wanted to. My dad is too cheap to buy cable, and I don't even have the ESPN app on my phone.

I bought the latest flight back I could find, just so I could squeeze every last drop of beautiful, glorious no-football-ness out of my day. I can feel my job starting to tug at my brain already, all the usual stress and anxiety. *Is Lopez finally gonna ease up on me now that we've won a game—a big game—with me playing at center? Will we be able to turn that single win into two wins, even three? If we don't, how fast will it take for everyone to whip right back to "fuck Johnny, we need Antonne" mode? And how much longer will I have to prove myself before he comes back from his injury anyway? Two weeks? Three weeks? One?*

I can feel all this noise lurking in the background of my mind, but I push it away, force it into a tight, football-proof box. I have one last day of nothing. A solid twelve or thirteen hours of jack fucking squat. And I'm gonna savor every last moment.

God, this feels amazing.

I head to the kitchen. I'm so fucking happy I'm actually whistling a tune. "Wish They All Could Be California Girls" by the Beach Boys. God, I love the Beach Boys. My dad is at the kitchen table, hunched over his phone, reading something. I swing open the fridge, grab some OJ, and start pouring myself a glass.

"Goooood morning!" I say, all bright and cheery and sunshiny.

My dad looks up from his phone, and I can tell immediately that something is wrong.

"What?" I say.

"Nothing," he says, looking quickly away. "Morning!"

"What is it?"

"Oh," he says, fumbling for words, which is very unlike my dad.

"Well, uh, I got this app, the ESPN app, and it's set up to give me alerts if something happens with your team, you know."

The motherfucking ESPN app. See why I don't fuck with that shit?

"Yeah?" I say.

"Well, apparently they just re-signed Paulson."

Paulson? *Paulson?*

"PAULSON?"

"Yeah," he says. "Paulson."

You remember Paulson, right? The guy from the preseason? The guy who should've been the backup instead of me? The guy who would've had my spot on the roster if he hadn't gotten miraculously injured? The guy who's a much more natural center than I am? The guy who loves Jesus and *Star Trek*?

Yeah. *That* Paulson.

"How . . . ?" I can't finish my sentence.

"It says he got the surgery on his groin, rehabbed a lot faster than everyone thought. You know that old dude they signed when Antonne got injured? That big slow guy who wasn't any good? What's his name again?"

"Yeah," I say, ignoring the question. "Right."

"They cut him to make room. Re-signed Paulson yesterday."

"Oh. Yeah. Of course."

"Look," my dad says. "You've been playing great, right?"

"Right."

"Right. So the team probably just figures that after this season you're gonna be gone. You know. Picked up by some other team to be their starter. So they re-signed Paulson as a fallback for you, for when you move on."

"Yeah," I say. "Sure. That makes sense."

Except it doesn't.

I've been playing well, but definitely not well enough to guarantee me a starting spot on another team next year. Plus, even if my team really is that worried about me leaving, there are still nine games left in the regular season. Why would they need to pick up Paulson now? It's not like other teams are gonna be fighting to sign a guy who just got out of rehab for a major groin injury.

Hell, it could mean anything. It could mean they got tired of wasting their money on an old guy who was too big and slow to add anything to the offense, so they figured they'd bring Paulson back instead. It could mean they're fed up with how I'm playing and want another option, but not certain enough about Paulson's health to risk flat out cutting me in the middle of the season. For all I know, it could mean they're just really nice guys and missed Paulson's quirky comments on the world of Vulcans and Christianity.

In fact, the only thing I do know right now is that I'm back to knowing absolutely dick about my future. And that my perfect, no-football Sunday just went right down the shitter.

Chapter 9
THE MEANING OF IRONY

Monday comes. I'm back at work. The doors swing open, and so do the floodgates of my mind.

I've always overthought shit. Always. But this isn't just me.

Something about this business, something about this League, brings out the worst of it. Something about pro football, even when you're starting, even when you're winning, even when you should be one of the game's golden gods, is just plain rotten. It fucks with your head. You never know where you stand, and you damn well don't know why. One second you're up, the next second you're down. The second after that, you're up again, even higher, all so they can smack you down even harder than before. It's enough to drive a fucker crazy.

I'd call it an emotional roller coaster, except that wouldn't do it justice. It's just another season in the NFL.

I head into the locker room. No one looks excited to be back. Not Brody, not Jeb, not the backups. For a few days they actually got a chance to enjoy life—lives they won't be able to lead for the rest of the year. No more friends, no more family. Back to the grind.

I'm sure Paulson must be around here somewhere. After I talked to my dad yesterday, just to be a good sport about it all, I went to Paulson's Facebook page to welcome him back to the team. Yep, it's Facebook official. I'm not an asshole.

I pass by Antonne, who's sitting and bullshitting with a couple guys from defense, a safety named Freddy and Jovan the Preacher. According to Teddy, Antonne did a lot of fucking, a lot of drinking, and a lot of partying over the break. The girl he was crushing on from Tinder didn't last past a couple nights—so much for romance. Without football games to give his life a sense of meaning, it's been all downhill from there. Guy looks like hell, rings under his eyes, like he got his ass kicked by a bottle. Not the physical condition you want to be in if you're still recovering from a serious back injury.

"Wait, wait, hold up," Jovan is saying. "So you can still, like, have sex and all even with your back all fucked up?"

"Yeah, man," Antonne says. "Just have the girl ride me, you know."

"Yeah, yeah," Freddy says. "But, like, what if you wanna hit it?"

"I can thrust, man."

Jovan and Freddy exchange a skeptical look.

"Did you *penetrate*?" Jovan says.

"Yeah," Antonne says. Then, after considering for a second: "One and a half times."

"What's the half?" Jovan says.

"It was too damn painful to make it a whole, motherfucker!"

They start cracking up. I make eye contact with Antonne, give him a nod. He kind of nods back but quickly turns back to his friends.

It was easy for Antonne to stay positive when everyone was kissing his ass, when the media and the players and even restaurant busboys were begging him to play again, to save the team. But after my last game, nobody's talking like that anymore. In the NFL, it doesn't matter how big you are, how much money you make, how many TV interviews you get, how many fans you have—if a team starts winning without you, you stop existing.

I figure I've got at least three more games before Antonne can make it back. I know that every single one of my starts will be agony for him. That no matter what he says publicly, he's hoping I fail. I can't blame him.

"Hey, Johnny! How was your break, buddy?"

There he is. Paulson. Back at his old locker, like nothing ever changed. All I can think is, man, I really hope it has.

"Hey, baby!" I say, smiling as big and wide as I can manage. "Welcome back!"

I give the guy a hug.

"Hey," he says. "It's just like I said. Gotta trust in God's plan, and everything will work out, you know? I'm just happy I can be back and contribute to the team, you know?"

Fuck, does he really believe all this shit? He's so nice it makes me want to heave.

"Absolutely," I say. "Hey, anything you can do to get Lopez off my back is good by me."

He laughs like this is the funniest thing he's ever heard.

"I can't wait, buddy," he says. "I can't wait!"

"Awesome," I say.

There's an awkward pause. I start to turn away.

"Oh hey," he adds. "Thanks for what you said on Facebook. I appreciate it. A lot."

"No problem, baby," I say. "Really is great to have you back."

I head over to my locker, barely able to suppress a sigh.

Fuck my life.

GOD, MY LIFE IS GOOD.

A wave of relief washes over me. Pure euphoria. Like I can actually feel the liquid joy pumping through my veins. Liquid joy: that's about one-quarter blood, one-quarter adrenaline, and one-half NFL job security.

We're in the Tuesday morning offensive-line meeting, and it's become very clear that, although Paulson might be back—for whatever reason, who the fuck knows—I'm still Lopez's guy, a guy with a job and a purpose.

I'm still The Man.

We review the game film, and Lopez is gushing in front of everyone about how I played. Well, gushing for him anyway. He diagrams a play he and I had discussed on the sideline. I wanted to block it one way, he wanted to run it the other, the usual. We went with my approach, picked up the pressure, and gained 17 yards.

"So congratulations, Johnny! You win that one! I bet that makes your day!"

"Why are you congratulating me?" I say. "We're on the same team! I'm not trying to beat you."

But even as I say it, I've got a big grin on my face. Truth is, I love to win. And I love hearing it from him.

"Look," he says. "We made progress here. You played well."

"It's because we worked together," I say.

Ah, it's so easy to be magnanimous in victory.

But it's more than just his compliments. It's the way he focuses only on me, asking my opinion on different coverages and reads, wondering if I have ideas about what we should adjust for the upcoming game. Suddenly we're the greatest football duo ever. It's bizarre, but the attention thrills me.

"Look at Lo and Johnny doing their thing!" Jeb calls out from the back of the room, laughing. "They're like father and son or some shit!"

Paulson is there, of course. Lopez welcomes him back, but after that, nothing. He talks to me. And Paulson just sits in the back of the room with that same perma-smile plastered across his face. Starting or not, I'm sure he's just happy to have a job again. I'm happy for him, as long as he doesn't take mine.

Antonne, on the other hand, is completely removed from the action. Lying on the floor, desperately trying to keep his back loose, eyes half closed as I get more and more comfortable in my starting spot.

Later in practice, he even takes a go at some drills, trying to do anything to stay relevant. Dumb, because all he's doing is increasing the risk of reaggravating his injury. Of course, I'm paying attention the whole time, because the last thing I need is for both him *and* Paulson to threaten my spot. And I can't help but feel a sense of satisfaction when he looks like absolute shit.

"How you feeling?" I ask when he comes out early from a drill to get some rest.

"Not there yet," he says. "But I'm getting there."

"Yeah," I say helpfully. "You look a little stiff, kind of tentative."

He looks at me blankly.

"Right."

He wipes some sweat away from his forehead, adjusts the headband holding back his huge mass of dreads, and very definitely moves a few feet away from me.

Whatever, I'm just trying to help.

"Hey, Johnny!" Lopez calls after practice, jogging over as I head back to the lockers with Teddy. Lo's belly flaps in the wind as he reaches us, and it's all I can do to keep from laughing at the guy.

"What's up, Lo?"

"Hey," he says. "I'd love to meet up with you to talk some shit over before the next game. Just a couple blitz looks, you know. Been wanting to do it for a while. You got time tomorrow night?"

"Ah, I'd love to," I say. "But I can't. I have a radio interview."

This statement is so ridiculous coming from me, former backup extraordinaire, that all three of us bust out laughing.

"Oh, look who's the shit now!" Lopez says. "The fuckin' star."

"Come on!" I say, laughing. "I'm just doing what your media people say!"

God, my life is good.

FUCK MY LIFE.

It's the next day. Lopez has been riding me since the moment I walked in, about anything, everything, and nothing at all. I'm surprised he didn't find me when I took my morning shit just so he could say my cheek-squeezing technique was all wrong.

In our afternoon offensive-line meeting he pulls up game tape from four weeks ago—four weeks ago!—my very first start. He cues it all the way up to a single play where I just barely missed a block. I took a bad set, a pretty simple mistake, and it ruined the play.

And Lopez replays it over and over again.

"Why didn't you get that, Johnny?"

"I don't know."

Rewind, replay.

"Fuck, we would've gone for forty yards on this one! Why didn't you get it?"

"Still don't know."

Rewind, replay.

"Look at that! We would've scored a TD! Fuck, why did you miss it?"

"Don't know."

Rewind, replay.

"Fuck! We would've won the game!"

"Yep, we would've."

All the other linemen just sit there, watching, amused. It's theater, their own personal entertainment.

"Uh-oh!" Jeb yells. "It's a family feud!"

Hell, Antonne looks happier and more sober than I've seen him all week.

Finally Lopez moves on. To Paulson, of course. And now they're best fucking buddies, like Pauly is Lo's long-lost son. Lopez flashes him a coverage on the overhead, and Paulson completely blows the read. Just gets it flat-out wrong.

Does Lopez explode? Does he raise his voice or even crease his chubby brow? Of course not. He gently explains things to Paulson like he's dealing with a wounded deer in a cartoon Disney forest.

"Just think back to last year, man," he says soothingly. "You were doing everything right, you had it all down. You got this, no big deal."

I lose it and slam my hand down on the desk.

"Why don't you just fire me already?"

The room goes quiet. Lopez just stares at me, doesn't say a thing.

At the end of the meeting, Paulson walks over. He looks genuinely sympathetic, even pats me on the back.

"Well," he says. "Looks like you and Lo are right where you left off."

"Yep," I say. "Some things never change."

I HAVE TO DRIVE AN HOUR outside the city to get to the radio station. We're not exactly talking *Mike & Mike* here. But hey, at least it's FM.

I sit across from two guys in the booth. You can see why they do radio. They're too ugly for TV. They look like twins, both with watery blue eyes hiding behind thick glasses, thinning straw-colored hair comb-overs, and faded flannel shirts that they probably trade back and forth every other day. The only difference is that one has a big bushy walrus mustache while the other one's decided to go for ratty sideburns.

When they stand up to greet me, I can't believe how short they are.

"So how's it been being a starter?" the main guy asks me on air.

"I've been fine," I say. "*You guys* are the ones who've been complaining."

The look on their faces is priceless. I only wish the twenty people listening could see. The media's so used to giving players shit, they never expect us to turn it around on them.

"What? Me? Complain about you?" the guy says. "It wasn't me, it was him!"

"No, no, no!" the cohost says. "It wasn't me, it was him!"

"It totally was not me, it was you!"

"No, no. It was totally you."

I think I just broke their twin bond forever. With loyalty like this, these two would do great in the NFL.

KATE AND HER FAMILY ARE visiting for the game this weekend. I haven't talked to her since I left Ohio, and we haven't been texting as much either. She's been traveling for work this week. She's busy, just like me. Whatever, no big deal.

I kinda dropped the ball with Sarah, too. Remember that nightmare dream-girl from the plane? I was supposed to text her when I got back into town, but with all the football shit, I just never got around to it.

Then Wednesday night, Sarah reaches out on Facebook. On Facebook! What is this, college?

"You *poked* me?" I message her. "Do people even do that anymore?"

Five minutes later she messages me back.

"Hey, at least I didn't go through and like all your pics like a total psycho."

I smile. I gotta hand it to her. She's persistent. I like that in a woman.

BRODY IS OUT.

That's right. Our starting QB is out for the season. He came up gimpy in practice on Tuesday, thought it was a cramp. It turns out he tore his Achilles. He's done for the year, just like that. Hey, the guy'll still get paid to be on injured reserve. And as much as I hate to say it, his injury might be my advantage.

Do I even need to repeat the line about the business again? We've all learned it by now, haven't we? Fine. One more time.

That's the business.

Why is Brody going out good for me? It all comes back to the chemistry. As a center, I need perfect chemistry with my quarterback. Brody and I could practice together all day—hell, we almost did—and, yeah, technically we'd get everything down. The snap, the count, all the basics. But the chemistry was just never there. We never got to the place where we just knew what the other guy was going to do before he even did it.

It's like a real relationship, you know? You can meet a gorgeous chick and want it to work as bad as anything. You can buy her flowers, candy, whatever. You can spend all your time together, clock an hour talking on the phone every single night. But if that spark isn't there, if the energy just isn't right, it doesn't matter how much time you spend together. *Hey, you're good-looking and single, I'm good-looking and single, come on, let's fall in love and make babies.* It doesn't work like that. You can't manufacture it, can't force that connection to exist.

Same thing is true in football with a center and a QB. A forced, practiced relationship might be good enough when a game isn't on the line. But we're not getting paid to play well when it's easy. We need to be great when shit gets hard, when a game plan falls apart, when everything comes down to improvising. And that's where chemistry comes in. Brody had that with Antonne. With me, not so much.

But for whatever reason, me and the backup, a third-year QB named McCray, do. We've barely even played together, hardly even snapped the ball, and it's there. We have this language, this ability to just kind of flow, to work both inside and outside the lines.

Some of it is that he's more athletic. He has speed, I have speed. We're a better stylistic fit than me and old-man Brody.

But most of it is personality. McCray and I both come from the Land of the Backups, like the Island of Misfit Toys. We know exactly how disposable we are, have a very strong sense of our own football mortality, so we both know how to have fun. We can relax and let the game come to us.

Thursday after practice, I head to the cafeteria to start loading up on food and water to replace the twelve pounds of sweat I just poured out on the field. I grab a tray, head over for my standard chicken and rice, when all of a sudden I feel a distinct pressure from behind me against my ass.

You read that right. From behind me, against my ass.

It's McCray. He's got his hands exactly where they'll spend a lot of their time during games: on my ass, waiting for the ball. The football, motherfucker.

"Set *hut*!" he shouts.

We're in the cafeteria, surrounded by some of the most hyper-masculine, homophobic men the good country of America has to offer. And we all just bust out laughing.

"*Sshhhh!*" I say, putting my finger to my mouth. "Save it for later, honey!"

More laughing everywhere.

Would it sound gay if I said that because Brody and I couldn't joke like that, we were doomed to fail? Should I add that he didn't listen to my problems or take me anywhere special on the weekends?

The funny thing is, though, it's kind of true.

It all goes back to some of the same issues with having an *actual* openly gay player like Michael Sam in the locker room. This is probably gonna sound stupid to all the PC police out there, but in an environment as ultramasculine as the NFL, there's almost no greater sign of comfort with a guy than being able to make a good gay joke with him. McCray knows I like women, I know he likes women—fuck, he's a bigger man-whore than Antonne—but we also trust each other. And thanks to that trust we can mock all the weird gender contradictions in our sport—seriously, he and I are "warriors" and it's his *job* to put his hands on my nuts—without feeling threatened.

It's not always easy to earn that kind of trust. It took me a solid month to get to the point where guys wouldn't flinch when I jokingly called them "baby"—and they had actually met my girlfriend! But with some-one like Michael Sam? A guy everyone *knows* is openly gay? Who could potentially be checking you out in the locker room? It would be impossi-ble to develop the strong bond a successful team needs.

If Sam ever smacked a guy like Dante on the ass—the official NFL version of a "high five"—Dante wouldn't take it as a sign of friendship. It would cause an all-out brawl.

That's why you won't be seeing any more "Michael Sam"s anytime soon. And it has nothing to do with whether or not they can play—I'm sure they already are playing, we just don't know it. But no one wants to be the guy who fucks up the chemistry on his team. No one wants to feel like an outsider who isn't welcome.

On the other hand, McCray, our completely straight new quarter-back, is already putting his hands all over my ass and I couldn't be hap-pier. Somehow, that all makes perfect sense in the NFL.

FRIDAY AFTERNOON. OUR WALK-THROUGH on the practice field, breaking down all the coverages and reads one more time before the game. And on one of the plays I fuck up. I go the wrong way.

"What the fuck was that??" Lopez screams.

"I went the wrong way, my fault," I say.

Lopez explodes.

"What the fuck was that! You don't know the calls? You don't know the plays? You didn't hear? What! The! Fuck!"

"No, I know them," I say. "I just went the wrong way!"

Lopez opens the gigantic hole in his face to keep ripping me a new one, when suddenly someone new enters our little game.

"What the fuck is going on?"

It's Jack. Lopez stops cold.

"I went the wrong way," I say.

Jack looks at Lopez, then back at me. Completely mystified.

"All right, so he went the wrong way. Let's keep going. Jesus."

Lopez grits his teeth, tucks his triple chin into his chest, and waddles off to the other side of the field as if nothing happened. I'm reminded that no matter how much he rides me, no matter how much he does or does not favor Paulson, I am the starter here. Me.

Membership has its privileges.

KATE AND HER FAMILY FLY in for the game Saturday afternoon. I only see her parents briefly when I stop by the hotel to pick her up for dinner. I give her mom a hug.

"See?" she whispers to me. "Told you you'd know what to do once you got out there."

I smile and awkwardly hug her.

"Johnny," Kate's dad says, all officially.

"Paul," I say, just as officially.

His name is Paul, if you couldn't tell. He's always thought I was an asshole. Probably always will.

Kate wants to have dinner just the two of us, so I take her to dinner at the Cheesecake Factory, her favorite. What can I say? No matter what city I play in, there's a Cheesecake Factory. The place is packed, as always, and Kate doesn't even wait till we sit down before she begins The Talk. I've been waiting.

"I've been thinking a lot about what you said back in Ohio, Johnny."

"Oh yeah?" I say.

"Yeah," she says.

The entryway is jammed with couples, families, little kids, old people, young people, black people, white people, brown people. Man, I think, everyone fucking loves cheesecake. It's the great American equalizer.

Mercifully our waitress seats us. Kate waits until we get a slew of appetizers before she continues.

"So like I said, I've been thinking about it," she says. "And, you know, I feel like you're just waiting around and hoping to find someone better."

"Okay," I say, munching on an avocado eggroll. Not aggressive, not defensive. Just calm. Neutral.

"So it's, like, no matter what happens, I'm, like, screwed, you know? You either find someone better, which is great for you, or I'm stuck with a guy who's just wishing he wasn't with me in the first place, you know?"

I dig into the bread basket. God, I love that brown bread. There are a few different ways to approach this situation—the conversation with Kate, not the bread. I could use this as an opening to break things off with Kate, which is something I've been giving a lot of thought to. Or I could lower the temperature, maintain the status quo, and save the Big Talk for another time. Like when I don't have a gigantic, potentially life-altering football game the following morning and I'm not enjoying a bevy of appetizers.

I choose to wait.

"Look," I say. "I'm not just waiting around for something better, not at all. Yes, things haven't been as exciting as *either* of us wants—you admitted that yourself, you feel that way too—but it's been hard, you know? How many couples have lived apart as much as we have?"

I know what you're thinking. Last time I talked to her, I specifically said that the problem wasn't the distance. It's an easy out, a way to save our night at Cheesecake Factory, and I take it. It works. She opens up like clouds after a storm.

"Does that mean you're thinking about moving in together after the season is over?"

I deftly parry.

"After the season?" I say. "Kate, you know me. I don't even know what I'm doing after tomorrow! I can't even think about after the season right now. Fuck, I can barely focus on these pot stickers, and they're fucking delicious!"

She laughs, relaxes a little. Maybe I seem like an asshole, but this is what we need right now.

Call me a masochist, but I actually enjoy a good serious relationship talk every now and then. I approach it analytically. Not like a shrink so much as a mathematician. I know what she responds to, what she doesn't. If something works, I do more of it. If something doesn't, I change tack.

As I'm finishing my appetizer, for example, I toss out something about us not "connecting." She doesn't like this. I can see her body language change immediately, her forehead tense, her shoulders hunch. I shift course immediately, return to talking about the condo in Columbus I may, someday, eventually, buy. And everything is fine again.

It kind of reminds me of how I deal with football, with my line, with my quarterback. How I'd like to deal with Lopez, if the fucker would just get with the program. Never attack, never blame, just stay cool, logical, and in control.

It's a good dinner. No Big Talk. I leave a nice 10 percent tip. That's a lot, for me.

We get back to my apartment. From the sounds I can hear, Teddy and his fiancée are back in his room, doing whatever. Kate and I sit on the couch, turn on the TV. She moves in close to me. Starts touching my leg. Subtle, I guess, but I know her well enough to understand where this is going.

"You realize we're not having sex tonight, right?" I say.

"Why not?" she pouts.

"Well," I say. "Because of what my grandpa said."

"Your *grandpa*?"

"Yeah. He said I should never have sex the night before a game. It wastes my energy or something."

"Holy shit, Johnny."

"What, it's true!" I say. "He was really good at football back in high school. He almost played in college, did you know that?"

ON SUNDAY, I PLAY MY best game of the year. Hell, as a team we play our best game of the year. And it's against one of the top teams in the League.

Everything is flowing, everything is clicking, everything is coming together. Maybe it's that new chemistry I've got with McCray. Maybe it's all that extra energy I have from not having sex with Kate last night. Maybe it has nothing to do with me at all. But whatever it is that's causing it, we're good.

So good that after the game Jack swears in his postgame speech that we're gonna go to the Super Bowl this year.

So good that Lopez walks up to Jeb, the leader of our line, and tells the guy he played like shit. Sounds a little counterintuitive, I know. If we did so great, why tell a guy he sucked? But for Lopez to yell at our star takes a lot of fucking balls. If we weren't playing fucking amazing, if Lopez's job wasn't completely safe, he could never do that.

Best of all? Jeb doesn't even argue with him. That's right, the same player who's been giving Lopez shit since day one just sighs and nods and takes it like a first-year rookie. I would've been less shocked if Lopez had told me he was renaming his firstborn son Johnny Anonymous and Jeb offered to breast-feed.

Hell, maybe we *are* gonna make the Super Bowl?

God, my life is good.

GOD, I'M IN SO MUCH PAIN.

It's Tuesday and I'm in the locker room, getting ready for our walk-through. Not much to do, won't need my helmet or my pads. I'm looking forward to the light day. My body is in perpetual agony; it's my natural state now. Like the sky is blue, like the sun is yellow, like the chicken and rice I gorge myself on every day is some off shade of brown. It just is.

And you know what? I kind of don't mind. It's the price I pay for being a starter. It's the price I pay to matter.

I lace up my cleats, these fancy black Nikes we only use for walk-throughs that we call Cadillacs because they ride so smooth. I stand up, and there's Lopez. He has this look on his face, something I can't read, something I haven't seen before. Is it satisfaction? Is it smugness? Is it sadness? I don't know.

He walks up to me, kind of puts his arm around me, his hand on the back of my neck. Gently, like a father.

"Hey, Johnny," he says. "Just wanted you to know that you've been great, how much I appreciate you stepping in. Antonne was gone, you came in, it was like we didn't miss a beat."

I look at him. There's really only one thing to say, so I say it.

"Thanks, Coach."

He stares at me as if he's waiting for me to say something more. Finally he just nods and walks away. He may not have said the words exactly, but he didn't have to. We both know what he meant.

Antonne is back, and I'm back to riding the bench. It's over.

Did Lopez expect me to get angry? To argue or act hurt or maybe gush with gratitude? I don't know, but whatever it was, I wasn't going to give it to him.

That afternoon at the walk-through, nothing is said. There are no announcements or speeches or handshakes or even bad fucking jokes. No discussions about how exactly Antonne managed to miraculously recover two or three weeks early, or whether that's good for the team, or even his own health.

The whistle blows for the ones to take the field, and Antonne simply goes with them, and I stay with the twos.

That's all. Nothing else.

That's the business.

Twenty minutes later, Antonne goes off on Coulter on the sidelines about some inconsequential mistake. Classic Antonne fire and brimstone, with an extra air of *I'm reasserting myself as the Alpha, so everyone get the fuck in line.*

Antonne storms off, leaving Coulter standing there shaking his head.

"Fuck, Johnny," Coulter says. "I wish you were back already."

"That's ironic," I say.

"What?" he says.

"You know, that just a few weeks ago, you were practically begging Antonne to come back again. And now here he is, and you're saying you want *me*."

Coulter looks at me, puzzled.

"No," he says. "I mean, like, what's *ironic*? Like, I don't get it?"

"Never mind," I sigh.

Fuck my life.

Chapter 10
MISS ME WHEN I'M GONE

I call Bernie, my agent, at the end of the day, break the news.

"Fuck 'em," he says. "We got what we wanted."

"Yeah," I say. Even though I feel like I got kicked in the teeth.

"Yeah, we did!" he says, forcing the excitement. "We got exactly what we wanted! Tons of game tape of you playing really great against some good players. Once the season's over, we're gonna shop you around to other teams, sell the fuck out of you."

"That's the plan," I say.

" 'Course, that all depends on if they're willing to release you at the end of the year, you know that. They could decide to hold on to you, keep you as a backup for next season. Then you're stuck making league min. The team's got all the leverage here, we just gotta see what they do. Wait a little. But you know that."

"Yeah."

"But hey. They decide to let you go, and we are in great shape, Johnny. We'll get offers all over the place. I will sell *the fuck* out of you."

"Yeah," I say. "Yeah."

ANTONNE LOOKS LIKE SHIT in Wednesday's practice. The team's in full pads, going all out at high speed, and he can barely keep up.

The offense is still running the plays that Jack installed to take advantage of my playing style, plays that feature a lot of running, a lot of movement. It would've been tough for Antonne *before* he got injured—he's more of a prototypical lineman, bigger, slower—but now *after* his injury? An injury he still clearly hasn't recovered from? It's not good.

When Antonne tries to run, he's stiff, four steps behind everybody else, and the rest of the offense is forced to slow down to compensate. There's no way we can get away with that in a real game. After three reps he's already sucking in air, hands on his knees, bent over at the waist. His face is crumpled in pain; he's wearing his agony like a cheap suit, on display for everyone to see. That's our leader.

And it's not just the speed or conditioning. The chemistry is gone. After all those weeks playing with me, the offensive line finally got used to my rhythm, how I operate. Now that Antonne is calling the shots again, they're completely out of sync. His snap count is different from mine. That has nothing to do with the injury, it's just naturally how he works. The difference is probably no more than a tenth of a second, but that's all it takes to create a chain reaction. Antonne keeps pace a split second too slow; the guys on the line jump a split second too soon. False start after false start after false start.

It'd be comical if it wasn't so painful to watch.

As far as I'm concerned, this feels like a well-earned fucking vacation. For every six plays the starters run, the second string only has two. My body needed this break, bad.

It's paradise, really.

"Yo!" a backup defensive end named Vinnie shouts during one of my plays. "We're fucking in pads for a reason, motherfuckers! Let's hit some fuckers! Come on!"

Vinnie's the most annoying kind of player in the League, what we call "Practice All-Americans." These guys are usually on the practice squad—meaning they're not on the active roster; the team's hired them *only* to practice with us, so practice is all they live for. They play every damn snap at a thousand miles an hour, all amped up like they're on the winning drive in the Super Bowl, a bunch of scrubs desperate to prove something to the coaches, the rest of the team, and themselves. Problem is, no one else really gives a shit.

"Hey, Vinnie," I say. "You're a fuckin' animal at practice, aren't you? You're a real fuckin' warrior."

Sneering, Vinnie flexes his ethnically Italian biceps. Thank you MTV, for *The Jersey Shore*.

"You like that, Johnny?"

"Oh, I'm terrified," I say.

"Oh hey, everyone!" Vinnie jeers. "Have some fuckin' fun, this is why we play the game!"

He laughs like a pathetic schoolyard bully. He's mocking my now-semifamous speech from my first game as a starter. You remember that game, right? The one we lost by 4 points? Yeah, that's the one.

"Ha," I say sarcastically, but no one's really listening.

Fuck. I miss being a starter.

I CALL MY DAD UP the next day. Kate and I haven't talked on the phone since her visit. Busy, you know.

"Antonne keeps telling the media he doesn't know if he can make it this weekend," my dad says. "Guy loves creating drama."

"Of course he's gonna play," I say. "He's practicing with the ones."

"You know, there were no sacks while you were starting," he says. "None. There were definitely sacks, at least a few, while Antonne was starting."

"It's true," I say. "They better hope they don't need me to take over for him this weekend, because I haven't gotten any decent reps."

"Fuck that," my dad says. "It would serve them right. I'd take you healthy over an injured Antonne any day of the week, no matter how much practice you got."

"Yeah," I say. Then I say what I've been wanting to say this whole time, what I've been holding back, what's been so difficult to admit to myself, to anyone, even my dad.

"You know, I kinda wanna see him fail."

"Yeah," my dad says. "Me too. I almost want to see your team lose."

We're both quiet.

"I mean, it's a shitty thought to have," I say. "I feel almost guilty. He's not a bad person. I actually like the guy, you know?"

"Yeah," he says.

More quiet.

"Hey," my dad says, kind of laughing. "Ball-peen hammer to the knee—I know a guy!"

"Ha-ha," I say. "There's a solid idea."

"Just kidding," he says.

"I know, Dad. I know."

FRIDAY'S OFFENSIVE-LINE MEETING. It's our last one before this weekend's game, so Lopez will be testing us on coverages to prepare. For the last month and a half, that's meant he tested *me* on coverages, firing one scenario at me after another, ripping me apart if I hesitate for an instant.

But what will Lopez do today? Will he go easy on me now that I'm not starting? Will he go even harder on me because Antonne's been playing like shit, and he needs to take his frustration out somewhere? Or will he just ignore me altogether?

That's the thing with Lopez, what drives me fucking crazy, I never know what to expect.

Teddy taps me on the shoulder. I look up.

"Hey, Johnny, you ever had a colonoscopy?"

"What?" I say. "No."

"Oh," he says, looking vaguely puzzled. "I've always wanted to get a colonoscopy."

"Fantastic."

Teddy shrugs, like I'm the weird one here.

"What's your problem?" he says. "It's not like you're starting or anything."

Lopez walks in, heads up to the front of the room. Closes his notebook, makes a big display of getting ready, building the anticipation, trying to get in our heads. Flicks on the overhead, the diagrammed coverage lighting up the giant screen in front of us.

Then he calls my name.

"Johnny, key left!"

My adrenaline starts pumping. I engage.

"Lion 52!"

The next thing Lopez should ask is "Why?" That's just how it goes, that's just what he says, that's our routine. But all of a sudden he gets kind of confused, stops short, breaks it off.

"Uh . . ." he says.

He looks around the room, sees Antonne sitting there, and then it washes over him: *that's* the player he should be talking to now. *That's* the player he should be testing before the game. *That's* the starter. Not me, Antonne.

Fumbling, Lopez changes the slide on the overhead. A new coverage for a new player.

"Antonne," he says. "Scat right!"

I STAND ON THE SIDELINES during the game, watching and waiting with the other backups. Keyed in on every possession, on every play, on every one of Antonne's stilted, hesitant moves. And there's no way around this: I'm hoping I'll get the chance to go in and save the day.

Lopez is pacing back and forth, chewing that pen to bits, his usual crazy energy. Every time it looks like he's just about to pop, he turns his eyes on me.

"Johnny, you gotta be ready!"

"I'm always ready, Lo."

"You gotta be ready to go in *any second,* Johnny!"

"I'm ready, Lo! I'm ready!"

Antonne looks like shit. Not just slow and stiff, but stupid. Like everything he used to know, all the coverages, all the calls, has just evaporated.

He's back at square one, making rookie mistakes. These are mistakes I never made, and I had never even played center before. After another three-and-out, Antonne hunches next to me, a weird look of panic in his eyes I haven't seen before.

"Johnny, you see what they throwing at me out there?" he asks. "What coverage that look like? Did that linebacker 'green dog'?"

"I don't know, man," I say. "It's really hard to read this shit from the sideline."

It's true. In a weird way, it's just as jarring for me to go back to the sidelines as it is for him to be in the game. Not used to seeing things from this angle.

"Fuck," he says. "It's moving fast out there, man. I'm rusty as hell."

Antonne keeps cramping up, complaining about how sore he is. In the third quarter I catch him looking woozy, swaying on his feet.

"You okay?" I ask.

"I just got a headache," he says, desperately sucking down a Gatorade.

"Yo, Colt!" he shouts at Coulter. "Colt! My forearms are cramping up big-time, man. You massage my left one while I massage the right, cool?"

"Say what?" Coulter says.

"Just massage this forearm, it's fucking cramping!"

Coulter does as he's told.

And I never set foot onto the field.

Shaking my head at the insanity, I spot McCray, the former Maverick to my Goose. He, of course, is still starting, still playing now that I'm gone. I give him a big, friendly slap on the back.

"Look at you," I say teasingly. "All out there doing stuff, running around and playing football and all."

"Yep," he says. "Gotta do it."

"Well," I say awkwardly. "Just keep after Antonne, we don't need him imploding."

He smiles blankly, stares out at the field.

"Yep," he says.

The clock winds down. We're gonna win this one easily, by 17 points.

The team we're beating is one of the shittier teams in the division, but still, it'll bring us one win closer to a trip to the play-offs.

It's a win. That's what matters.

I'm about to leave the field when I see a guy on the bench, sulking with a towel over his head, a third-string lineman who didn't dress for the game. There are fifty-three guys on the team, but only forty-six players actually dress for the games, depending on who the coach needs. This week, this guy, this dumb fucking rookie, is one of the seven who got to stand there in street clothes, doing nothing all game.

Nothing. Just like me. And it hurt his feelings.

"What," I say to him. "You're pissed? Is that it?"

"Yeah," he says, all surly and defiant.

"You're getting paid to literally do nothing!" I shout. "What are you complaining about? What, you wanna wear the pads so you can feel all big like you're in the NFL?"

"Yeah, I guess," he says, kind of sheepish now.

"Awesome," I say.

I walk into the tunnel by myself as the coaches and the media and the rest of the players swarm the field. Some people just need to grow the fuck up.

MONDAY. OUR DAY OFF. I sleep in. The best day of the week.

That afternoon, I hang out with Sarah, from the plane, for the first time. Not a date, because I'm still technically with Kate. We're just hanging out, but man, she has some great tits. They're so big that as we walk, the friction from their bouncing pops open the top button on her shirt. Definitely real!

We head downtown for lunch. No mall. Too soon.

"Oh, Johnny! Johnny, can we stop there? Please? Just for a few minutes?"

She points at a pet store. I sigh.

"Okay," I say, smiling. "If you want to torture yourself."

Kate, my girlfriend, has wanted me to get a dog for years. I've never given in. I mean, think about it. Forget the usual fears about commitment and settling down—although all that still holds completely true—I'm a fucking *football player*. I lead one of the most nomadic lifestyles imaginable. I travel every other week. I live out of my goddamn truck, for fuck's sake. What am I gonna do, lug a dog around with me too?

Not a chance.

Then, on our way out of the store, just as the bleeding is about to stop . . .

"Do you see what I see?" Sarah says. "That little pug is *gorgeous!*"

She points at this little mess of a dog asleep in its cage.

"Come on," I say. "Let's go."

I look up to see another puppy staring me right in the face.

He's a French bulldog. No bigger than the sloppy pug, but somehow different. He's tiny, French, and a total pussy of a dog, but I can't look away.

He's all white except for big black spots over his eyes, bright, and alert. He's not barking, acting stupid, or doing anything desperate. Just playing it nice and cool. I tap on the glass. Most dogs would hesitate, but he pounces and plays. Tries to lick me through the glass.

Ah shit, I think. *This is gonna be trouble.*

I ask the lady working there if we can take him out of the cage, hang out a little bit.

"Of course!" she says, smiling knowingly, like she already senses a sale.

Hold on, lady, I think. *I don't break so easy.*

Fifteen minutes later, I'm a Lego set that fell down the stairs.

"Hey, how much for this little guy?" I ask her.

"Oh, the French bulldog?" she asks. "He's twenty-one hundred dollars."

"Ugh!" I say.

"But today he's on sale for twelve hundred."

On sale? Shit! That's even better news than the dog!

"Tell you what," I say. "I'll give you eight hundred dollars for him."

The sales lady hesitates, shifts on her feet. I get the distinct impression that Sarah, who's standing next to me, is completely embarrassed that I'm haggling over a puppy. Oh well, so much for that relationship.

"Ummm," the sales lady says. "I'm gonna have to talk to my manager."

"Oh, you don't have to do that," I say, smiling my most charming smile.

She sighs.

"How about nine hundred?"

"Deal!"

I bend down and look at my new dog. I've already decided to name him Riley, after an old childhood friend.

"Hey, Riley! Hey, buddy! Welcome to the life of an NFL backup!"

He lets out a little bark and kisses my nose. This might be the start of something great.

The pet shop gives me a leash, but the little guy is so tiny his little legs can't even keep up. So I pick him up in the palm of my big hand and carry him. People stare at us like two animals at the zoo. And you know what? I don't blame them.

"Look at you guys!" Sarah coos. "It's like you were meant for each other!"

She's right. Fuck the NFL. Nothing screams badass like a six-pound dog.

THE WORST PART ABOUT NOT starting anymore? It's not the boredom. It's not the sitting on the sidelines during games. It's not the way no one pays attention to me anymore.

It's having to take reps with the scout team.

What's the scout team? Every week in practice, our defensive coaches study the film of the other team, and the scout team has to run their plays against our starters. If we're gonna play Denver, I have to run the Broncos' offense that week. If we're gonna play Miami, then it's the Dolphins' script. And so on. All so our defense can get used to playing against whatever offense the other team usually runs.

Of course, the plays the coaches draw up for us are generally horseshit, designed mostly to make their own defensive schemes look great.

But by far the worst thing about being on the scout team is dealing with the prima donnas on defense. See, only a small fraction of my job is *really* helping them get ready. As far as they're concerned, my main job is making them feel good about themselves. So I gotta play just hard enough to make it look good for the coaches, without ever really challenging the starters. Push back against the D line a tiny bit, but never really finish. Pull up just at the right time, and *always* let them look impressive. Basically, be their walking tackling dummy.

One afternoon after my demotion, I decide I've had enough.

Today, I'm gonna be an asshole. Today, *I'm* gonna be a Practice All-American, just to fuck with the idiots on D. And also because I'm really sick of watching Antonne do all the stuff I used to do but a whole lot worse. I gotta do something with all my energy, because it sure as hell isn't getting used up in games.

So every single play, every time a defensive lineman comes at me, I block him. It's that simple. I'm not playing dirty or even hitting hard. I'm just actually playing. I'm trying. I'm doing my job, or at least what it's supposed to be. And that's too much for them.

Our precious defensive starters don't make a single play.

They glare at me, growling at me while we're lined up, before I snap the ball.

"Fuck you, bitch."

"What the fuck is wrong with you?"

"We gonna fuck you up!"

The other guys on the scout team, my fellow backups, are getting nervous. The right guard elbows me before a snap, whispers through his face mask.

"Why do you keep pissing them off, Johnny?"

They just want to get through this, keep everyone happy, business as usual. Well, fuck that. I'm sick of the business as usual that makes me look and feel like shit. If I'm not happy, no one's gonna be happy.

Bad idea.

At the end of practice, during one-on-one drills, the defensive line-men all get their revenge. One-on-ones are exactly what they sound like—one D lineman going up against one O lineman, the D tries to get by, the O tries to block. You typically use them to refine technique, work on pass-rush moves. Yes, you hit each other, but you don't hit each other hard. That's not what the drill is for. They're for skill, not power. In other words, don't fucking bull-rush in one-on-ones. It's an unwritten rule.

One that they violently break with me.

I line up against the first defensive lineman, a nice big fucker at six foot five and 340 pounds. And when I snap the ball, he comes at me, no move, no technique, no skill. Just two hands to the chest and run. He smashes into me with every last ounce of his massive frame, full speed, high momentum, head-on.

Fuck.

Don't get me wrong, I can take it. But after a long day of practice, it hurts.

And it's not over yet. They each get a turn. That's just how the drill works. These bastards line up, one after another, and each one gets a piece of me. After the third time, I actually start to laugh.

"Come on," I say to the guy lined up across from me, this fucker who's staring at me with blood in his eyes. "We both know you're about to bull-rush me just because I made you look like a bitch before. Get over it!"

"I ain't doing shit," he says, gritting his teeth. "Now shut the fuck up and snap it."

So I snap it. And he takes off. And he bull-rushes me.

I've probably ground up more cartilage in the last ten minutes than the last two weeks combined. And I fucking loved it.

THAT NIGHT I GET BACK to the apartment. Riley has peed on the kitchen floor. Twice, by the looks of it. Two nice big healthy puddles of yellow.

But honestly? It doesn't bother me at all. The floor is tile, so it's easy to clean up. He's already gotten better since I first brought him home—yesterday he didn't pee inside once—and I've decided to take him to a trainer this weekend. I've tried to discipline him a few times, the whole whack-on-the-ass-with-a-magazine thing, but he's just so damn small and so damn cute that I can never bring myself to do it.

"Come on, Riley," I say. "You have to go outside! Pee-pees outside!"

He wags his tail and barks and looks up at me with his shiny brown eyes, and it makes me happy. I reach down, scoop him up, and carry him outdoors for a walk, and, yes, for pee-pees outside.

I'm becoming an annoying dog person, and I love it. I've taken a million photos of him, told a million too many stories. Last night I actually sat down and googled "How often does a French bulldog poo?" just to make sure he's on a healthy schedule. I swear he has a machine gun for an asshole.

There's just something about taking care of Riley. I know it sounds cheesy as hell, but I like how I'm his everything. From being fed to going on walks to going pee, he always needs me. Well, more or less on that last one anyway. After a long day of being angry and hitting guys, he turns me into a complete softy. Most of all, I like how he takes my mind off the rest of my life.

I told Kate all about him, and it's weirdly kind of reinvigorated our relationship. I like talking to her about my daily adventures with my dog. It's fun to have something to bring us together beyond my constant struggles with the NFL. Instead of "Fuck this!" and "Fuck that!" it's "Can you believe Riley chewed Teddy's cleats to shreds today? He's adorable!" Kate's decided that Riley is a sign that I might finally be thinking of settling down and embracing responsibility. And, of course, her.

And my dad? First thing he says when I tell him I got a dog is "Ah, you're fucked." But then I tell him about the amazing deal I managed to negotiate, and that improves his outlook immensely. Plus, my dad gets it. He gets how much I needed this—needed something *consistent*.

Apparently, that something was Riley.

FRIDAY'S OFFENSIVE-LINE MEETING. Our last one before this weekend's game.

Lopez quizzes Antonne almost the entire time. On coverages, on calls, on everything. Antonne does fine. He's improving, shaking the rust off, but he's still far from what he used to be.

But here's the revolutionary part: when Antonne does fuck up, Lopez doesn't go after me.

A couple months ago, before I had my chance to start, I would've been Lopez's scapegoat for everything. Even if a play didn't involve me, even if I wasn't anywhere near the goddamn field, he would've found a way to pin it on me, to direct all the sarcastic anger he couldn't unleash on the untouchable starters on his favorite target, Johnny Anonymous.

No more. Now that I've been through the fire, Lopez treats me different. I can't be certain, but I think the guy might actually respect me a little. He doesn't kiss my ass like he does with the starters, but I don't need him to. He simply treats me like I'm normal, like I belong here. He laughs at my jokes, says hi in the halls. But mostly he just leaves me the fuck alone. Maybe it's because he doesn't have to worry about me actually playing anymore. Whatever it is, I'll take it.

In the meeting, Lopez rolls some film from the last game. Our quarterback gets sacked, and it's clearly Antonne's fault. He left his man for Teddy, hung him out to dry, and Teddy got beat.

Lopez, of course, lays into Teddy. Not Antonne.

"What the fuck was that, Teddy?" Lopez shouts. "Letting that fucking guy get by you like that? You ever put a fucking helmet on before? What the fuck!"

Teddy takes it. Unlike me, he hates to argue.

"Yep," he says, nodding. "My fault, Lo, my fault. Sorry, won't happen again."

Brilliant strategy, actually.

Lopez moves on. Teddy turns and glares at me.

"If you were still playing, that would be *you* getting fucking screamed at."

"Yeah, that sucks," I say. "Hey, you ever had a colonoscopy before?"

"Fuck you, Johnny."

BEFORE OUR GAME SUNDAY NIGHT, Lopez gives me one of his patented fatherly talks, puts his arm around me, his hand on the back of my neck.

"Hey, you been going real hard last few weeks, and I don't want you to let up. Can't lose focus, can't get soft. You gotta be ready all the time, gotta always be on your game."

"Always ready," I tell him.

The offense plays like shit again, especially the offensive line. Our game plan is flawed, and the other team's defense does a great job predicting our plays. Our guys play horrible, completely unmotivated, making a lot of stupid mistakes. We generate a pathetic 47 yards in rushing.

We win anyway, by 9 points.

"Great game from the defense and special teams," Jack says in the locker room after the game. "Imagine how great we would've done if the offense had actually done its job!"

Oh. By the way, I got to play.

On our last series, a total of three plays, just to run down the clock. Our third-string quarterback taking one knee after another, and me snapping him the ball—all so the mighty starter Antonne wouldn't have to strain himself doing shit that didn't matter. Pure garbage time.

But I was ready.

Chapter 11
LOSERS

Tuesday morning. I finish taking my post-weigh-in glory shit and head to the locker room. Turning the corner, I nearly get blasted in the head by a small, fast-moving projectile cutting through the air.

"Heads up!"

Thwap!

I duck at the last second and it hits the wall behind me.

"What the fuck?!?" I yell.

I bend over, reach down, and pick it up. It's a Wiffle ball, wrapped tight in athletic tape to make it go faster, farther.

"Johnny!" Ollie the kicker jogs over from the other side of the lockers. "Sorry, bro! Just playing some intense Wiffle ball here, you know, letting off some steam!"

That's right. I just got done relieving myself of six pounds of turd I had to hold in so I could make weight and keep my job, and Ollie and the special teams guys are busy playing a super-intense game of Wiffle ball.

"Let off steam?" I say. "You guys barely even fucking do anything! You're the last people who need to let off steam."

Special teams guys are some of my favorite people in the world. They might be on a football team, but they play a different game than the rest of us.

Don't get me wrong—their jobs can be incredibly stressful. Whole seasons can ride on that last-second field goal. The ones I've met are incredibly professional, and very hard workers. There's only room for a couple special teams players on each team, so the competition for their spots is incredibly intense. Pound for pound, the kicker on my last team may have been one of the top athletes on the squad. I mean, he probably only weighed about 170 pounds, but still, those few pounds were very athletic.

But compared to everyone else on the team, their jobs are very, very focused. They kick a ball, or they snap a ball. So in practice, they kick a lot of balls and snap a lot of balls. Beyond that, they have a lot of time on their hands. They come in later than the rest of us, hit the steam room for an hour or two. Do a few curls in the weight room if they're up for it. Spend an hour or so chatting up the cute chicks in the front office. Then during practice, while everyone else is busting their ass, they just kind of hang out, watch, maybe get in a few rounds of "football golf" to get that ol' heart rate up. They're not being lazy, per se. They just don't have anything to do.

Fuck. Why didn't I ever learn how to kick?

Ollie almost looks hurt as he takes the tape-ball from me.

"You kidding, bro? I was just in the steam room for, like, an hour straight. I totally needed to let off . . . *steam*."

"Look at you," I say. "You are a *master* of puns."

Greg the punter and Eric the long snapper come and join our hilarity.

"Johnny, get a few swings in!" Eric says. "Greg is taping it with his iPhone, we're gonna put it on YouTube."

"Yeah, yeah," Greg says. "Make a Vine!"

"A Vine?" I say. "What the fuck does that even mean?"

The three of them look at each other like this is the stupidest question ever.

"You know," Eric says. "It's funny. People watch it. It's *viral*, man."

"Yeah," Greg says. "*Viral*, dude."

I sigh, give them my classic eye roll.

"Come on, Johnny," Ollie says. "Take a swing. What the fuck you got going on anyway?"

You know what? They're right. What *do* I have going on?

Eric hands me the yellow plastic bat. I step over to the "home plate," a dirty towel balled up on the floor. Ollie pitches and Greg catches as Eric shoots the action.

"Okay," I say, digging my toe into the floor. "Let's see what you got here."

Ollie winds up and throws—way too fucking high.

"Hey, don't give me that bullshit!" I shout. "You're a fucking professional!"

He sends me one right down the middle. I whack it—a fast grounder that skids across the plush locker room carpeting, past one row of lockers, past another row, and another, and another, and finally coming to a stop.

Right at the feet of Lowry. The general manager.

The tall bastard bends down and picks up the tape-covered ball. He doesn't say a word, just arches a brow and stares at us.

We stand there awkwardly for a moment.

"Hey, Lowry!" Ollie shouts. "Come on, take a swing! We're putting it on YouTube!"

"Yeah," Eric yells. "We're putting them on Vine!"

Lowry stares. Then slowly grins.

"I'm in," he says. He tosses Ollie the ball, looks at me. "Johnny . . . you got outfield."

Fuck it. He's the boss.

IT'S NOT JUST ME AND the special teams guys—everyone seems relaxed this week. We won our last few games, our record's 8-4, and the play-offs feel all but guaranteed. They're not, of course. We still got four more games to go and shit could go south. But that's not how it *feels*, you know?

Everything is clicking, we're in a rhythm, we're all happy during practice, laughing, fucking around, actually enjoying our jobs. Acting like a *team*. Players, coaches, trainers, interns, everyone.

Everyone except Antonne.

Antonne, to use a technical football term, looks like ass. When you return from an injury, the goal is to keep getting better, continue to heal. You might not come back at full strength, but each week you get a little closer to 100 percent. If anything, though, Antonne looks worse.

Every day the lines under his eyes get a little deeper. Every day his movement is a little tighter, a little slower, a little more cramped.

It gets so bad I actually feel sorry for the guy. Me, the one who was guiltily hoping he would fail just a week ago. That's the business.

"Hey, baby," I say to him Wednesday morning after he practically sleepwalks through a workout. "What the fuck is going on with you?"

He turns away, sighs.

"I don't know, man," he says. "It's like I'm just not myself out there, you know? I just, I don't know, it's like I'm not the same player."

The word in the locker room is that he's been going out almost every night. He's not dating, he's not on Tinder, he's just getting drunk—black-out drunk. I heard that last week he went out with a few guys and got so wasted he just ended up standing in a corner by himself, staring quietly at the wall.

Most players on the team go out maybe one night a week, on Thursdays or Fridays, before light practice days. The job is so physically demanding, there's no way you can drink or do a lot of drugs, even if you wanted to. I'm so constantly exhausted I don't know how they even manage one.

Of course there's always a few younger guys who party a ton. Like everything else in the NFL, it breaks down racially—there's a black group of partiers and a white group of partiers. The black partiers usually start off at a strip club and spend the night drinking, while the white partiers start drinking together at home . . . and then end up at the strip club later. It's very yin-yang.

The majority of these guys are all highly functioning—you wouldn't even know they went out a lot if they didn't tell you. They're young, so their bodies can handle the strain. They're making a ton of money for the first time, and living the NFL lifestyle they always dreamed of. But it can turn into a problem if they're not careful, and I know a couple guys where that's happened.

That may be the case with Antonne. Antonne is in his early thirties. His body definitely cannot take this right now.

"You gotta take better care of yourself if you want to recover," I say. "What did you eat last night?"

"Uh, a whole bunch of wings."

"Shit," I say. "All fat and grease, that's horrible for you. With the amount of stuff we do, the strain your body goes through, you gotta eat clean. You know that, man!"

"Yeah, yeah," he says, looking down at the ground. "You're right."

I feel like a parent scolding a little kid for not eating his vegetables. But I know vegetables aren't the real problem here. I take a deep breath, prepare myself to ask a question I do not want to ask because frankly, it's just not my business.

"You drinking?"

"Uh . . ." he says sheepishly. "Well, I like to go out, you know."

"You gotta stay hydrated so your muscles can repair themselves," I say. "What, you want an IV every day?"

He doesn't say a word.

Now look. I know I sound like Dr. Fucking Oz right now. And I know I'm not going to get this guy to stop getting hammered. No one can do that but him. But maybe I can help him feel a little better, maybe even regain some of his lost confidence. I can at least try.

The Players Association offers substance abuse programs for players with a drug or drinking problem, but I don't know anyone who's ever had the guts to take them up on that offer. One of my buddies had a massive coke problem when he was younger, almost lost everything. But he managed to turn his life around through pure willpower.

Then there's Williams, one of the starters on the O line. A few years ago Williams went to rehab for drinking and drugs, one of those fancy places called "Crystal Meadows" or something. So now we have this massive black dude with an old-school high-top fade and a gigantic gold grille in his mouth walking around spewing all this self-help BS about "the power of positive thinking" and "self-actualization."

But honestly, as players we're mostly on our own. The amazing truth is that it's actually really easy to get away with drinking and doing street drugs as an NFL player.

That doesn't mean performance enhancers, like steroids or human growth hormone—we get tested constantly on those. Every week of the regular season the NFL chooses about ten players from our team to test at random. They test us multiple times during the off-season too—they'll send a guy to test you at your house and everything. They'll do a piss test and sometimes a blood test, and they take it incredibly seriously. The guy makes you strip off your shirt and pull your pants down to your ankles, then watches you while you urinate. I had a tester who was so neurotic about guys cheating that he actually kneeled down in front of me and looked directly at my dick while I was pissing. (Although I guess there could've been other forces at work as well.)

But recreational stuff, like weed or cocaine? The League tests for that once a year, over the summer—either during the summer session or at the beginning of training camp. That's it, once. The rest of the year, as long as you're not doing steroids you're home free. If anything, I'm always shocked at the guys who still *do* get caught.

Why does the NFL test so little? It's damn well not because players aren't using. Sure, there aren't many flat-out addicts, and they stay away from the hard stuff—like I said, the game is just too physically demanding for anyone with a major problem. But tons of guys smoke weed casually all the time, both white guys and black guys, before they go out, if they're just hanging out at home relaxing. It's just no big deal.

On my last team, one of the defensive players actually took his NFL headshot stoned out of his fucking mind. This is the same photo they use for all the media guides, on TV, everything. The dude's eyes were bloodshot, his mouth was hanging slack, it was a huge joke on the team. The day after we took the photos I saw him in the locker room.

"Hey, man," I said. "Did you see your headshot? You, uh, kind of look a little high."

He grinned—and I noticed his eyes were as red as ever.

"Well then, I probably look the same as I do right now. Because I am *totally* fucked up."

Honestly, I think the NFL executives just don't want to know. If they did, they'd probably have to put half of us into some kind of program.

When it's all said and done, as far as I'm concerned Antonne has no one to blame but himself for the mess he's in. An injury's no excuse to lose control. Other guys have had similar injuries, and come back faster and been fine. Shit, I've had worse injuries and *I've* come back and I've been fine. Antonne makes huge money, and it's his job to earn it.

But the season is a fucking grind. I understand that now better than I did before. Recovering during the middle of it? That's a huge test. Physical and mental. And part of me gets what Antonne is going through. He might have a ton of money, but his life is shit. After all these years on the same team, in the same city, he still doesn't really have a life here, isn't even close to anyone on the squad. The only thing Antonne does have is football, and he's scared and angry because his injury might take that away.

The one difference between the two of us is that I learned how to deal with my anger and fear in ways that don't depend on football. I talk to my dad. I go to the mall. Hell, I just bought myself a tiny little dog. But like a lot of other guys in the NFL, Antonne hasn't. So when he doesn't have football to get out his frustrations, he drinks.

For the rest of the week, I carry a spare water bottle for Antonne with me at all times. Whenever I see him, I throw it at him: "Take a swig, baby."

And the same answer: "No, I'm good, bro."

And I jam the bottle into his face and squeeze.

"All right then," I say.

Instant hydration.

OUR TEAM TAKES ITS NEWFOUND carefree attitude into the next game. Before we head out through the tunnel and onto the field, you know what we got blasting in the locker room? Not rap, not heavy metal, not even classic rock.

Nope. It's smooth contemporary jazz.

Turns out Jovan the Preacher is a big fan. Dante even tries rapping along, something about the white man always trying to keep him down or something. Really loses its edge against the backdrop of Kenny G's sweet saxophone.

Then, surprise surprise, we go out and promptly get our asses kicked up and down the field.

The massacre starts with a simple, unavoidable fact: the team we're facing is better than us. Their quarterback is better than our quarterback, their offense is better than our offense, their defense is better than our defense. More talented, more athletic—and better coached. They throw a defensive wrinkle at us that we're not expecting, and Jack and Lopez have no idea how to handle it.

Somehow we manage to hang on through the first quarter anyway. They're beating us, but only by 3 points.

Then McCray gets sacked. Again. And again. And again.

Three times. Not in a row, but it might as well have been, that's how horrible it feels to see your quarterback get driven into the fucking turf. Over and over and over because your offensive line doesn't know what the fuck it's doing.

When McCray gets flattened, when he feels the crunch of a gigantic body slamming into him at a hundred miles an hour, tastes the dirt and the spit and the blood as his head gets smashed into the ground, our whole team sees that, and it's like a switch gets flipped. Like we realize that it might not matter how happy and relaxed and smooth-light-jazz we've been feeling, these other guys are simply better than us.

Our confidence crumbles.

Antonne stumbles off the field after the series from hell and practically collapses on the bench. He's looked horrible so far, getting no push against the defensive linemen, huffing and puffing from all those run-heavy plays that Jack designed for my style of play, but still hasn't taken out of the offense.

Throwing his towel over his head, Antonne sits there like a broken man.

"I'm just not the same player anymore," he says to me. "I just don't know what to do."

Try cutting the booze, I want to tell him.

But I don't even have time. Five seconds later, our defense forces a turnover, strips the quarterback. We get the ball back, and suddenly we've got a crucial opportunity to get the momentum back. If we're gonna take advantage of their mistake, we gotta move fast. Go *now*. Hit them hard before they even know what's coming at them.

The offense sprints out to the field.

Except for Antonne, who keeps sitting there. Head covered with his towel. Not moving a muscle. Doesn't know we have the ball. Doesn't even care.

The coaches, Jack and Lopez, just stare at him, no idea what to do.

Is this it? I think. *Is this my shot to get back in? To play?*

I grab Antonne's shoulders, shake him hard.

"Hey, man, you're up!" I say. "Get your ass in the game!"

Antonne looks up groggily, squints at the field, puts his helmet on, and slowly jogs back into the game.

Our offense goes three-and-out. The other team gets the ball back and scores within minutes.

What would've been a loss, even on a good day, turns into a rout. The players blame the coaches, who blame the players, who decide, what the fuck, let's blame the coaches again. Everyone turns on each other.

At halftime, no one is talking. Everyone is just sitting there, all in their own private universe of pain. Finally, McCray tries to give the team a pep talk. It's so forgettable I literally can't remember a single thing he said.

In the second half, Antonne tries to turn things around, force himself to be the player he once was. But instead he just winds up doing *too* much, running too hard, spreading himself too thin. And he accomplishes nothing at all.

"Your boy Antonne is losing his mind out there," Lopez says to me.

If Lopez is confiding in me, you know it's bad.

I TALK TO MY DAD on the phone the next morning.

"Antonne looked like shit out there yesterday," he says.

"Yeah," I say. "I'm almost starting to wonder, I don't know . . ."

"What?" he says.

"What if he plays *so* bad they have to pull him and start me again? I mean, I know it's almost impossible, but fuck, you saw how *awful* he looked out there, right?"

"Forget about it, Johnny," my dad says. "I want it to happen as much as anyone, but there's no way. The general manager would look like an idiot for paying big bucks to this guy who isn't performing. And Antonne would be embarrassed in front of everyone. He'd never be able to play again."

I try to stop myself from hoping, try to listen to my dad, but I can't. It's not just the money anymore, or even the revenge. It's the football. I miss it.

"Bernie says he thinks he'll be able to shop me around to another team next season," I say, wishing I could hide the desperation in my voice. "Sure, my size will be an issue, it always is, but I've got the game tape now. People can see what my speed can do, the advantages it has. I mean, teams build offenses around players and what they can do all the time, right? They adjust. Maybe they could do that for me."

My dad hesitates.

"Johnny, I'm just not sure that's realistic," he finally says. "Hey, I just remembered—I found a chain of restaurants, some fast-food places, and the price point is perfect. I was thinking of buying them . . . I could use a partner to develop them with me."

"Wow," I say, surprised. He's mentioned going into real estate with him before, but this is new—this is specific. "It's just, I'm so focused on the season . . ."

"I'm not telling you to quit football," he says quickly. "Just consider it a potential investment—for the future."

I tell my dad thanks, and I hang up the phone.

THE REST OF THE WEEK is one massive shitstorm.

Our record is now 8-5. If we had won, we'd be 9-4. That's just a one-game difference. We *should* win the rest of our games easily. We *should* control our own destiny. Play-offs *should* be a lock.

But that's not how it feels, and sometimes how it feels becomes the reality.

Everyone fucked up in the last game. Every single coach, every single player. And every day this week, we all get it, we all hear it, we're all to blame.

Me? I just sit back and laugh. Fuck 'em all, right?

"So," I whisper to Teddy before Tuesday's O-line meeting. "Are we ready for a show?"

For once, Teddy can't laugh with me. He's still starting, the sorry bastard. Just this morning Lopez called him in for a private meeting, told him he's "not even half the man" he was at the beginning of the season. His attitude sucks, he's playing like shit, typical football stuff. So yeah, Teddy's not feeling too good.

"Fuck off, Johnny," he says.

I chuckle despite myself. Not my problem anymore, fuckers.

Lopez walks in, cues up the game tape. And realizes he has an issue. See, Teddy's the only guy who actually played in the game who Lopez can really lay into, because Teddy's the only guy who's not a career starter. But Lopez already did that this morning. He already blew his Teddy wad. Premature evisceration.

Lopez scans the room. He has to move on to other players, but how do you criticize the uncriticizeable?

Finally, he sighs. Points the little remote at the projector and clicks.

A play flashes on the screen. Jeb whiffs on a block, just takes the wrong angle, lets his man get right by him.

Lopez looks out at the players accusingly, and loudly clears his throat. "Ahhhhhhem!"

Turns back to the screen, points the remote, another click. This time Coulter, a false start.

This time, the throat clearing is about one octave louder and two seconds longer.

"*Aaahhhhhhhheeemmmmm!*"

Back to the screen, click goes the remote. Williams with a missed assignment.

"AAAHHHHHHHHHHEEEEMMMMMMM!"

We all sit there with blank looks on our faces. The throat clearings register with no one. That must be one gigantic fucking loogie.

Back to the screen. Click. Antonne makes a bad read, points at the wrong linebacker.

Lopez turns to the room. And looks right at Antonne. No throat clearing this time, nothing dramatic, just a cool, calm question.

"So. What happened here?"

The whole room is silence. Antonne shifts in his seat a little, says nothing, does nothing. After a few seconds, I actually start to miss the sound of Lopez's phlegm.

"Well," Antonne finally says. "I guess it was just a mix-up."

Lopez just stares. If *I* had made the mistake, he would've torn my balls off. But still. He singled out his star center in front of everyone, and by doing that he made a statement: *I'm watching you. I might not be able to do anything about it right now, but I know you're not performing. Get your shit together.*

As we all start filing out, Antonne just sits there, alone.

Williams walks over to him. He hands Antonne a blue pen with a logo on it—for the same rehab clinic Williams went to a few years ago.

"Hey, Antonne," Williams says. "You should give that place a call."

Antonne tenses up. His eyes, bloodshot, stare straight ahead into nothing. He looks like he's about to explode.

Fuck, Williams is a prick. Yeah, Antonne clearly has a problem. But to call him out like that in front of the rest of us?

I walk over, pat Antonne on the shoulder.

"Relax," I say, looking directly at Williams. "Williams is just pissed because he keeps falling off the wagon."

Antonne smiles. The sad fact is, though, Williams is probably right.

WE LOSE OUR NEXT GAME by 10 points. It's a team we should've easily beaten. Our record is now 8-6, and our spot in the play-offs is at risk. We're officially in trouble.

BERNIE GIVES ME A CALL after the loss. He's been sending out feelers to other teams to see if anyone would be interested in me after this season, hasn't been hearing much back. Not that it matters. There's no sign my current team wants to release me.

Ironic, huh? I spend the entire first half of my season praying to God my team won't cut me, and now I actually kind of hope they will.

"What," Bernie says to me, "you're already tired of not being the man? After just a few weeks?"

"Eh, what do I care," I say. "I'll just be a goddamn backup forever."

I sigh. The honest truth is that I don't know what I want to be. I'm fucking sick of thinking about it, though.

"Listen, Johnny," he says. "My son graduated from college last year. Had a three-point-seven GPA. A fucking *three-point-seven,* at an Ivy League school. I know, because I paid a fucking mint for his tuition. You wanna know how much he's making in his new job?"

"How much?"

"Fucking fifty-three thousand a year. That's it. And you know what? With this economy, he was happy to get that."

"Wow," I say. "Shit."

I feel horrible for the kid. You could do a lot worse than making $53,000, but still—he's not even making an eighth of what I make. All for playing a game.

"It's not easy out there, Johnny. You got it pretty damn good."

TUESDAY MORNING. TEDDY AND I are walking through the main hallway with a pack of other players on our way to a big teamwide meeting.

When suddenly we encounter a slightly sexy, incredibly skanky, and not-at-all scintillating scene. This is the kind of thing that most of the sad, horny men of this great nation would give their left arms to be a part of, and the very thing that *all* our die-hard male fans will be jerking themselves off to on this happy new year.

Our cheerleaders' Christmas card shoot.

Ho. Ho. Ho.

There's a giant green tree, glowing red lights, shiny silver tinsel, and brightly wrapped gift boxes everywhere, all in the team's colors. And standing, kneeling, and lying posed among it all is a collection of the nakedest bunch of Santa's little helpers you've ever seen in your life. They're dressed in red and green velvet Santa hats, little bits and pieces of white fur trim placed here and there to cover necessary body parts, an odd sequin or two, a little glitter, and not much else.

It looks like the set of a very special Christmas porno. *Frosty Does the NFL.*

Ho. Ho. Ho.

They're being directed by a weaselly-looking photographer with a thick porno mustache who looks like he hasn't showered in a week, barking things like "There you go, Vivian! Could you move that bow out of the way? I want to make sure we get that gorgeous ass of yours on camera."

And I have to admit, it's a pretty great ass.

But what makes this really special is the meeting we're headed to. A meeting that, we've been told via text, is going to be our first-ever seminar on domestic violence.

That's right. On the way to a meeting about how we should treat women, we are treated firsthand to exactly how we should *not* be treating women. Courtesy of our own team.

Ho. Ho. Ho.

WE WALK INTO THE LECTURE HALL where we have all our team meetings, including the one about sensitivity at the beginning of the year. Given what happened with Ray Rice, I'm guessing that the NFL feels like *that* lecture didn't quite take. So now we're having yet another meeting, here at the end of the season. I'm sure this one will work a lot better. Yeah, right.

A woman stands at the door, nodding to each of us as we enter. She's blond, solid-looking, in her midforties, and she has a "go fuck yourself" look on her face as she stares us all down, one by one.

This, I think, *must be the speaker.*

I sit down at my seat, Teddy and Coulter next to me, and I realize for the first time in my life I'm wrong. That lady was just one of the organizers. Instead of her, a big Latino guy who looks like a security guard or a high-priced mall cop gets up in front. He's with NFL security. And he's the one who's going to speak to us about domestic violence.

He begins by describing to us all the special training he's had in domestic abuse.

"Now I haven't been specially trained in anything about domestic abuse . . ."

Right.

"But that's what I'm gonna be talking to you about today."

Off to a great start here.

"My family is from the Southwest," he says. "Dad was a blue-collar worker, drove a truck; Mom cleaned houses. Real old-fashioned, old-school stuff. And in *my* home, what my dad said was law. Period. That's just how it was. And the situation wasn't easy, it was hard. I don't want to pass judgment on my father, but if you take a look at what this manual on domestic violence says . . ."

He holds up a small, slim manual on domestic violence. Our new bible on morality.

"You'll see that what I grew up with sounds a *lot* like abuse."

He tells us that the NFL wants us to be role models. To create a positive ripple effect in our communities. To make the world a better place for everyone. He tells us that this seminar is designed to be interactive, so we should all speak up and engage with him whenever we want. No one says a word.

Coulter leans over and whispers to me.

"I've been married for eight years and have three kids. I haven't hit my wife once. Why would I start now?"

"Yeah," I whisper back. "Can't they just go back to the three personality tests I took at the combine and see I'm not gonna beat my wife?"

Teddy starts to nod off. Even Paulson, the usually perfect student, closes his eyes for a nap. This speaker is losing his audience. Fast.

"So," the security guy says. "Anyone out there sext?"

That wakes motherfuckers up pretty damn quick. Eyes open wide, a few sideways glances, some mumbling and muttering. Dante the Diva tentatively raises his hand.

"Is there, uh, something wrong with that?" he asks.

A few chuckles. But everyone is listening.

"Not all the time," the security guy says. "But it becomes abuse if she sends you naked or explicit photos and you share them with your friends."

Nervous laughter breaks out all over the room. A couple guys elbow each other knowingly.

"Good," security guy says. He knows he has our attention now. "What about Tinder?"

Antonne sits bolt upright.

"Watch out there, man!" Jovan yells at him.

"Also not illegal," security guy continues. "*Unless* you end up with an underage girl who posted a fake profile."

Antonne relaxes. A little.

"Here's another situation for you," the security guy says. "What if you're with a group of guys, buddies from the team or whatever, and one of them is a six-foot-eight, three-hundred-fifty-pound lineman. And the girl he's talking to is five feet tall and ninety pounds."

He looks at us expectantly.

"Yeah?" I say. "That's like every day of our lives."

"Well," he says. "All she has to do is *feel threatened* for it to legally be assault."

This absolutely blows people away.

"She also can't have a blood-alcohol level above .87."

Chaos breaks out.

"Fuck!" Jeb says. "Nothing would ever even happen! We'd never have sex again! It's like we can't even walk outside without getting sued!"

The security guy proceeds to go through an endless list of one "don't" after another. Every possible situation that could involve any form of abuse, neglect, or corporal punishment, whether with a woman, a child, a stranger on the street, or possibly even a small animal. He emphasizes that we're not just responsible for ourselves, but we're also responsible for one another. As near as I can tell, we may be responsible for the behavior of the entire human race.

It all lasts fifty miserable minutes. By the end, we're left with one basic conclusion. If any of us ever wants to get laid again, every conversation we have with a woman for the rest of our lives will go something like this.

"Hello, my name is (last name first, first name last). Have you had anything to drink? No? And no marijuana or drugs? You aren't intimidated by my size, are you? You're not impaired or having fun in any way? No? Excellent. Would you be interested in having sexual intercourse with me at a (specified time, date, and location)? Please sign this disclaimer here, here, and here. Thanks, have a nice day."

Suddenly, all those skanky cheerleading Christmas elves hanging out in the lobby are sounding a whole lot better.

THAT NIGHT WHEN I GET HOME, I take Riley outside to pee. I've come to enjoy this part of my day. He usually takes at least ten minutes to make up his mind on where to go. This is the perfect amount of time to catch up with Kate, who's helping me look for condos again. Somehow, almost without me noticing, she and I are 100 percent back together again. Now that I think about it, I'm not sure we were ever really officially apart. Our relationship is far from perfect. But at least it's familiar.

"Make sure you take more photos of the next place, okay?" I tell her.

"I know, I know!" she says.

"Pee-pees *outside*! Pee-pees *outside*!" I say to Riley.

He looks up at me and wags his tail. Nothing. We've been outside in the freezing cold for thirty minutes, I'm wearing nothing but my boots, my boxers, and a peacoat—and still no pee-pees outside.

"You're already outside," Kate says. "Why do you keep telling him 'pee-pees outside'?"

"That's what my dad always said to our dog when I was growing up," I say. "I'm trying to make it a verbal trigger for him, a ritual. I say 'pee-pees outside,' he goes pee-pees outside, I pick him up and congratulate him, we celebrate together, and then we go inside. Riley! *Riley!* Pee-pees outside! *Pee-pees outside!*"

Nothing.

"Maybe he just doesn't have to go," she says.

"No!" I say. "I won't let him win!"

"You're freezing! Just go back inside!"

"*I won't let him win!*"

"You're crazy!"

"Pee-pees outside, Riley! PEE-PEES OUTSIDE!"

After five more minutes of no pee-pees outside, I take Riley back inside. Now *I* have to pee. I set Riley down in the living room next to Teddy, who's playing his perpetual video game. I go to the bathroom and pee. I walk back out to the living room. Riley looks at me. Then Teddy looks at me.

"Uh, I tried to stop him," Teddy says.

Riley barks and wags his tail happily.

"What did you *do*, Riley?" I yell. "What did you *do*!?!"

Riley says nothing, but it's clear what he did: he peed all over the carpet, right next to Teddy.

"PEE-PEES OUTSIDE!" I shout uselessly. "*PEE-PEES OUTSIDE!*"

Riley barks and wags his tail happily. I get the paper towel and my bottle of 409, get down on my hands and knees, and start cleaning up his mess. I could almost swear the cute little bastard has a smile on his face. He knows the truth as well as I do.

I have lost, and he has won.

FRIDAY. IT'S TWO DAYS BEFORE our second-to-last game of the regular season. Winning won't be easy, but it would really help our desperate play-off prospects.

And Antonne has a total breakdown in our final walk-through.

His body language is shit all day. When he lines up in the offense, he doesn't just make the *wrong* reads—he doesn't try to make *any* reads. He just keeps his head down, snaps the ball, trying to get it all over with.

Jack and Lopez exchange a look, unsure what to do. The last thing they want is to call out the leader of their offensive line in front of the whole team.

"Antonne!" I shout from the sidelines. "Get your head up! You should be in 'man'!"

Antonne looks up groggily, hardly even aware of where he is.

"Huh? Oh, right."

He changes his read and snaps the ball. They barely have a chance to run the play before Lopez jumps in and blows it dead.

"Teddy!" he yells. "*Teddy*! What the fuck are you doing?"

"What?" Teddy says, looking around, blinking.

All signs indicate that this'll be a typical Lopez-Teddy interaction: Lopez screams at Teddy, embarrasses him a little, Teddy agrees and apologizes, and we all move on.

"Do you have any fucking clue who you're supposed to be picking up here?" Lopez says.

"Oh, my fault, Lo," Teddy says. "I didn't, uh—"

But apparently Antonne doesn't see things that way.

"*Yo!*" he screams, completely out of the blue. "If you guys don't shut the fuck up and get this over with, I'm gonna punt this fucking ball to the other side of the field!"

Everyone just kind of turns and looks at him. Then at each other. Like *Okay, I guess this is our center now?*

Jack blows the whistle.

"All right, people," he says. "Let's move it along, next play!"

We get in three more listless, uninspired plays before the walk-through ends.

"It's about fucking time!" Antonne says.

He grabs the ball right out of Lopez's hands and punts it to the other side of the field. Just like he said he'd do. Then heads back to the lockers alone.

Jack stands there, shaking his head.

"Your center's not all there today," I tell him.

"Yeah," Jack says. "I know."

WE LOSE OUR NEXT GAME by 19 points, getting absolutely destroyed on the road by a much better team, a team that will definitely be going to the play-offs. Our record drops to 8-7. We're right on the brink.

We have one more game in the regular season. One last shot to make the play-offs as a wildcard. And I can finally admit to myself that I want to play in that game.

I don't care if I'm a starter or a backup. I just want to contribute. I want to help my team win. I want to play the game I love.

The only question is whether or not I'll have the chance.

Chapter 12

WINNER

We have one game left in the season. We have one week to get ready for that game.

This game will determine whether or not we make the play-offs. If we win that game *and* a few other teams *also* lose their games this weekend, we're in. If we lose that game, it doesn't matter what happens in the rest of our division, we're out. Year over. All done.

It's the Game to End All Games.

So the coaches do the smartest, most helpful, most coachiest thing they could possibly do in a high-pressure Game-to-End-All-Games situation.

They freak the fuck out.

"All right! We're going back to basics!"

Jack is up in front of everyone in Tuesday's all-hands-on-deck team meeting. Jack really isn't much of a yeller; Lopez is the one who likes to lose his shit. But this morning, Jack is doing his very best Lopez impression.

The words come fast, loud, and angry. His face is red, his fists are clenched, and his mouth is rapid-firing clichés like a football machine gun.

"We're gonna teach the receivers how to catch and the quarterbacks how to throw!" he shouts. "We're gonna teach the running backs how to run and the kickers how to kick! We're gonna teach you to score, we're gonna teach you to defend, we're gonna teach you to stop turning the ball over on offense and start getting turnovers on defense! We're starting over from scratch! Why? BECAUSE EVERYTHING IS ON THE LINE!"

Jack is right about the stakes. Making the play-offs is the most critical way to measure a season. We make the play-offs, and all the fuckups, even the losses of the regular season, are all forgotten. Our huge skid at the end of the year? If we win this week and make the play-offs, the story becomes *Look at the way they fought through adversity till the very last moment! Just when shit looked darkest, these guys pulled it together and beat the odds!*

But if we lose, all anybody will remember is the losing. How in the middle of the season we had a spot in the play-offs almost guaranteed, and we gave it all the fuck away.

If we don't make the play-offs, coaches who thought their jobs were safe, especially first-year guys like Lopez, have to start worrying—about finding a new team, about selling their house and uprooting their family to a whole new part of the country.

If we don't make the play-offs, starters who had big, fat, untouchable contracts suddenly need to worry about getting traded or maybe even cut altogether as the front office starts to "rebuild" or "try a new philosophy" in the wake of all the fans' righteous outrage.

And backups? We lose out on the extra bonus we get for making the play-offs. For a guy like me, that ends up being about $15,000 for the first game and gets larger the further you go. That's a lot of money, especially if your career could end at any minute.

Making the play-offs is the difference between being winners and being losers. And at the end of the season, *that* is the only thing that matters in the League. Not how we treat our women and children, not if we're gay or straight, not even if we cheat or play by the rules. But whether or not we win.

Oh yeah, one other thing. We have to worry about all that shit over Christmas.

That's right. The Game to End All Games is on Sunday, December 28.

Now look. We're professionals. We're competitors. Hell, for the sake of argument, let's even say we're warriors. But we're also human beings—and it has been a very long season. Our coaches have worked us hard, harder than even old vets like Jeb can remember ever working. The injuries, the late-game collapses, the pressure from the fans and the media, they've taken a toll on everyone. And right now, with one last week to go, a week we should all be home with our families, we are fucking over it.

Everyone, that is, except me. I actually *want* to play.

This shit is so ironic I think even Coulter might be able to figure it out. Then again . . . Nah.

TUESDAY AFTERNOON. OUR LAST OFFENSIVE-LINE meeting of the day and everyone's still waiting for Lopez to show up.

"All right," Teddy says. "Here it is!"

He holds up his notebook. Inside is a crudely drawn calendar for this week. The days are each numbered. Christmas is marked, simply, "Christmas," with a sketch of a little green tree. Then there's December 29, the day our season could come to a close. "END OF THE YEAR!!!!!!!" it says in big red letters. All around the date he's drawn stars and firecrackers and hearts and smiley faces. The only thing missing is glitter.

"It's our official countdown calendar!"

"That right there is a goddamn Picasso," I say.

He smiles.

"Cool!" he says. "I like that guy."

Jeb holds up three scrawled-on papers of his own.

"More hate mail," he says. "From our fans."

"Fuck that, man," Antonne says. "I just can't care anymore, even if I wanted to. Can't take another meeting or practice, or another fucking drill. I mean, shit, I'm already about to lose my job. I've been playing like shit."

He laughs, one of those awkward laughs you make when you realize you just said something you shouldn't have.

"I hate all this bullshit," Williams says. "I *especially* hate the hate mail."

"Yo," one of the backups calls out. "What's the Top Five Things You Hate in Life?"

"I know!" Coulter says. "I hate people who take selfies while they're on vacation all the time, then post that shit on Instagram."

"Hell yeah," Antonne says.

"Like this one chick," Coulter continues, "it's like she's on vacation *all the time*. She posts that shit and it's, like, 'No fair! Let me go on vacation too! That's all I want is vacation right now!' "

"I hate bitches that just after your money," one of the backups says. "It's, like, they knew you before you got big, before you hit the League, but they didn't give a fuck about you. But now you got money? They act like they been in love with you, like, forever."

There's general agreement that we all hate "bitches" who are "after our money."

"I hate being tired all the time," Jeb says. "Like our last coach, he'd give me plays off during practice sometime, let me skip some of the workout sessions, you know? These guys just want you to work all the time. I ain't trying to be lazy, you all know that, but I ain't twenty-five no more. I gotta rest if you want me at a hundred percent for the games!"

"Fuck right!" Williams says.

"I hear that," Teddy says.

"Yeah, totally," Paulson says.

Suddenly inspiration hits me like a shot of adrenaline to the heart.

"Okay, wait!" I say. "I've got a *great* one."

They all look at me expectantly.

"Yeah?" Antonne says.

I'm so excited I actually stand, my eyes open wide.

"I absolutely *hate* people who are happy all the time."

Nothing but blank stares.

"You know," I say, trying to sell it. "Like happy *all the time*. For no good reason?"

A few awkward glances are exchanged. Finally my roommate bails me out.

"Yeah, Johnny," Teddy says. "Happy people suck. Or whatever."

I shrug.

"Well," I say, sitting back down. "I think so."

Lopez finally walks in and cues up the game tape. He's a few minutes late. We all quiet down. We know we're supposed to focus, we know we're supposed to *want* this. This is the fucking play-offs. This is what it's all about—the will to win.

But it's like Antonne said. It's not that people *don't* care. They're so tired, they *can't* care.

Lopez is about to start. Then, offhandedly, like it's something that just as easily could've slipped his mind, he looks at me.

"Hey, Johnny," he says. "Me and Vaughn got a little something cooked up for you."

The guy he mentions, Vaughn, is our offensive coordinator. I arch my eyebrow.

"Huh?" I say. "What do you mean?"

He smiles, almost like he's proud of himself.

"We're gonna install you as a jumbo tight end," he says.

I bust out laughing.

"Okay," I say. "Right."

"I'm serious," he says. "We're gonna get you into the game as a tight end. We're installing it in practice tomorrow."

I stop laughing. Lopez is looking at me, almost puzzled that I'm not taking him seriously. Every single fiber of my being, every ounce of my 279 pounds, is screaming at me not to trust him, not to believe a word he says. But he's not kidding. He means it.

I'm gonna get to play in the game.

Hell, maybe being a happy person doesn't suck so bad after all.

WEDNESDAY ARRIVES, AND THE COACHES actually install the play. Lopez wasn't just fucking with me. Imagine that. The NFL—or at least one of its representatives—told me the truth.

I'm going to be a jumbo tight end.

Now don't get me wrong. Unlike my switch to center, this isn't a permanent shift to a completely new position. This won't mean I'm starting again, or even that I'll be playing for the whole game. This is just a trick play we can run in goal-line situations. A play that uses me at a position, tight end, where my size can be an advantage for once, where guys tend to be big, but not as big as me. I'm gonna be a gimmick.

Or as I like to think of it, a secret weapon.

"All right, Johnny," Vaughn, the offensive coordinator, says before practice, "here's what we're thinking . . ."

And he tells me all about it, how they're gonna use me as an extra blocker to power the ball into the end zone, and I listen.

"Don't you think they'll game plan for this?" I ask.

He looks at me like I'm absolutely fucking nuts.

"Johnny, no one's gonna game plan for you."

And I laugh.

I love it. It doesn't bother me that I'm not starting, that I'm not gonna be the focus of attention, or the guy leading the big charge on our final game-winning drive. I don't need any of that. I just want to play.

I know now that that's enough. That's what makes me happy. That's why I'm a player in the NFL.

It's why I put up with all the politics and the hypocrisy, all the injuries and the fucked-up diet, all the loneliness and the traveling and the uncertainty and the fear. It's not because of the "money for nothing" or even the revenge.

It's because I love to play. And in the last game of the season, I finally will.

Later that day, I hear through the grapevine that my old team has been having a lot of problems with the guards on its offensive line. Remember the guy who shared an agent with one of the coaches, the one they cut me for? Well, he's not working out too well for them.

I text Bernie.

"Hey, you see what's going on with my old team? That guard situation?"

"Yeah," he texts back.

"Wouldn't it be funny if I ended up back there?" I write. "Those fuckers would have to kiss my ass and roll out the red carpet."

I press send and smile from ear to ear.

Well, okay. So the revenge still makes me happy too.

THURSDAY NIGHT. THE GAME TO End All Games is in three days. But it's Christmas.

Even our team can't ignore that.

Kate and I are driving to Lopez's place for Christmas dinner with the O line, and then to a party for the whole team at a bar downtown. That's right, Kate's in town, and we're back to our passive-aggressive bickering like we never skipped a beat.

"Riley is clearly used to peeing on the sidewalk," she says. "He's a city dog! We should definitely be looking more for a place for us in downtown Cincinnati."

Note the strategic use of "we" and "us." She still wants to move in together, and now she's even using my dog to send me signals. After weeks of trying, I've actually trained Riley to ring a bell with his cute little nose whenever he wants to pee outside. Something tells me he'll be able to adapt wherever I decide to live.

"Uh-huh," I say. "We'll figure it out."

I have no desire to engage. I actually don't have the heart to tell her the truth: that, for now at least, the dream of me buying my own place is dead. The fucking bank won't give me a loan. That's right—with only one more year left in my NFL contract, they're worried about my job security. Amazing, huh? A guy making hundreds of thousands of dollars can't even get a mortgage for a two-bedroom condo in Ohio.

Honestly, though, I almost can't blame the fuckers. I worry about my job security too.

"Oh wow!" Kate says. "What a nice house!"

We pull up at Lopez's place, an old Tudor in one of the wealthier suburbs outside the city. There's a large, well-manicured lawn with an ancient, sprawling oak in the front and a shiny silver Lexus parked in the driveway. Christmas lights decorate the house, and dozens of candles have been carefully arranged on the snow-covered front lawn to spell "Happy Holidays."

"Wow," Kate says as we walk up with some other players. "That's really sweet that he went to the trouble to do that."

"Yeah, I don't think Lopez was the one who actually put those out," I say.

No matter what some of the players might say behind his back, something tells me Lopez doesn't really do yard work. The dude is clearly getting paid.

"Welcome to our home!" Lopez's wife, Tanya, announces as we walk through the door.

Lopez nods, awkwardly shakes my hand. He's standing next to his wife, looking extremely uncomfortable in a bulging shirt and tie that both look way too small for his overflowing flab. She, on the other hand, is about four and a half feet tall. Another tiny blonde with another gigantic lineman. What a surprise.

The rest of the line is there too, all these massive mountains of muscle and fat squeezed into suits and fancy shoes, some of them with their girlfriends or wives, some alone. Antonne is there by himself, his eyes bloodshot, lost in his own world. Not only has he not quit drinking, but word is that he's been smoking a lot of pot too. With the League's nonexistent testing policy, he's in the clear—and high off his ass.

Everyone else is being a good athlete, sipping ice waters, speaking in hushed tones, politely making small talk about weather and the game conditions we can expect on Sunday. Yeah, tons of fun.

"You got any beer back here?" I ask Tanya, motioning to the kitchen.

"Of course!" she says, bubbling over with holiday cheer.

One minute later I'm cracking open a Pabst—thank God my coach has good taste in beer—and so is Teddy. And Coulter. And Jeb. And Paulson. All the guys except Williams, who remains true to his sober self-help ways, and Antonne. For about five minutes.

"If I start with one, that'll become two real quick," he says. "But fuck. It's Christmas!"

Everyone loosens up, and the party becomes a party. We all break out our white elephant gifts. Teddy's brought a life-size, *usable* latex model of Jenna Jameson's pussy. Put the thing on the floor and you can actually fuck it. One of the other backups gets it, but Teddy's fiancée is pissed because it's pretty clear he wanted it for himself. Knowing Teddy, there's a solid chance he thought that's how the white elephant thing works.

I end up with Jeb's contribution, a surprisingly nice Armani bag that I'd never buy on one of my mall trips. And Antonne, for better or worse, ends up with my offering: a pricey bottle of Glenfiddich eighteen-year-old scotch whisky, which he proceeds to down in shots.

"Fuck!" he says. "This shit is terrible!"

"Yeah," I say. "That's because you're supposed to put it in a glass and sip it."

The only guy who doesn't look like he's having a great time is Lopez. He stands off to the side, watching the action, not even drinking a club soda.

Tanya, his wife, walks up to me, puts her hand on my arm.

"Johnny, this is your first time here, right?" she says, subtly guiding me over to where her husband stands alone. I try to pull Kate with me, but she's busy talking to Teddy's fiancée.

"Uh, yeah," I say to Tanya. "It sure is."

"Bill," she says to her husband. "Why don't you show Johnny your memorabilia collection in the den?"

It's strange hearing someone call Lopez by his first name.

"Huh?" he says, like he's just been woken up from a weird dream. "Oh yeah. Sure."

Lopez leads me down the central hallway to the back of the house. I notice that the few scattered pictures hanging on the wall are all of him and his wife. No kids of their own.

He opens the door to his den, a small, cozy room. It's completely covered in photos, every square inch taken up by pictures of the teams he's coached, the players he's shaped over the years.

And it hits me: *These* are his kids. *This* is his family.

He takes me on a tour, telling me about all the different players on all the different teams, mentioning each one by name.

"You know this guy?"

"Nope."

"Great kid, great player. How about him?"

"Never heard of him."

"Great leader, small like you, even smaller, one of the best guys I ever coached."

"Oh," I say. "Cool."

I spot a team photo that's a tiny bit bigger than the others, slightly fancier frame—a college team he coached that won their conference championship.

"Wow," I say. "Championship. That must be really awesome."

"Oh, yeah," he says, barely even noticing. "It was cool."

He'd rather show me someone else. Another player. A shot of the two of them together.

"How about this guy? You know him?"

"Lopez," I say, "I'm sorry, but I don't think I know any of these guys."

"He's the best player I ever coached," he says, like he didn't even hear me.

"Oh yeah?"

"Yeah," he says. "He called me a few years ago, just out of the blue. Said he wanted me to know I was a great coach, that he really respected me. I told him thank you, said I respected him too, said he was the best I ever coached. He killed himself the next day."

A sad, thick silence hangs in the air.

What killed him? Was it the game? All the head injuries? Or was it something else? Something completely different? Nothing to do with football at all?

I don't know. I doubt Lopez does either. The best kid he ever coached, one of his many sons, is dead. That's all we know.

"Lo," I say. "That's horrible."

He shrugs. What more is there to say?

"Yeah," he says. "Well, I guess we should get back out to the party, huh?"

"Yeah."

We turn toward the door, and there, hanging directly above it, is a picture I had missed on the way in—a big color photo of a smiling Jeb in a heavy wooden frame. Jebediah, the Old Vet. The superstar. The same guy who just three months ago told Lopez he'd never cut it in the NFL.

In the picture Jeb looks so happy it's all I can do to keep from laughing.

"Where the hell did you get *that*?" I say.

"Oh that?" Lopez says, smiling with obvious pride. "Jeb gave it to me himself, few weeks back. Real class act, that guy."

SUNDAY. THE GAME TO END All Games is here.

Hours before it all begins, I head out to the field for my pregame ritual. I stretch my legs, warm up. I walk across the field, alone. I take in everything around me. The die-hard fans arriving at their seats, the players fist-bumping friends from the other team, the friends of the owners taking selfies in the end zone. The media, the refs, the ball boys, the trainers. The paint from the hash marks smeared against my toe, the smoke from the hot dog grills in my nose.

I soak it all in, make it my own, just like I do before every game. But somehow, this game, it's different.

Heading back to the locker room, I see Paulson, my Jesus-loving former rival, on his way in. He looks at me, shakes his head, rolls his eyes.

"Man," he says. "I really hope they don't make the backups get any reps in. I'm exhausted."

I just smile and laugh, pat him on the back.

I'm different. Today, I want to play. Even if it's only for a few minutes, I want to play. To make an impact. To be a part of this team. To have some fun out there on that field. I want to play.

I wish I could tell you that's what happened.

I wish I could tell you our team went out there and won that game. That we were down by 6 points on the last play of the game, that our offense was right on the goal line, that our coaches decided to put me in and use the trick play they had installed earlier this week. I wish I could tell you I scored the winning touchdown. That after all the pressure, frustration, and hope, we made it to the play-offs.

But I can't, because this isn't a fairy tale. This isn't a Hollywood story. This isn't a happy ending.

This is the NFL.

Our team came out flat, exhausted. The other team outplayed us at every step of the way. There was never any need for that trick play, never a chance to "win the game." The score never got close enough.

The coaches did put me in at the end for about thirty-five seconds, but it was just to run down the clock, just to finish it up and make it all go away, like they'd used me so many times before.

But this time is different, because I'm different.

Even though it's just garbage time, even though it's completely mean-ingless to everyone else in that stadium, I don't roll my eyes when I jog out onto the field. I don't sigh before I snap the ball. I don't look at the ticking clock and hope it'll all end so I can just go home.

I enjoy it. I listen to the crowds, feel the leather of the ball on my fingertips. I sense my mother looking down at me from somewhere out there.

And I picture myself playing. Looking out over the defense, making the read, and shouting the call. Snapping the ball, my legs driving me forward to meet my opponent, my muscles tensing. My arms, my torso, at the exact angle for perfect leverage, slamming into him, the crunch of our pads, the crack of our helmets. Driving him into the ground, bend-ing his will to mine, taking complete control as everything around me vanishes. No fans, no coaches, no winning or losing.

Nothing except me and the fun of the game, and my mom watching over me.

I picture it all, because I don't *care* if they won't let me play. This is mine, all mine, and they can't take it from me.

I wanted to play, because I love to play. I know that now. And I'm gonna appreciate every minute of it, because this is the League, and who knows if these minutes will be my last.

The game ends. We lose. Season over. I call my dad up on the phone.

"Well?" he says. "How was it? How do you feel?"

"Absolutely perfect," I answer. "I'm the best fucking backup in the NFL."

TUESDAY MORNING, DECEMBER 30.

I weigh in for the very last time. A nice, solid 282 pounds. At this point, now that I've proved I belong on this team, does reaching 285 mean as much? No, probably not. But for some reason, I'm still proud that I managed to stay so close to the target weight, that magic number, all year long.

Pathetic, right? But that's what I'll do for this game.

I take my final glory shit. Also nice, also solid, also very heavy.

Fuck, that feels good.

Yesterday I packed up my truck. Kate helped, or at least she started to. Then I yelled at her for doing a shit job folding my fancy Egyptian cotton bedsheets—she just wadded them up into a big ball and threw them on the floor!—so she let me handle the rest. I can still fit everything into the Durango, even with all Riley's toys and the goddamn electric massage easy chair my sister gave me for Christmas. I strapped that bitch to the top of the roof, done and done. I'm ready to move yet again, back to Ohio, back to my pad above my dad's garage.

I just hope Riley won't pee all over everything on the long ride home tonight. I wonder if I can set up his little pee-pee bell in the backseat? No, that won't work. He'll ring it every five minutes to get me to stop the car. Fuck, that dog owns me.

I finish up my exit interview with the HR lady. That's right, we have exit interviews, just like any other employee for any other gigantic corporation. And ours are just as annoying and pointless. Same silly questions about job satisfaction, respect in the workplace, productive employment environment, blah blah blah. I just answer yes to everything, barely even listen to what she asks.

I walk down the hall with my gym bag. The place already practically empty. Most of the players gone, even Jack, the head coach. It happens that fast.

I'm about to head out when I decide there's one more thing I want to do. I turn around, dive back into the maze of offices. Eventually, I reach the one I want. Offensive-Line Coach. Bill Lopez.

I knock on the door, don't hear a thing. Who knows, maybe he's already gone too? I try the knob. It's unlocked. I open the door.

Lopez is sitting there, at his desk, his head in his hands. He looks up at me. His eyes are red and watery.

"Hey, Lopez," I say.

"Hey," he says.

"How you doing?"

"Eh, you know," he says. "I guess there's next season."

"Yeah," I say.

He looks down at his desk again. I stand there for a few seconds.

"Okay then," I say. "I'm gonna get going."

I start closing the door, and he looks up.

"Johnny," he says. "You're kind of a dick. But you're always busting your ass, and I respect you for that."

I nod.

"Thanks, baby."

And close the door behind me.

EPILOGUE

By the time this book comes out, I'll be stuck in the guts of another season as the Best NFL Backup Ever™. It's a tough fucking job, but someone has to do it.

Actually, that's not true. No one has to do it. Professional football could end tomorrow, and we'd all be just fine. Hell, a lot of us would be better off. But they're paying me a shitload of money, and it turns out I actually have a whole lot of fun playing this stupid, meaningless game. So I guess I'll keep doing it.

Thanks, you know, for being such a fan.

As of this writing, I'm still with the same team. I can't say the same about some of the other guys you got to know in the book.

Dante the Diva receiver got dropped. He asked for too much money and they called his bluff. He'll end up somewhere, I'm sure, probably making more money in a year than you or I will ever see in our lifetimes, so yeah, don't shed any tears.

Coulter, a starting offensive lineman, got dropped too. Like Jeb, he's getting old. Unlike Jeb, he doesn't make the Pro Bowl every year. He hung it up, decided to retire and spend some time with the kids he missed so much during the season.

Even the starters aren't immune to the grind of the NFL. It's just a matter of time for all of us, no matter where you fall on the depth chart. That's the business.

Ironically, the other backups are all back. Paulson started reading the Bible cover to cover again for probably the five millionth time. And my roommate, Teddy? Now that Marcus is all healed up, he'll be back on the bench with me.

"Fuck, Johnny, you were right," he said on the first day of the summer session. "I *love* just being a backup."

"See?" I said laughing. "That's what I've been trying to tell you!"

Williams, Jeb, and Antonne, they all made it. During the off-season, Antonne actually had a kid, a little boy. He's not close to the mom—they aren't married and probably never will be—but he adores his son. Antonne's found his anchor. He's not drinking nearly as much, the darkness is gone, the depression has lifted. He's playing like a star again, though I'll be ready if he's not.

The special teams guys continue to be special teams guys. Taking long showers, posting videos, letting off steam. Maybe the biggest surprise for me last season was when Eric the long snapper actually made it to the Pro Bowl. That happy-go-lucky fucker? I didn't even know long snappers could *make* the Pro Bowl! But apparently underneath it all the guy is actually really good. He hasn't botched a snap once in six years.

And Lopez, my mentor and my tormentor, my father figure and the bane of my existence? He's back for his second year as an NFL coach. We started right where we left off. Our first week back, Williams fucked up one of the drills.

"Fuck!" Lopez shouted. Then he paused and smiled. "Well, I might as well just blame Johnny, seeing that's what I do for everything else."

So at least he can admit it. Progress.

Not making the play-offs was a blow to the entire coaching staff, there's no question. And it's probably a big reason they cleaned house with players like Coulter. But Lopez had a lot of adversity to deal with his first year, losing so many starters to injuries, needing to rely on a first-time center like me to lead the line on the field. That was shit he couldn't control, and even his bosses couldn't fault him for it. He'll get at least one more year to prove himself.

But if we miss the play-offs again? All bets are off—not just for him, for all the coaches.

There have been changes in the rest of my life as well.

On the drive back home, Kate and I started arguing in Illinois, kept arguing through Indiana, and by the time we hit Ohio we had broken up. We've broken up before, but this time I think it's really over. You know, for at least another three or four months.

The truth is, my relationship with Kate had been dead for a long time. I just didn't have the strength to admit it. My life was changing constantly, and I was moving from one city to another; I had no idea if the NFL would hire me or spit me out on the street, and even less idea what I would do with my life *after* football. I needed some kind of security, some kind of stability, and Kate provided that. I'll always be grateful.

But once the season ended and I gained some distance from all the turmoil in my life, I realized it was time to move on, for both of us. Because she was right. I never would've been satisfied staying with her. And that wasn't fair to either of us.

Plus, now I have Riley.

Sure, go ahead and laugh, but that dog has helped me adjust to the NFL more than any sports psychologist ever could. Taking care of Riley has filled a void in my life I didn't even know existed. I can go to work, Lopez can scream at me for an hour straight, and I can go home, look at that silly, adorable little dog, and everything is okay again.

Best of all, I can proudly say that Riley now goes pee-pee outside only. On occasion he will poo inside, this is true. But his turds are so small and solid they take five seconds to clean up. I consider it a win.

Walking Riley down the street in Ohio this spring even helped me meet my new girlfriend, Stacey. She saw a giant man with a tiny little dog and just had to stop and say hello. We've been together ever since, and our relationship has all the excitement, all the challenge and adventure that my relationship with Kate was missing. Yes, Stacey is tiny. Yes, she's got big boobs. But she's a brunette instead of a blonde and she wears thick-rimmed glasses sometimes. So I feel like my tastes in women are really evolving.

Although I have at least another year to go in the League, I also feel like I finally have a plan for what I'll do after football. My dad and I just bought a small restaurant franchise in Cincinnati together—as an investment, just like he said. The facilities needed a lot of work, and during the off-season I've managed the project. Shockingly, there's something about being in charge that I really, really enjoy.

What I like most, though, is working with my dad. We're partners on the building, fifty-fifty. After all we've been through together, something about running a business with him just feels right.

Then there's football.

So far in my second year with the team, I've stayed connected to my love of the game. The joy, the simple pleasure of being out on the field playing the kind of football I grew up with. Everything I had lost when I started writing the book is all back, and I hope it's here to stay.

If it wasn't for the hellish injuries, nagging coaches, pompous general managers, overpaid diva players, and the demanding, entitled fans, then, baby, I would play this game forever.

Which is why I plan on getting out of this game before I fall apart. None of the things I hate about the NFL will ever go away, but my injuries will be with me forever. The longer I play, the worse they'll get, and the greater the chance that something will happen to me that doesn't just keep me out of the game, but hurts my life too.

Hopefully, I'll know when the time is right to finally give it up.

But for now, at the start of my new year, I'm savoring doing something I love and getting paid for it. I know it's a gift, and I feel like I've earned it.

On my last day of the summer session, just days before writing this, I pull out of the team's parking lot in my truck and pass by the parking lot attendant. He's an old-timer I've seen a million times before, but who's never said a word to me.

I give him a little wave, about to press my foot to the gas, and he smiles at me.

"All right, Mr. Anonymous," he says. "Have a good day."

I smile back. I think people officially know who I am.

ABOUT THE AUTHOR

JOHNNY ANONYMOUS is a four-year offensive lineman for the NFL. Before that, he played for a major college program and in his senior year was named one of the top linemen in the nation. In his spare time, he's earned a master's degree in sarcasm from Getting Fucked University. During the off-season, he moonlights as a professional asshole. Under another pseudonym, he's also a contributor for the comedy powerhouse Funny Or Die.